LEADING

FOR

INCLUSION

How Schools Can Build on the Strengths of All Learners

LEADING
for
INCLUSION

How Schools Can Build on
the Strengths of All Learners

Phyllis Jones
Janice R. Fauske
Judy F. Carr

EDITORS

Teachers College, Columbia University
New York and London

Published by Teachers College Press, 1234 Amsterdam Avenue, New York, NY 10027

Library of Congress Cataloging-in-Publication Data

Leading for inclusion : how schools can build on the strengths of all learners / Phyllis Jones, Janice R. Fauske, Judy F. Carr, editors.
  p. cm.
 Includes bibliographical references and index.
 ISBN 978-0-8077-5258-6 (pbk.)—ISBN 978-0-8077-5259-3 (hardcover)
 1. Inclusive education--United States. 2. Children with disabilities—Education—United States. 3. Mainstreaming in education—United States. I. Jones, Phyllis. II. Fauske, Janice R. III. Carr, Judy F.
 LC1201.L42 2011
 371.9'046—dc23

                                                                    2011027418

ISBN 978-0-8077-5258-6 (paper)
ISBN 978-0-8077-5259-3 (hardcover)

Printed on acid-free paper
Manufactured in the United States of America

18 17 16 15 14 13 12 11   8 7 6 5 4 3 2 1

If you are neutral in situations of injustice, you have chosen the side of the oppressor. If an elephant has its foot on the tail of a mouse and you say that you are neutral, the mouse will not appreciate your neutrality.

—Desmond Tutu

Contents

PART IV: FACILITATING SYSTEMS OF SUPPORT

Introduction

The book is intended primarily for people who make leadership and administrative decisions in schools: administrators, lead teachers, aspiring leaders, primarily school-based leaders, and all who support those folks. The book adopts a broad view of which students should be the focus of whole-school inclusion policy and practices, and moves beyond traditional groups of students with labels that identify disabilities. Discrete groups of students form the focus of Part III, and although they may not capture all the different groups of learners in every school, they do embrace a much wider group of underrepresented students than may usually be found in a book on educational inclusion.

The book adopts a systems view of supporting effective inclusionary practices. Across the four Parts of the book, a holistic systems development perspective is presented. Chapters focus upon policies and practices that involve systems for planning, development, implementation, and evaluation in the context of collaborative practices. Throughout, the book includes examples and tools the reader may adapt and use to lead greater inclusive practice across the school. Naturally, all names are pseudonyms to maintain confidentiality of the teachers, students, and families with whom the authors work. Additionally, we have applied People First Language throughout this book to acknowledge that all students are young people first. People First Language has emanated from the field of disability to counter the negative terms that reflect ways in which people with disabilities are viewed (Snow, 2009). Quite simply, People First Language puts the person before the label. We support the use of People First Language to recognize that the way we talk to and about students reflects the value placed on the personhood of those students. Here is a general summary of the four Parts of the book:

- The three chapters in Part I discuss central concepts and practices of inclusion and leadership from a practice and policy perspective.
- The three chapters in Part II explore examples of strategies that leaders can use to promote inclusion in schools.

- The five chapters in Part III focus upon lessons learned around a selection of discrete groups of students and are framed to support a broader understanding of school inclusion.
- The two chapters in Part IV emphasize the interconnectedness of the school community and fluidity of that relationship, recognizing that the school community is a living, changing, and dynamic entity. The role of data and implications for systemic decision making is explored.

Researchers who wrote chapters in this book come from the five separate departments—Reading, Childhood Education, Psychological and Social Foundations, Measurement and Research, and Educational Leadership and Policy Studies—that comprise the College of Education at the University of South Florida, Sarasota-Manatee. In addition, a faculty member from the Department of Special Education at the University of South Florida, Tampa, a faculty member from the Warner School of Education at the University of Rochester, New York, and a consultant from the Center for Curriculum Renewal in Sarasota, Florida, collaborated in the writing and editing process.

The rich diversity of contributors to the book is one of its defining elements. The compilation of the book became about balancing content and voice and style of presentation; about making space for differences; and about celebrating discrete contributions to the inclusion debate with the aim of shedding a perspective on school inclusion policy and practices that represents the reality of diversity across school. Through doing this, all writers participated in a shared process of learning—just as is the case in schools where teachers and administrators work together to promote greater inclusive policies and practices.

ACKNOWLEDGMENTS

Thank you to Brian Ellerbeck at Teachers College Press for his continued support and counsel. A special thank you to Kristina Moody, who joined the process at the end with an eagle eye for detail. We extend our deepest gratitude to the teachers, administrators, and students in the school districts with whom we have had the good fortune to work and learn together.

Part I

POLICIES AND PRACTICES TO PROMOTE INCLUSION

In this part we summarize major concepts that introduce central themes of the book, including inclusion, leadership, and leadership for inclusion, as well as systems capacity building. A working definition of inclusion is developed that acknowledges that schools are full of students who do not fit neatly into tidy boxes, but who are interesting, intricate, multifaceted, and often unpredictable, who transcend traditional groups of learners. To meet the needs of such students, schools need more and more to understand, respond, and be proactive concerning the diversity of student learning profiles. Leadership is a key factor of effective inclusive policies and practices, and Chapter 1 explores the complex concept of inclusion and the moral imperative to embrace, model, and promote inclusive practices in schools. It calls for a systems view of inclusion in schools, a view that is immersed in the notion that members of the school community are engaged in a systemic relationship, where one action influences a myriad of other actions. Chapter 2 emphasizes the interconnectedness of the school community and the fluidity of that relationship, recognizing that the school community is a living, changing, and dynamic entity. This chapter promotes a systems view of inclusion in schools, a view that embraces the notion that members of the school community can be engaged in a systemic relationship where one action influences a myriad of other actions. Chapter 3 examines the legal background of inclusive education and the value of creating communities of belonging through interpretation of policy. Case law is included to chronicle exclusion and inclusion of students with disabilities, as well as discuss the courts' interpretation of the key policy terms. Emerging from this discussion of case law are the central issues of social justice, the difference principle, the constitutional basis of racism/ableism, and the racial formation theory. As the Part ends, we demonstrate that there is a need for school leaders to reflect on law and policy as frameworks for praxis in schools and explore how members of nondominant communities are constructed as racialized groups, viewed as social "projects" to be fixed, or denied access to certain privileges.

CHAPTER 1

Creating Inclusive Schools

Phyllis Jones, Julia M. White,
Janice R. Fauske, and Judy F. Carr

A small urban school district north of New York City serves a diverse population of students with myriad ethnic, linguistic, economic, sociocultural, and educational realities. The makeup of the district differs significantly from the predominantly White, middle-class community of 30 years previous. A curriculum audit 5 years ago noted too-quiet classrooms focused on compliance. Students worked alone in workbooks or photocopied learning packets, and when the rooms got too noisy, students were told to put their heads down on their desks to help enforce teachers' demands for quiet. Students' hands were behind their backs as they moved in single-file lines from one place to another for recess, lunch, art, or fire drills. Teachers monitored students more than they taught them, and both behavioral referral and academic data reflected low expectations for student performance. On graduation day that same year, one elderly, long-term school board member looked at the group of graduates, turned to the superintendent of schools, and asked, "Why are so many of the seniors not here for graduation?" "Because 50% of the students who started ninth grade with this class are no longer enrolled as students," was the superintendent's reply. It was a "light bulb" moment.

The district described here is typical of many across the nation experiencing decline, challenges, and despair. Fortunately, this district, and a few like it, initiated an audit of their practices and curriculum and engaged in deep and thoughtful reform that gave voice to the teachers, students, and parents, and garnered the collective force of human resources to act in the best interest of the children. The intent of this book is to explore how this transformation of schools and districts happened, by examining many factors that contributed to the challenges, exploring the troubles in schools as well as with individual groups of students, and offering ideas for responding with passion, expertise, and energy to educational needs of students and adults in the school community. Many of the "troubles" in schools can be traced to a history of decisions, both explicit and implicit, that shaped our attitudes as well as our schools. Examining these historical decisions is the first step to improving our schools.

The history of education in the United States is a "majoritarian story" that "privileges White men, the middle and/or upper classes, and heterosexuals by naming their social locations as natural or normative points of reference" (Solorzano & Yosso, 2002, p. 28). The privileged evoke power and locate the norm as themselves, attributing difference to others, and then treating "classifications of difference as inherent and natural while debasing those defined as different" (Minow, 1990, p. 111). Thus, many of the differences that matter in schools—the status differences that serve to exclude and deny children equality of educational opportunity—are imposed by the privileged (Markus, 2008). Children in schools who have this difference thrust upon them—ability, status, race, social class, gender, ethnicity, sexual identity—thus become stigmatized through learning what is the norm, and then by learning how they are "disqualified according to it" (Goffman, 1963, p. 80). This theory can reasonably be extended to ableism, heterosexism, sexism, ethnicism, and classism, in which students are essentialized and their imposed unequal social status is reproduced through their being identified as in need of "special care" (Winant, 1998). Thus is the "dilemma of difference," in which the "stigma of difference may be recreated both by ignoring and by focusing on it" (Minow, 1990, p. 20).

Desegregation, integration, Regular Education Initiative, mainstreaming, inclusion: These are some of the many names that have been attached to the idea of students being "allowed" to enter the standard or dominant school community (e.g., a "general education classroom"). Each of these terms is rooted in the concept that there are "Others" who must receive consent in order to enter these classrooms: Students must be at a certain level in learning English, students must be "ready" to participate in the general education curriculum, or students must behave in particular ways deemed appropriate by the school. Students might well be granted access to the school building, but if students perform in the lower quartile of the state accountability assessment tool, if students have significant disability labels, if students are not proficient speakers of English, or if students do not conform to the dominant, meritocratic social order, these students are most likely to be forcibly segregated in one place or another at some point during their time in the building. Each of these students manifests a difference that matters (Minow, 1990) and each is marginalized because of this comparison to the social construction of "normal."

What is lacking in the terms listed above is the notion that all students belong and all students have automatic full citizenship in their school communities. There should not be any preconditions or prerequisites placed on students before they are "granted permission" to be a part of their own learning communities. Inclusive practice demands that those working in schools challenge the attitudes and conditions that determine who is seen as worthy of being educated and who is denied full participation in schools and meaningful access and equal opportunity to education.

SOCIAL EXCLUSION, SCHOOL EXCLUSION

Schools provide special care to various populations of students with the intent of providing equality of opportunity. Legislation provides the framework for the system of education, case law interprets the meaning of the legislation, and administrators—from federal to school—implement the policy. Instead of providing a seamless system in which all students receive what they need to access education meaningfully, though, students are classified and provided programs that accentuate their differences while simultaneously trying to mitigate the impact of the unequal social structures that have created and reinforced these imposed differences.

The children caught in the crosshairs of these imposed differences—for whom special programs are constructed—are pathologized, are viewed as deficient and as burdens by school organizers; these supposedly "deficient" students are thus marginalized, excluded, and tracked into hierarchical divisions of school labor under the guise of meritocracy (Apple, 1995, 1996; Armstrong, Armstrong, & Barton, 2000; Erevelles, 2005; Ferri, 2009; Kliewer, 1998; Kozol, 1991). Educational policy is informed by the medical model—students who do not conform to the majoritarian story need prescriptive instruction to "cure" their deficits. For example, the basis of IDEA (The Individuals with Disabilities Education Improvement Act of 2004) is categorical; students must manifest one or more of the 13 "disabilities" enumerated in the law before the allocation of federal funds is possible to states, districts, and then schools, for students' individualized educational programs (IEPs). The education of diverse students is largely "exceptionalistic" in that the problems exist within the student and must be remedied through programs that will fix the individual's problem—in this way the victim is blamed (Ryan, 1976). Students must "fit into the dominant structures, when it is those structures that ought to adapt to the needs of diverse students" (Moses & Nanna, 2007, p. 65).

Inclusion is a worldwide phenomenon that has its roots in human and civil rights. It transcends schooling to encompass social policies and practices (D'Alessio, 2007), and it transcends disability to include the many different groups of people who are marginalized and underrepresented in society. The nature of the inclusive debate is dependent on philosophical perspectives, professional disciplines, fields of knowledge, and geographical issues. The intent of this book is to present a thorough discussion of the capacity of school leaders to affirm, envision, nurture, and evaluate inclusive practices for students who are underrepresented in the school. Mittler (2000) offers a poignant reminder that however grand the discourse around inclusion is, the reality of inclusion occurs in the classroom. The classroom, the school, the teachers, the resources, the environment, the other students, the other professionals, and the parents are key stakeholders in inclusion. Each of these stakeholders can impact how successful an inclusive placement is in the classroom for individuals or groups of students. School leaders have the power to influence, lead, motivate, and coach all of these key stakeholders. In the practice of inclusion, school leaders set the philosophical tone of acceptance in the school and, because of this, are the main audience for this book. Quite simply, the more prepared a school leader is for inclusion, the higher the chances are of seeing effective inclusive practices consistently maintained across a school (Fleming & Love, 2003).

TOWARD A BROAD DEFINITION OF INCLUSION

When inclusive education is fully embraced, we abandon the idea that children have to become "normal" in order to contribute to the world. . . . We begin to look beyond typical ways of becoming valued members of the community, and in doing so, begin to realize the achievable goal of providing all children with an authentic sense of belonging. (Kunc, 1992, pp. 38–39)

The work of Kunc (1992) gives a context for shifting principles of inclusive practice away from notions of everyone needing to be the same, toward notions that each person is to be valued. The idea that all students belong to an inclusive learning community has become a central tenet of discussions about inclusion. Lynch (2001) discusses understandings of inclusion focusing upon a "pluralism of learners with a pluralism of needs" (p. 10) being influential. Both of these authors dispel the notions of sameness and normativity in authentic inclusion. Recognizing and eschewing the paradigm of normativity are central to the purposes of this book.

The social imperative for engaging in the quest for greater inclusive school communities is echoed by Kasahara (2006), who helps move the imperative for inclusion beyond the walls of the school:

If we are serious about growing as citizens of inclusive societies, we must engage in a dialogue with people valuing and embodying diverse perspectives and experiences. We must explore the meaning of "inclusive society" together, and seek to understand the kinds of education, system, culture, and support we need to achieve the vision. (p. 5)

This view is echoed by the Institute for Inclusion (n.d.) and its discussion of inclusion as a way to build a stronger society through the explicit valuing of difference among the members of that society. The complexity and challenges inherent in the process of creating an inclusive school are captured by Udvari-Solner, Villa, and Thousand (2002). In their seminal work, focused upon access to academics for all students, they highlight how inclusive schooling

propels a critique of contemporary school culture and thus encourages practitioners to reinvent what can be and should be to realize more humane, just and democratic learning communities. Inequities in treatment and educational opportunity are brought to the forefront, thereby fostering attention to human rights, respect for difference and value of diversity. (p. 142)

Thus another purpose of the book is to reinforce the humane and democratic ideals of schools in a societal and global context.

Recently, in public schools, inclusion has been a term applied most commonly to students identified as having special needs, students labeled as "special education students." A broader definition of the term is necessary to embrace the dynamic of difference, "a reciprocal process that occurs when individuals of different cultures interact" (Emery, 1997, n.p.). This book explores understandings and practices of teaching as well as leading for a diverse range of student groups. This includes students who present as different because of their gender, first language, ability, and sexual orientation. It also includes students who present as different in schools through their social, economic, migrant, or refugee status.

Inclusion is a system of policy and practices that embraces diversity as a strength, creates a sense of belonging, equal membership, acceptance, and being valued, and involves fundamental civil rights. Inclusive teaching and learning occurs in natural settings, with extensive and appropriate instructional supports, modifications, and accommodations that are meaningful to students and teachers. Inclusion services throughout the school are collaborative and integrated where the school and local community grow and evolve.

THE CONVERGENCE OF MULTIPLE ECOLOGIES

School leaders whose intention is to create schools that are more inclusive work in a system built upon difference, categorization, separation, and segregation. They face the challenge of initiating and maintaining a supportive learning environment in schools where established policy and practice may fall short upon implementation. While this book draws upon the powerful research base of each discipline and approach, its intention is to integrate and apply the research to a more holistic understanding of students and inclusive practices. This demands a critical approach to inclusion and asks for creativity in the application of research to other learners in the school. For example, research-based effective practices for students who are LGBTQ (lesbian, gay, bisexual, transgender, and queer/questioning). Or, the research on teaching students who use English as a Second Language (ESL) may be highly appropriate for students who are migrant.

This book describes systemic approaches for embracing a more holistic view of schools as intentionally more inclusive. It does this by presenting multiple perspectives of learners and systems, which can support such learners in a sensitive and proactive way. The complex ecologies of people who participate in schools—from students and their families to staff and community members—creates both a challenge and a dynamic opportunity for authentic exchange and learning that can shape lives within and across the school context. This book explores Stokes's (1997) "Pasteur's Quadrant" by highlighting studies of current systemic approaches for integrating these groups of students in schools. This underscores both effective and deleterious practices by emphasizing specific interpretations of inclusion and a language of belonging that can inform school leadership, curriculum development, equity of access and achievement measures, and the creation of an inviting and supportive school setting (Stokes, 1997).

The authors synthesize current knowledge and practices surrounding inclusion of marginalized groups of students and offer analysis of the contextual educational responses to the needs of these students. Exploring elements of social context and the convergence of multiple ecologies has guided the content and purpose of the book by uniquely bringing together scholars from different fields in education: leadership, social foundations, language/literacy, special education, and research/measurement. These scholars share expertise for creating systemic, school-level responses to the differing needs and converging ecologies of marginalized groups of students.

We have explored systemic practices that support greater inclusion in schools, highlighting the crucial role of school leaders in defining and acting upon an inclusive vision, mission, systems, and practices. The important role of positive language in setting an ecologically systemic culture of respect will help frame a critical analysis of contemporary school culture, which encourages separation and categorization of students, and then offers this as being the only way to organize schools. Key research, about how we understand, talk about, and teach groups of students who are traditionally underrepresented in schools, is used to challenge current systems of school organization. School leaders are encouraged to view their school communities in a way that focuses on what can be and should be, in order to capitalize on student differences in making the school community and systems stronger and more effective for all students.

CREATING TRULY INCLUSIVE SCHOOLS

Truly inclusive schools require forms of leadership that respond to the social imperative to embrace, model, and promote inclusive practices in schools. Who are we as leaders, and how do we reflect upon and examine our own experiences, beliefs, and practices? By what criteria and processes do we examine the schools we lead with regard to equity and inclusion? How do we live out the moral imperative for change? The remaining chapters of this book provide context, structure, and examples to promote and support the reader in responding to these essential questions.

REFERENCES

Apple, M. (1995). *Education and power*. New York: Routledge.

Apple, M. (1996). *Cultural politics and education*. New York: Teachers College Press.

Armstrong, D., Armstrong, F., & Barton, L. (Eds.). (2000) Introduction. In *Inclusive education: Policy, contexts and comparative perspectives* (pp. 1–11). London: David Fulton.

D'Alessio, S. (2007). "Made in Italy": *Integrazione Scholatica* and the new vision of inclusive education. In L. Barton & F. Armstrong, F. (Eds.), *Policy, experience and change: Cross cultural reflections on inclusive education* (pp. 53–72). Dordrecht: Springer.

Emery, T. (1997, Spring). Embracing the dynamics of difference: Cultural competence in children's mental health. *Networks: National Technical Assistance Center Newsletter*. Retrieved June 5, 2010, from http://www.lib.utexas.edu/etd/d/2003/davists032/davists032.pdf

Erevelles, N. (2005). Rewiring critical pedagogy from the periphery: Materiality, disability, and the politics of schooling. In S. Gabel (Ed.), *Disability studies in education: Reading in theory and method* (pp. 65–84). New York: Peter Lang.

Ferri, B. (2009). Doing a (dis)service: Reimagining special education from a disability studies perspective. In W. Ayers, T. Quinn, & D. Stovall (Eds.), *Handbook of social justice in education* (pp. 417–430). New York: Routledge.

Fleming, J., & Love, M. (2003). A systemic change model for leadership, inclusion, and mentoring (SLIM). *Early Childhood Education Journal, 31*(1), 53–59.

Goffman, E. (1963). *Stigma: Notes on the management of spoiled identity*. New York: Simon & Schuster.

Institute for Inclusion. (n.d.). *Institute for Inclusion: Our definition of inclusion*. Retrieved May 31, 2010, from http://www.instituteforinclusion.org/index.php?option=com_content&view=article&id=28

Kasahara, M. (2006). Teacher training for inclusive education database project: Final report. Unpublished manuscript. World Bank, Washington, DC. Retrieved July 20, 2010, from http://web.worldbank.org/WBSITE/EXTERNAL/TOPICS/EXTSOCIALPROTECTION/EXTDISABILITY/0,,contentMDK:22197866~menuPK:6522289~pagePK:210058~piPK:210062~theSitePK:282699,00.html#sec1

Kliewer, C. (1998). *Schooling children with Down syndrome: Toward an understanding of possibility*. New York: Teachers College Press.

Kozol, J. (1991). *Savage inequalities*. New York: Harper.

Kunc, N. (1992). The need to belong: Rediscovering Maslow's Hierarchy of Needs. In R. Villa, J. Thousand, W. Stainback, & S. Stainback (Eds.), *Restructuring for caring & effective education: An administrative guide to creating heterogeneous schools* (pp. 25–40). Baltimore: Brookes.

Lynch, J. (2001). *Inclusion in education: The participation of disabled learners*. Paris: UNESCO.

Markus, H. (2008). Identity matters: Ethnicity, race, and the American dream. In M. Minow, R. Shweder, and H. Markus (Eds.), *Just schools: Pursuing equality in societies of difference* (pp. 63–100). New York: Russell Sage Foundation.

Minow, M. (1990). *Making all the difference: Inclusion, exclusion, and American law*. Ithaca, NY: Cornell University Press.

Mittler, P. (2000). *Working towards inclusive education: Social contexts*. London: David Fulton.

Moses, M. S., & Nanna, M. J. (2007). The testing culture and the persistence of high stakes testing reforms. *Education and Culture, 23*(1), 55–72.

Ryan, W. (1976). *Blaming the victim*. New York: Vintage Books.

Snow, K. (2009). *A few words about People First Language*. Retrieved May 20, 2010, from http://www.disabilityisnatural.com/images/PDF/pfl-sh09.pdf

Solorzano, D., & Yosso, T. (2002). Critical race methodology: Counter-storytelling as an analytical framework for education research. *Qualitative Inquiry, 8*(1), 23–44.

Stokes, D. (1997). *Pasteur's Quadrant: Basic science and technological innovation*. Washington, DC: Brookings Institute.

Udvari-Solner, A., Villa, R., & Thousand, J. (2002). Access to the general education curriculum for all: The universal design process. In J. Thousand, R. Villa, & A. Nevin (Eds.), *Creativity and collaboration: A practical guide to empowering students and teachers* (pp. 85–103). Baltimore: Paul Brookes.

Winant, H. (1998). Racism today: Continuity and change in the post–civil rights era. *Ethnic and Racial Studies, 21*(4), 755–766.

CHAPTER 2

Collaboration as Transformative and Inclusionary Leadership

Janice R. Fauske

Curtis Lee assumed the role of principal in July when teachers were away and the staff was a skeleton crew. About 20% of Washington Elementary's student population scored one in the state standardized tests in reading and math, which have a range of one (low) to five (high). It was not the lowest scoring school in the district, but it was close. Principals had come and gone, especially over the past 5 years. Curtis had been assistant principal at a school that had started with similar scores and had watched the school turn itself around under Principal Juanita Gomez, his mentor. Curtis studied Juanita as she made positive changes at the school, but harbored doubts about his own ability to lead such a turnaround on his own. Rumors were that teachers at Washington were frustrated, overwhelmed, and angry. They supposedly complained bitterly about the students' lack of ability. Although Curtis had heard that teachers in his previous school showed similar frustrations and negativity, he saw none of that when he was appointed assistant principal in the third year of Juanita's tenure as principal. He found a staff that was eager to grow and learn, a staff that was willing to work together and share new strategies. His first year as assistant principal coincided with the first year that every student in that school scored above one or achieved AYP under Juanita Gomez's leadership. Curtis wanted the same kind of turnaround for Washington Elementary. He learned from experience that he could only achieve his goal for students with mutual support from teachers and staff, by rewarding teachers' inquiry and thoughtful risk taking, setting clear expectations, and providing opportunities and support for professional growth. He believed that he and the staff could create the context for student success, and he laid out a plan based on Principal Gomez's example.

This chapter describes a systems view of inclusion in schools, a view that is immersed in the notion that members of the school community are engaged in a systemic relationship where one action influences a myriad of other actions. Specifically, the chapter explores the role of leader, of systemic leadership. School communities are coalitions of individuals and groups with enduring differences who come together for shared purposes that can transcend those differences, sometimes permanently, but often temporarily, in order to achieve shared goals. The school community is a living, changing, and dynamic entity with interconnected members, or stakeholders. Acknowledging this dynamic nature of the school community requires school leaders to underscore the elements of systems thinking and its implications for leader behavior. This dynamic educational community also requires that school leaders be continual learners who can approach the school community adeptly using a variety of lenses for understanding the human dimensions of a system. The school community includes the multitude of psychological, social, political, and cultural elements that define the humanity of the school as an organization. An organization is, in fact, its people. The extent to which individual and group purposes align with the purposes of the school and its community can enhance or impede the collective movement and ultimate success of the school in achieving shared goals. When the goal is the practice of inclusion, initiating a dialogue about a collaborative systemic approach to inclusion and establishing shared language related to the processes is vital.

This chapter first explores definitions, perceptions, and connotations of language used to describe forms of collaboration, coalitions, systems, and systems thinking. It then explains additional terms for clarity. A leadership framework for approaching the school community is outlined next, within the three dimensions of examining schools, including organization, social, and symbolic; these dimensions are reflected in a tool that can be used to dissect inclusion and related leadership practice for levels of implementation. The extended hypothetical example of Curtis Lee's principalship is offered to illustrate the effect of successful inclusive practices as a focus on systems renewal. The chapter describes a scenario of success where a school leader has created systemic changes focused on student performance. The text outlines the implications for school leadership, with specific strategies for influencing the school community of learners, monitoring change, and building trust, with emphasis on building capacity for school leaders to reciprocally influence those community entities that influence the schools. Moving on, the chapter explores strategies for changing schools, in relation to continuous improvement, and offers a step-by-step protocol for nurturing interactive, evocative dialogue about shared beliefs, values, and assumptions. The importance of language and symbols in setting broad-based expectations and systems for behaviors among school community members is also shared.

THE LANGUAGE OF COMMUNITY

Our use of language is fraught with assumptions, symbols, history, and connotations as well as the denotations that are both intended and unintended by the speaker or author. Exploring the assumptions embedded in our discourse can help us embrace the intended or challenge the unintended messages. The clear and precise use of language is pivotal in creating an environment of trust, mutual respect, and integrity based on meaningful, reflective, and professional dialogue. Several educational researchers have described essential elements for this dialogue; Burbules (1993), for example, contrasts *inclusive* and *critical* orientations. These both represent stances that people can take in reflective dialogue: On the one hand, the dialogue is accepting and inclusive; on the other hand, it is critical in the sense that ideas and assumptions are challenged. These opposing stances are the foundation of building community based on dialogue about tough professional challenges (Achinstein, 2002).

> It is the way teachers manage conflict—whether they suppress or embrace their differences—that has the greatest impact on the group and its potential for learning and change. Many teacher educators have found that the optimal means for encouraging critically reflective thinking in teachers is through communities of peers engaged in dialogue about educational issues and dilemmas or problems. (Wade, Fauske, & Thompson, 2008, p. 409)

Dialogue among teachers, staff, and school leaders is central to the notion of creating communities of inquiry and systemic thinking about school processes. Thus a primary function of language is building a community—a linguistic community (Young, 1990)—in which participants have a shared understanding about common purposes and processes and an opportunity to explore the translation of these into the practice of the school and classroom.

Often educators assume that other educators clearly understand their meaning when they speak about education. However, educators working shoulder to shoulder in the same school can have vastly different interpretations of terms and expectations (Marshall & Gerstl-Pepin, 2005). Inclusion and inclusive practices are explored in Chapter 1 and in this chapter. The concepts of systems, systems thinking, and communities of practice are clarified to support shared understandings and conversations in school. Systems in sociological terms are coalitions of people with shared language and goals who come together to achieve a shared purpose or task. Systems are not structural entities, but rather are the people themselves and their shared information/language and resources (Wheatley, 2005). A system can be open or closed to its environment or surrounding context (Scott, 1998; Wheatley, 2005). Schools are assumed to be open systems that interact and interconnect with their sociopolitical contexts. Schools interact daily with their environments, their contexts, in a variety of exchanges with community members, business, law enforcement, and parents, just to name a few. This environmental interconnectedness allows systems to thrive and avoid entropy, with school leaders acting as brokers among entities and groups in the broad school community (Wenger, 1998; Wenger, McDermott, & Snyder, 2002; Wheatley, 2005).

Systems thinking is applied as an analytical approach to schools that emphasizes the connectedness of multiple elements and persons within the school community. It seeks to look at the whole picture instead of breaking education matters down into smaller pieces for analysis. This type of analysis allows exploration and examination of complex, interconnected issues or problems. Systems thinking, applied to schools, acknowledges the complexity of tasks, relationships, and context of the school and classroom.

The dynamic nature of systems is related to the human dimension and to the information flow, primarily language, which is the substance of human interaction. Because language is central to human interaction, systems can be described as linguistic communities. Linguistic communities define a number of coalitions and groups that influence schools and schooling. Chapter 3 has outlined political dimensions of inclusion. Policy has used language to include or exclude people from groups, for example, those who are "like" thinkers, or those who have alternate views. Similarly, the use of language in schools shapes thinking about inclusion and the school leader has a major influence in how inclusion is framed. Language and labels determine who is included and who is not. Language is powerful, and the ability to use the robustness of language to shape thinking cannot be ignored (Marshall & Gerstl-Pepin, 2005). Because leadership has been positively linked to student performance as well as to the morale and productivity of the school (Leithwood, Louis, Anderson, & Wahlstrom, 2004; Leithwood & Mascall, 2008), a leader's actions and language become paramount in initiating change and sustaining the energy necessary for an inclusive school environment.

Language in schools includes policies and procedures surrounding curriculum, student behavior, teaching strategies, and a plethora of spoken and written professional and personal discourse. School leaders can examine the language of their school, particularly inclusion, to assess the linguistic community as an indication of the inclusiveness of a school. This assessment can highlight formal discourse and raise awareness of the informal discourse. For example, a school leader can focus on the use of People First Language across the school. Naturally, doing so also results in introspection and self-assessment of one's own language and action as leader.

Curtis spent most of his first summer gathering information from all those who came to the building and calling many of the teachers and staff. He listened to their concerns and asked about Washington Elementary's proudest moments. From what he learned, Curtis sensed a shared pride and commitment to the school and the students as well as a basic commitment to quality education. Poor student performance suppressed these positive factors. Teachers were frustrated at having to include certain groups of students in the overall school assessment. Educators viewed students who were transient, had special needs, or had limited English as a population negatively affecting the AYP. The language that some used to describe these students reflected deficit thinking and blamed the students.

At the opening of one school meeting, Curtis took a risk. After welcoming the faculty and staff, Curtis reflected aloud upon his conversations over the summer, and he spoke from the heart about his commitment to the school community. He reflected upon what he learned in those conversations about the challenges that the staff faced, and described the commitment that many displayed toward the school and its students. He applauded those who had sought out training in Response to Intervention (RTI) and other professional development as well as those who had reached out to parents for support of their students' success. He described the kind of collaboration and teamwork that was necessary to reach all the students, especially the lower scoring population. He ended his opening remarks with a strong statement and expectation: "My goal is that every student in our school will score above a one by the end of this year." The response was a mixture of energy and shock with an ample dose of skepticism. Curtis ended the meeting by pledging his commitment to support teachers/staff and "do what it takes" to meet this goal.

In this scenario, Curtis first sought to understand the language of school community members, then identified shared goals and reflected the shared message, while setting expectations and shaping a collective goal. His presen-

FIGURE 2.1. Circular Model for Enacting Systems Renewal

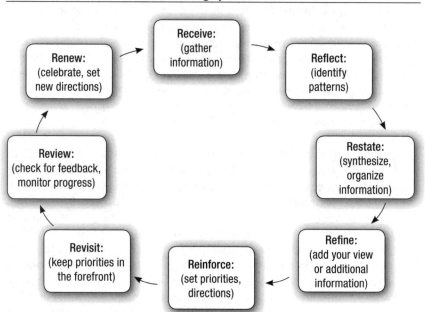

tation to staff makes explicit the interconnectedness of people and elements within the school. He gathered and considered the language of stakeholders, reflected back and highlighted themes, focused attention and energy on the positive, and made a commitment to a goal/theme that emerged as a shared concern. Figure 2.1 is a leadership tool for initiating and managing information flow, focusing on the ongoing renewal of schools as systems. It is a step-by-step protocol for nurturing interactive, evocative communication about shared purposes. The circular process is a form of action research that begins with gathering information and insights from a broad segment of the school community. The school leader reflects on and restates what he hears, and he analyzes the data for patterns and themes that reveal belief systems in the school. These patterns might include a shared doubt that some children can succeed in math, for example, or a shared view that the school is strong in writing strategies. There are usually both positive and negative patterns and themes. Generally, the school leader can refine the negative patterns into shared goals for improvement, and can refine the positive themes into elements promoting pride and cohesion. The school leader can also refine the patterns and themes by infusing information from best practices or other research direction resources (i.e., book study groups, peer observations) to expand and reinforce the goals for improvement. As the process continues, the school leader keeps the shared patterns and themes in the forefront by revisiting them regularly and by prioritizing collaborative work related to them. At the close of the year (or sooner as needed), the school leader and teachers review their work and progress, make adjustments, and celebrate successes. The process, of course, is iterative and may not proceed exactly step-by-step, looping back and forth instead. Still, it is a systemic approach to continual change and refocusing energy that can help school leaders themselves, as well as their schools, stay focused.

COCREATING COMMUNITIES OF PRACTICE

In theoretical terms, Curtis cocreated a community of practice with the stakeholders of his school (Scharmer, 2007; Wenger, 1998). The education literature has often called these communities *professional learning communities* (Dufour & Eaker, 1998; Hord, 1997; Louis & Kruse, 1995; Waters & Cameron, 2006) or *communities of inquiry* (Carr, Fauske, & Rushton, 2007). Darling-Hammond (2009) endorses professional communities as a means of empowering the school community, broadly conceived as inclusive of school personnel as well as parents, students, and other community groups or members. Many researchers have studied professional learning communities in educational settings, and numerous practitioners have implemented these kinds of communities. Scharmer (2007) has used the term, *communities of practice,* to connote the dimension of cocreation highlighted in that conceptualization and to acknowledge the collectivity of creating communities of practice. Fullan (2005) calls for building vertical and horizontal networks as a key step in initiating and supporting change in schools; these relational networks are necessary to sustain the community of practice over time. In addition to cocreating a community of practice, Curtis purposefully enacted both networks and activated human and related resources on behalf of the school. Certain patterns, conditions, and elements have emerged to define professional communities and provide criteria for assessing the success of such practices. Figure 2.2 offers a checklist for school leaders, which is adapted from several of the studies cited above.

The dual notions of cocreating communities of practice and building networks for sustainability goes well beyond the traditional structure of distributed leadership and site-based management (SBM). Although shared decision making is essential in creating an inclusive environment, Marshall and Gerstl-Pepin (2005) found it to be limited in effectiveness because of ambiguity about task, and because it often perpetuates the status quo views of difference. Consider the SBM of schools with high proportions of students with special needs, where there is little opportunity to access adequate

FIGURE 2.2. Communities of Practice Self-Assessment for School Leaders

Self-Assessment Questions	Evidence (people, groups, processes)	Next Steps
Have I provided a process for sharing best practices among teachers? across classrooms and grade levels? with parents?		
Have I facilitated an environment of distributed leadership? Do I solicit information and feedback from teachers and staff? from district personnel? from community representatives? from parents?		
Do I invite and reward innovation and inquiry?		
Do I share information freely and in a timely way?		
Do I model high expectations and authentic engagement for teaching and learning in my daily interactions with the school community?		
Am I consistent in my message about the meaning of inclusion and differentiated instruction? Do I allow competing ideas or activities to interfere with my commitment to inclusion?		
Do I actively seek out resources to support teacher growth?		
Have I provided processes for nurturing teachers and others in the school community?		

resources to meet needs. The SBM team in this school might be blamed for poor performance, when actually improving performance is beyond their control (Marshall & Gerstl-Pepin, 2005, p. 144). Conversely, the SBM team in a high-performing school might be praised for success that they did not initiate. At the district level these possibilities are aggravated by inattention to inequities across schools that can only be addressed by allocating more resources to the needier schools. In addition, simply working through existing teams and structures may not produce the desired result or level of energy needed for change because they perpetuate the status quo, re-plete with existing conflicts and limited thinking (Amin & Roberts, 2008; Wenger, 1998). The act of cocreating, where all participants can play a part, is the catalyst for change and improvement. Cocreation of communities of practice implies iterative and continual self-assessment and mutual agreement across the school. It requires authentic engagement and embraces difference in the decision-making process. It is dynamic, creating synergy and empowering all voices in the community.

Transformational Leadership

School leaders who create synergy can bring about improvements through shared vision building; continued professional dialogue and adequate resource support can transform schools. *Transformational* school leaders can have a tremendous influence on schools by emphasizing the value of shared work and by encouraging stakeholders to think beyond self-interests—to be people oriented while maintaining quality, as they pursue a collective vision and purpose of their work (Yukl, 2001). Attending to symbols and language and information sharing is one aspect of transformative leadership. Chapter 8 further explores this issue in relation to English as a Second Language (ESOL) students. In addition to the symbolic/language-based aspect, two others—social and organizational—must be addressed in order to enact inclusive thinking and practice in schools (Marshall & Gerstl-Pepin, 2005). Correcting the school's social and organizational dimensions of transformative leadership requires a leader's careful, honest scrutiny of staff attitudes and behaviors, as well as school operations. Shapiro and Stepkovich (2011) have described this kind of scrutiny, saying it enacts an ethic of critique, which drives ongoing assessment of status quo practice in schools that often disenfranchises those who are seen or labeled as "different." They offer a three-level analysis of ethical leadership, which includes perspectives of justice, caring, and critique. An ethic of justice evokes a leadership response of fairness and the absence of prejudice in actions and behaviors. An ethic of caring describes a leadership response that is people centered, valuing the well-being of students as well as all others in the school community. An ethic of critique involves analyzing the inherent and potential social injustices in schools and striving to make changes that resolve these injustices. Ethics in school leaders, staff, and teacher, then, can be defined as acting on, or enacting, attitudes and behaviors that reflect high regard for ethics of justice, caring, and critique while recognizing and embracing differences with respect and sensitivity. Observing high ethical standards can guide cocreation of communities of inclusive practice.

The ethic of caring is highlighted by a process of growth and change, where the school community is asked to work harder and smarter on behalf of students. Setting high expectations and inviting the staff to meet challenges through additional training, or by trying new strategies, can induce stress; these actions create pressure to perform. Stress and angst is a common response to change initiatives and can exacerbate differences in practice and opinion. Hargreaves (2001) described a kind of tension that emerges in the struggles that teachers and parents encounter when cultures clash within a school. Consider, for example, a teacher's middle-class expectations for attendance, homework, and performance clashing with a family expectation for children to care for siblings so both parents can work, leaving no time for attending school or completing homework. There are many other examples of differing views including notions of discipline, nutrition, and culturally specific behaviors, such as looking teachers in the eye. In Hargreaves's study the ongoing stress of these interactions exacts a cost in emotional labor for all stakeholders. By attending to potential and actual emotional labor when implementing change, school leaders will realize greater success and will engender mutual trust and support that can pervade the school community—teachers, staff, students, parents, and community members alike.

For systemic change and continual improvement in communities of practice, the need for nurturing and support are clear. Emotional labor from committed professionals can be nurtured by providing ongoing recognition for effort as well as resources and intrinsic support; these are largely functions of language and symbols, which can create both expectations and rewards for implementing inclusive practices.

Inclusion as Transformative Practice

Inclusive practice can take various forms and dimensions: academic inclusion (curricular access and participation, both policy and practice based), social inclusion (race, ethnicity, class, gender, sexual orientation, political stance, and religious beliefs), and organizational inclusion (access and opportunities for advancement, extracurricular activities, leadership, and authenticity of involvement) (Marshall & Gerstl-Pepin, 2005, p. 115). Schools have a variety of strategies and processes to support greater inclusive practices across the school. We present one tool for assessing the school's response to diversity and the level of inclusive practice in Figure 2.3. This is a matrix based on a typology created by Wade and colleagues (2008, pp. 416–420), which is adapted from discussions of multicultural education by Banks (2002, 2004), Nieto (2000), and Sleeter and Grant (1999). Figure 2.3 builds from the major categoriesin this typology, but has been broadened to focus on the three kinds

FIGURE 2.3. Assessing a School's Level of Inclusion

School Response	Description	Language	Assumptions About Practice
Business as usual	School functions as usual, does not differentiate practice.	Language largely ignores differences, presumes school is doing right thing.	Practices aim to help student learn the "system" through assimilation.
Remediating deficiencies	School practices promote assimilation.	Language locates deficits in the students and responsibility with teachers.	School is responsible for fixing the problem (e.g., teaching students to speak English).
Difference orientation	School practices value difference, but seek assimilation.	Language respects differences while presuming the goodness of the existing "system."	Practices use difference to help students assimilate (i.e., teach in native language to learn status quo content).
Human relations based	School practices promote tolerance, friendship, scrutiny of current practices.	Language honors differences, presumes changes are needed in current practice.	Practices focus on creating positive relationships among students and staff.
Transformative	School practices create inclusive spaces for teaching and learning.	Language focuses on social justice, mutual acceptance of difference.	Practices involve revision of curriculum and broadening strategies to integrate difference into the system.

of inclusion across various categories of diversity (Marshall & Gerstl-Pepin, 2005). This tool can help a school leader assess a school's responses to diverse students by assessing and classifying kinds of instruction and their underlying philosophies regarding inclusion for each category of inclusion: acadmic, social or organizational. This assessment is based largely on the language used by teachers and school personnel to describe these students and their attempts to teach these students. Thus the tool highlights the import of words, labels, opinions, and stances toward inclusion.

This tool offers a matrix for a developmental analysis of current practice in school on a continuum with transformative practice as the ultimate state of being, creating not only a system that promotes mutual acceptance, but also an inclusive system where differences are woven into the fabric of the school community. It also allows school leaders to see successes as well as need for improvement more clearly among academic, social, and organizational dimensions of inclusion.

Over the course of his first year, Curtis's commitment was tested many times. He consistently passed the test by providing training and support, rallying parents, and badgering the district for support. He held to his goal and high expectation, not letting teachers "off the hook." He led by example in his tireless work for student success. He created a small committee to generate a professional development plan based on feedback from surveying teacher needs. Teachers wanted more specific teaching strategies and better tools for managing student behavior. The committee recommended training in Response to Intervention (RTI) and Positive Behavior Support (PBS). Curtis arranged after-school professional development sessions and dedicated as much teacher workday time as he could to follow sessions.

Not all teachers chose to participate in all sessions, but by midyear almost half the teachers had attended at least one session for each area. In May of his first year, he was disappointed to see only marginal increases in student scores. Still, the movement was in a positive direction. Curtis wondered what should be his next steps and remembered his mentor Juanita's actions during this juncture of her turnaround at his previous school—to energize teachers in sessions where they defined the challenges, set strategies and benchmarks, and set a plan for continued dialogue about the strategies that most teachers had found effective.

He met with the school leadership team and asked them to highlight the "pockets of excellence" at the school that focused on instruction as well as connections to parents and support from the community. Together they laid out a comprehensive plan for training and development that included steps for teachers as well as staff and families; interaction/support from the community; and securing resources from the district and state. Curtis's main assignment in the plan was to garner support and resources—to get the word out that the school was changing. Dialogue that focused on student success continued between Curtis, teachers, staff, the leadership team, parents, and others in the school community.

The scores at the end of his second year as principal were much more encouraging, with over half of the students scoring above two and 75% of the students showing improvement. In spring of his third year he awaited the score report with great anticipation. That spring every student scored at least 2 (but only 10% were at level 2; 90% were 3 or above). In a cookies and milk reception Curtis celebrated the school's success. He praised teachers and students, sent out a newsletter and an editorial to the local newspaper, and recognized those who had participated in professional development with a certificate and a letter for their files. Amid cheers and tears, the school community rejoiced at their success and pledged to continue growing.

Curtis sat in his office after the celebration, assessing his approach, and called Juanita to share the news. He reflected on the journey of support versus pressure, of building trust through consistency. Before he retired for the night, he set new goals for the next 3 years.

Consistency and Trust

Trust is defined as consistency and predictability, based on repetition of outcomes and behaviors over time (Galvin & Fauske, 2000; Ring, 1996). Consequently, longitudinal relationships become important in sustaining communities of practice (Bryk & Schneider, 2002; Fullan, 2005). Implications of time and trust building for school leadership are clear. The school leader can build trust through consistent emphasis of mutually created goals and strategies, keeping the resources and energy of the school and its community efficiently focused. In the example of Curtis Lee trust in leadership and in the process of change emerged over time. School leaders can create safety nets for emotional labor and generate a sense of joining a journey, which is alternately rocky and smooth but always shared. School leaders thus can nurture the school vision and mission, as well as personnel, while simultaneously supporting and rewarding best practices.

In addition to consistency and predictability over time, being free to innovate, which is accompanied by a feeling of being valued, promotes trust among stakeholders; greater trust can in turn generate increased satisfaction in work, strong professional relationships, and ultimately a sense of joy surrounding the work environment and experience (Drucker & Senge, 2001). Fullan (2008) echoed the idea of joy or love as one of his six secrets of change, along with focusing on systems change, connecting colleagues with shared purpose, building human capacity, engaging in learning and professional growth as being the work of the community, and honoring transparency. Fullan expounds on his first secret of change for leaders, "Love Your Employees," (p. 21) and calls for building "high-quality" relationships with employees that are grounded in love (pp. 21–37). These notions of joyfulness and belonging exemplify a living, dynamic social system that is genuinely inclusive. Wheatley (2005) describes organizations, such as schools, as behaving similarly to living organisms when encountering changes. She suggests breaking the bounds of traditional professional organizations and work by organizing our work environments more as we organize our lives:

> If organizations behave like living systems, the following description of change should sound familiar: Some part of the system (the system can be any size—an organization, a community, a team, a nation) notices something. It might be

in a memo, a chance comment, or a news report. It chooses to be disturbed by this. *Chooses* is the important word here. . . . If it chooses to be disturbed, it takes in the information and circulates it rapidly through its networks. As the disturbance circulates, others grab it and amply it. The information grows, changes, becomes distorted from the original, but all the time it is accumulating more meaning. Finally, the information becomes so important that the system can't deal with it. Then and only then will the system begin to change. It is forced by the sheer meaningfulness of the information, to let go of present beliefs, structures, patterns, values. It cannot use its past to make sense of this new information. It truly must let go, plunging itself into a state of confusion and uncertainty that feels like chaos, a state that always feels terrible.

Having fallen apart, letting go of who it has been, the system is now and only now open to change. It will reorganize using new interpretations, new understandings of what's real and what's important. It becomes different because it understands the world differently. And, paradoxically, as is true with all living systems, it changed because it was the only way to preserve itself. (pp. 85–86)

In schools, teachers and school leaders often cling to structure, policies, procedures, and language that constrain rather than free us to be innovating and creative. Consider the role of school leader as initiator of systemic chaos, the creator of high expectations and modeling of authentic inclusions, and the enforcer of best inclusive practice. How quickly might those expectations spread through the system? How much meaning could the models and behavior accrue? How would the school recreate itself to accommodate the new information? Imagine the possibilities of living and working together in a joyous, inclusive community of practice.

REFERENCES

Achinstein, B. (2002). Conflict amid community: The micropolitics of teacher collaboration. *Teachers College Record, 104,* 421–455.

Amin, A., & Roberts, J. (2008). The resurgence of community in economic thought and practice. In A. Amin & J. Roberts (Eds.), *Community, economic creativity, and organization* (pp. 11–34). Oxford, UK: Oxford University Press.

Banks, J. A. (2002). *An introduction to multicultural education.* Boston: Allyn & Bacon.

Banks, J. A. (2004). Teaching for social justice, diversity, and citizenship in the global world. *Educational Forum, 68,* 295–305.

Bryk, A., & Schneider, B. (2002). *Trust in schools: A core resource for improvement.* New York: Russell Sage Foundation.

Burbules, N. (1993). *Dialogue in teaching: Theory and practice.* New York: Teachers College Press.

Carr, J., Fauske, J. R., & Rushton, S. (2007). *Teaching and leading from the inside out.* Thousand Oaks, CA: Corwin Press.

Darling-Hammond, L. (2009). Teaching and the change wars: The professionalism hypothesis. In A. Hargreaves & M. Fullan (Eds.), *Change wars* (pp. 45–68). Bloomington, IN: Solution Tree.

Drucker, P., & Senge, P. (2001). *Leading in a time of change: A conversation with Peter Drucker & Peter M. Senge* [VHS]. San Francisco: Jossey-Bass.

Dufour, R., & Eaker, R. (1998). *Professional learning communities at work: Best practices for enhancing student achievement.* Washington, DC: National Education Service.

Fullan, M. (2005). *Leadership & sustainability: Systems thinkers in action.* Thousand Oaks, CA: Corwin Press.

Fullan, M. (2008). *The six secrets of change: What the best leaders do to help their organizations survive and thrive.* San Francisco: Jossey-Bass.

Galvin, P. F., & Fauske, J. R. (2000). Transaction costs and the structure of interagency collaboration: Bridging theory and practice. In Bruce Jones (Ed.), *Educational leadership: Policy dimensions in the 21st century.* Stamford, CT: Ablex.

Hargreaves, A. (2001). Emotional geographies of teaching. *Teachers College Record, 103,* 6, 1056–1080.

Hord, S. (1997). Professional learning communities: What are they and why are they important? *Issues About Change, 6,* 1.

Leithwood, K., Louis, K., Anderson, S., & Wahlstrom, K. (2004). *How leadership influences student learning.* New York: Wallace Foundation.

Leithwood, K., & Mascall, B. (2008). Collective leadership effects on student achievement. *Educational Administration Quarterly, 44(4),* 529–561.

Louis, K. S., & Kruse, S. D. (1995). *Professionalism and community.* Thousand Oaks, CA: Corwin Press.

Marshall, C., & Gerstl-Pepin, C. (2005). *Reframing educational politics for social justice.* Boston: Allyn & Bacon.

Nieto, S. (2000). *Affirming diversity: The sociopolitical context of multicultural education.* New York: Longman.

Ring, T. O. (1996). Networked organization: A resource based perspective. *Studia Oeconomiae Negotiorum, 39,* 6–52.

Scharmer, O. (2007). *Theory U: Leading from the future as it emerges.* Cambridge, MA: Society for Organizational Learning.

Scott, W. R. (1998). *Organizations: Rational, natural and open systems.* Saddle River, NJ: Prentice Hall.

Shapiro, J. P., & Stepkovich, J. A. (2011). *Ethical leadership and decision making in education: Applying theoretical perspectives to complex dilemmas.* New York: Routledge.

Sleeter, C. E., & Grant, C. A. (1999). *Making choices for multicultural education: Five approaches to race, class, and gender.* Upper Saddle River, NJ: Merrill.

Wade, S., Fauske, J., & Thompson, A. (2008). Prospective teachers' problem solving in online discussions. *American Educational Research Journal, 45,* 398–442.

Waters, T., & Cameron, G. (2006). *The balanced leadership framework: Connecting vision with action.* Littleton, CO: McREL.

Wenger, E. (1998). *Communities of practice: Learning, meaning, and identity.* Cambridge, UK: Cambridge University Press.

Wenger, E., McDermott, R., & Snyder, W. (2002). *Cultivating communities of practice*. Boston: Harvard Business School Press.

Wheatley, M. (2005). *Finding our way: Leadership for an uncertain time*. San Francisco: Berrett-Koehler.

Young, R. (1990). *A critical theory of education: Habermas and our children's future*. New York: Teachers College Press.

Yukl, G. (2001). Leadership in organizations (5th ed.). Saddle River, NJ: Prentice Hall.

CHAPTER 3

Policy Matters:
Law, Policy, Practice, and Their
Relationships to Inclusivity

Julia M. White

Joey is entering the first grade. He has multiple disabilities that are considered "severe" by the school district. Joey was fully included in kindergarten, but the school that would be his home elementary school has determined that his needs are too significant for the general education first-grade classroom to accommodate. At his latest Individual Education Plan (IEP) meeting, school staff told Joey's mother that he would not be able to achieve a regular diploma and recommended that he be placed in a self-contained, multiage class at his home school that focused primarily on life skills, and that he would ultimately attend the "multiple and severe cluster school" for the region and receive an IEP diploma, which is basically a certificate of attendance. Joey's mother did not accept this assessment of her child or his placement, but was told that the self-contained class was the only option "for kids like Joey" at this school. Joey's mother was concerned about academics, Joey's opportunities to interact with children without disabilities, and the school's disregard of the law's mandate that Joey should be educated "to the maximum extent appropriate" with his nondisabled peers.

However, Joey's mother, who works two salaried jobs, does not have the financial resources to hire an attorney or take time off work to fight the school's determination of Joey's placement. Instead, she chose to place him in a school in another district, a 45-minute bus ride away, where he is still in a self-contained classroom, but participates in specials, lunch, and some cotaught academic classes with his nondisabled peers. Joey's mother now works with the regional higher education inclusion task force, the local advocacy center, and Joey's school to advocate for increased professional development in inclusive practice for all schools in the region.

Policy, and its interpretation and implementation, are integral parts of inclusive practice. Laws and regulations exist that support the schooling of all children equitably and fairly in schools, and it is incumbent upon school administrators to implement these policies in ways that provide equality of access to, opportunity for, and participation in school experiences through which all students can attain meaningful educational benefit. The vignette at the beginning of this chapter illustrates one school's denial of the provisions of equality of access to all students and another school's evolution toward inclusive practice. These schools, led by leaders who view the same student in somewhat different ways, are examples of how special education, which is distinctly identified as a "service" under the law, is transposed into a "place" where services are provided: the self-contained classroom. While one school views Joey as uneducable and would deny him any access to the general education classroom, the other school views him as conditionally educable and provides some access to the general education classroom. In both schools, Joey is considered an outsider, not fully belonging in the general education classroom in either place. Neither school truly works to build a school community that addresses children like Joey in respectful ways to negotiate perspectives and construct an environment that fosters recognition and belonging for all students.

In this chapter, I examine how policy matters—how policy structures how schools think about the meaning of education, what constitutes knowledge, how schools measure achievement, and how schools can work within the frameworks of policy toward a more socially just approach to creating learning communities that are true places of belonging for all students. The chapter begins with the legal history of inclusive education, from international treaties to local policy. Then it offers a social justice lens through which to critique the enactment of policy in schools, and tells how this lens can in turn inform a potential framework for school leaders to create schooling that is more inclusive.

THE LEGAL HISTORY OF INCLUSIVE EDUCATION

Education is a human right, as affirmed in Article 26 of the United Nation's *Universal Declaration of Human Rights* (UNDHR), which includes the full participation of all students, regardless of "race, color, sex, language, religion, political or other opinion, national or social origin, property, birth, or other status (UNDHR, 1948, Art. 2). Indeed, all human rights instruments prohibit discrimination in these areas. In response to concern over "inadequacies in education systems around the world and the growing recognition of the vital importance of basic education for social progress" (World Declaration on Education for All, 1990, preface) and to a report that 113 million children of school age worldwide are excluded from schools (Lynch, 2001, p. 3), the World Conference on Education for All was convened in Jomtien, Thailand, in 1990. The Jomtien Conference produced the *World Declaration on Education for All*, which stressed that one of the purposes of education is "to further the cause of social justice" (p. 3). This declaration affirms the international instruments that address the fundamental human right to education. Inclusive education is based on equality—equal access, equal opportunity, equal protection, and equal participation. "Differences that matter"—such as race, class, gender, religion, national, sexual orientation, and disability status—should not be viewed as a deficit and subsequently cause children to be segregated based upon a deficit model; rather, all students should be welcomed into their learning communities as full participants who have much to offer their peers. Inclusive education requires a "paradigm shift from the notion of 'learners with special needs' to the concept of 'barriers to learning and participation'" (Muthukrishna, 2000, para. 1).

Overview of International Human Rights Instruments

In the United States, 37% of people with disabilities drop out of school (U.S. Department of Education, 2006). The U.S. national completion rate, including all types of completion (diploma, GED, and so on), in 2006 was 74%, which means that a quarter of students did not complete school (Stillwell, 2010, p. 3). Among different student demographics 36.5% of Latino students, 38.6% of African American students, and 18.9% of European-American students do not complete school (Stillwell, 2010, p. 7). In addition, drop out rates, defined as 16- to 24-year-olds not enrolled in high school and lacking a high school credential, are 4% for middle-income, 2% for high-income, 9% for low-income students, and 33% for gay and lesbian students (Laird, Cataldi, KewalRamani, & Chapman, 2008, pp. 27–29; Lambda Legal, 2002, para. 13). Dropping out of school increases the chances that individuals will be under- or unemployed, receive social welfare benefits, be involved with substance abuse, and will be involved with the judicial system. People who are perceived to have "differences that matter" face marginalization, are stigmatized, and are oppressed socially, economically, and politically. Education is an economic, social, cultural, and political issue and is arguably the most important factor to ending the disenfranchisement of persons belonging to marginalized communities. Every United Nations human rights instrument includes language that lends itself to a justification of inclusive education for all students.

The fundamental human rights enshrined in international human rights instruments include, among others, the rights of nondiscrimination and equality under the law, freedom of movement, employment, and education. Following the establishment of fundamental rights in the UDHR, international conventions, treaties, and laws were instituted to protect these fundamental human rights, to hold States Parties accountable for the treatment of their citizens, and to prevent further international genocide in the aftermath of World War II. The other seminal United Nations human rights instruments are: the *International Covenant on Economic, Social and Cultural Rights* (ICESCR, 1966/1976); the *International Convention on the Protection and Promotion of the Rights and Dignity of Persons with Disabilities* (CRPD, 2006); the *International Convention on the Elimination of All Forms of Racial Discrimination* (ICERD, 1965/1969); the *International Covenant on Civil and Political Rights* (ICCPR, 1966/1976); the *Convention on the Elimination of All Forms of Discrimination against Women* (CEAFDW, 1981); and the *Convention on the Rights of the Child* (CRC, 1989/1990).

Article 7 of the United Nation's *Universal Declaration of Human Rights* (UDHR) clearly constructs equal protection under the law as a human right, which certainly applies to the law of most countries that mandate compulsory (and often free) education for all children:

> All are equal before the law and are entitled without any discrimination to equal protection under the law. All are entitled to equal protection against any discrimination in violation of this Declaration and against any incitement to such discrimination.

"Equal protection of the law" is also found in Article 26 of the *International Covenant on Civil and Political Rights*.

The right to education. Under the *International Covenant on Economic, Social and Cultural Rights* (1966/1976), States Parties should

> recognize the right of everyone to education. They agree that education shall be directed to the full development of the human personality and the sense of its dignity, and shall strengthen the respect for human rights and fundamental freedoms. They further agree that education shall enable all persons to participate

effectively in a free society, promote understanding, tolerance and friendship among all nations and all racial, ethnic or religious groups, and further the activities of the United Nations for the maintenance of peace. (Art. 13.1)

The *International Convention on the Protection and Promotion of the Rights and Dignity of Persons with Disabilities* (2006), the most recent human rights instrument and the first of the new century, deals specifically with education through Article 24, which recognizes the right to education "without discrimination and on the basis of equal opportunity" and encourages States Parties to "ensure an inclusive education system at all levels" (Art. 24.1). This article encourages States Parties not to exclude persons with disabilities from the general education system on the basis of disability (Art. 24.2.a), and to ensure that persons with disabilities "receive the support required, within the general education system, to facilitate their effective education" (Art. 24.2.d) "in environments that maximize academic and social development, consistent with the goal of full inclusion" (Art. 24.2.e). Article 5(v) of the *International Convention on the Elimination of All Forms of Racial Discrimination* and Article 10 of the *Convention on the Elimination of All Forms of Discrimination against Women* both reaffirm the right to education in their particular contexts. The *Convention on the Rights of the Child* also mandates the "right of the child to education . . . on the basis of equal opportunity" (Art. 28.1).

The United States has signed all of these treaties. The Bush administration stated that it would not sign the *Convention on the Rights of Persons with Disabilities* since it felt that the Americans with Disabilities Act was sufficient; however, on July 30, 2009, 6 months after President Obama took office, the United States signed the convention. The United States has ratified (which means that it must be incorporated into U.S. legislation) the *International Convention on the Elimination of All Forms of Racial Discrimination* and the *International Covenant on Civil and Political Rights*. The United States has signed, but not ratified, the *Convention on the Elimination of All Forms of Discrimination against Women* and the *International Covenant on Economic, Social and Cultural Rights*. Along with Somalia, the United States is the only other member to not ratify the *Convention on the Rights of the Child*. Along with Iran, Nauru, Palau, Qatar, Somalia, the Sudan, and Tonga, the United States has not ratified the *Convention on the Elimination of All Forms of Discrimination against Women*. Even if a state has signed, but not ratified a treaty, the state must make a good faith effort not to violate the treaty. The U.S. State Department announced in June 2009 that the United States is currently reviewing these two conventions for submission to the U.S. Senate for ratification (Verma, 2009). The United States is not currently reviewing the *International Covenant on Economic, Social, and Cultural Rights* for ratification, as the United States has traditionally taken the position that economic, social, and cultural rights are desirable social goals, but not fundamental rights (Amnesty International, n.d.). In light of the current debate on universal health care in the United States, it appears as though the current Obama administration is deciding not to engage with the Senate over this covenant. Even though States Parties can ratify treaties with reservations or clarifications, before changing U.S. legislation to reflect a treaty, there are concerns in some groups that ratifying these treaties would diminish U.S. sovereignty.

Human rights, sexual orientation, and gender identity. In December 2008 the Dutch and French delegations to the United Nations introduced a resolution to the United Nations which became a *Statement on Human Rights, Sexual Orientation, and Gender Identity.* As of March 2009, 67 member states, including the United States, have signed this statement (Wood, 2009). This statement reaffirms the universality of human rights and the principle of nondiscrimination enshrined in the human rights instruments discussed above, which includes the right to education and the freedom from exclusion.

Overview of National Human Rights Law and Policy

Although international law recognizes education as a fundamental human right, the U.S. Constitution does not recognize education as a fundamental right. Throughout the history of the United States, populations that manifest "differences that matter" have been denied participation in at least some aspects of American life. Before the 15th Amendment to the U.S. Constitution (1870), race counted in who was allowed to vote. Before the 19th Amendment (1920), gender counted in who was allowed to vote. Before the 24th Amendment (1964), ability to pay a poll tax counted in who was allowed to vote. The Voting Rights Act of 1965 (42 U.S.C §1973) eliminated all voting qualifications for any citizen of the United States. The Naturalization Act of 1790 (1 Stat. 103) granted citizenship to aliens who were "free white persons" alone, and not until 1965, through the amendments to the Immigration and Nationality Act (P.L. 89-236), were racial and national origin quotas for immigrants abolished.

Early in the twentieth century, individuals who were deemed "different" were denied access to schools and at times, up to the mid-twentieth century, they were denied access to public spaces. The Wisconsin Supreme Court (*Beattie v. Board of Education of Antigo,* 1919) upheld the Antigo Board of Education superintendent's refusal to enroll Beattie, a young man with a disability that caused him to drool and to have facial contortions, because "this condition nauseated the teachers and other students" (Yell, 2006, p. 62). Ugly laws, or, more accurately, "unsightly beggar ordinances" (Schweik, 2007, p. 59), allowed authorities to criminalize loiterers, beggars, or individuals who occupied public spaces on the basis of their appearance:

> No person who is diseased, maimed, mutilated or in any way deformed so as to be an unsightly or disgusting object or improper person to be allowed in or on the public ways or other public places in this city, or shall therein or thereon expose himself to public view, under a penalty of not less than one dollar nor more than fifty dollars for each offense. (Chicago Municipal Code, repealed 1974)

Many municipalities other than Chicago had these ordinances, but Chicago's was the last to be repealed. Historically, difference does matter, and policies such as these reflect how the "normate" (Thomson, 1997) looks at and thinks about difference. The term *normate* was coined by Garland Thomson (1997) as a means to disrupt and challenge the social construction of the word *normal*. These policies, around human variations that have been labeled as disability, constructed by "haves," relate to how the difference itself is positioned as a problem, not about the relationship of the policy to the construction of the problem.

Today, almost all areas of American public life are legally available to any citizen, except for one group. It wasn't until 1973 that homosexuality was removed from the *Diagnostic and Statistical Manual of Mental Disorders-II* (DSM-II), used by physicians, psychologists, and schools to identify psychiatric and mental disabilities. Today, the most recent edition of this manual, the DSM-IV-TR, continues to pathologize difference, in classifying Gender Identity Disorder in children, adolescents, and adults (302.6, 302.85) as a mental disorder. Gays and lesbians who publicly acknowledge their homosexuality until very recently have been prohibited from serving in the U.S. military under a now repealed federal law (10 U.S.C. § 654), known informally as the "Don't Ask, Don't Tell" policy. Accordingly, the presence of open gays in the military "would create an unacceptable risk to the high standards of morale, good order and discipline, and unit cohesion that are the essence of military capability" (10 U.S.C. § 654(a)(15)). So, while *Lawrence v. Texas* (2003) decriminalized private sexual behaviors between consenting same-sex adults, the military continues to criminalize gay soldiers.

Education practice. The history of education of students from minority populations in the United States can be characterized by Spring's (1994) methods of deculturalization, including (1) segregation and isolation, (2) forced change of language, (3) content of curriculum reflects culture of dominant group, (4) content of textbooks reflects culture of dominant group, (5) dominated groups are not allowed to express their culture and religion, and (6) the use of teachers from dominant group (p. 49). It was a crime to teach a slave to read and a crime for a slave to learn to read. Students from Native American communities were forced to attend American boarding schools where they were not allowed to speak their own languages, forced to participate in Christian rituals, and forced to assimilate into European American life. Even today, Native American students are the least likely of all student groups to graduate from college (Waterman, 2007). Chinese, Japanese, Korean, and other Asian students were sent to segregated schools alongside African American and Mexican American students.

The philosophical roots of inclusive education can be found in the seminal school desegregation case, *Brown v. Board of Education* (1954). This case found justification in the 14th Amendment of the U.S. Constitution, which states:

> No state shall make or enforce any law which shall abridge the privileges or immunities of citizens of the United States; nor shall any state deprive any person of life, liberty, or property, without due process of law; nor deny to any person within its jurisdiction the equal protection of the laws.

The *Brown* decision overturned *Plessy v. Ferguson* (1896), which had previously set the precedent of "separate but equal," and asserted that separate schools for students of color were not equal: "In these days, it is doubtful that any child may reasonably be expected to succeed in life if he is denied the opportunity of an education. Such an opportunity, where the state has undertaken to provide it, is a right which must be made available to all on equal terms" (*Brown v. Board of Education*, p. 493). While this decision hinged on desegregation based on race, it clearly paved the way for litigation to include students with disabilities and English language learners into regular classrooms, generalizing the scope of the case from race to ability and language, thus cementing it into the realm of human rights. The language of *Brown*, while adhering to the rights set forth by the Constitution, clearly follows a human rights agenda. The court concluded, "in the field of public education the doctrine of 'separate but equal' has no place. Separate educational facilities are inherently unequal" (p. 495).

Recent education legislation and court decisions. After *Brown*, the civil rights movement continued and a host of legislation related to civil rights was passed, including the Voting Rights Act of 1965, the Civil Rights

Act of 1964, and the Elementary and Secondary Education Act of 1965, reauthorized in 2001 as P.L. 1070-110, known as No Child Left Behind and referred to hereafter as ESEA. Titles III and IV of the Civil Rights Act (42 U.S.C. § 2000.c et seq.) pertain to education, as Title III prohibits barring individuals from public facilities based on race, religion, gender, or ethnicity, and Title IV deals with school desegregation. In 1973 the Equal Educational Opportunity Act (20 U.S.C. § 1703) was passed, which prohibits the denial of equal educational opportunity and prohibits the "deliberate segregation" of students on the basis of race, color, or national origin. ESEA currently covers a wide range of issues in education. Title I of this act sets out the mandates for "improving the academic achievement of the disadvantaged," Title III covers "language instruction for limited English proficient and immigrant students"; Title V, Part D, Subpart 21 contains the "Women's Educational Equity Act"; and Title VII deals with "Indian, Native Hawaiian, and Alaska Native education."

The *Brown* case was a campaign of decades—attorneys and activists searched for cases to test desegregation and worked within communities to mobilize parents and raise support for these test cases (Kluger, 1975). Similarly, the parents of children with disabilities in Pennsylvania and Washington, D.C., fought the segregation of their children and ushered in a new area of civil rights: disability. *Pennsylvania Association for Retarded Children (PARC) v. Commonwealth of Pennsylvania* (1971) was the first right to education lawsuit filed on behalf of children with disabilities. In this case, children labeled with mental retardation were "denied access to a free public program of education and training" (I.1). An important part of this case is expert testimony that states "all mentally retarded persons are capable of benefiting from a program of education and training . . . a mentally retarded person can benefit at any point in his life and development from a program of education and training" (II.4). This case also dealt with least restrictive environment issues, in that "placement in a regular public school class is preferable to placement in a special public school class and placement in a special public school class is preferably to placement in any other type of program of education and training" (II.7).

In *Mills v. Board of Education of the District of Columbia,* seven students (all were African American, some lived at home and some lived in institutions) with disabilities were denied a free public education in Washington, DC. The court found that the District of Columbia was "excluding, suspending, expelling, reassigning and transferring 'exceptional' children from regular public school classes without affording them due process of law" (p. 2). *Brown* is cited in this case to provide rationale for the equal opportunity of all students to be educated in a desegregated public school.

Incorporating findings from *PARC* and *Mills*, the Education of All Handicapped Children Act (Pub. L. No. 94-142, reauthorized in 2004 as the Individuals with Disabilities Education Improvement Act (IDEIA, Pub. L. No. 108-446) was passed in 1975. IDEIA mandates that students be provided with a free appropriate public education in the least restrictive environment. The text of IDEIA does not mention the word *inclusion,* but the law states that a student should be "educated in the school that he or she would attend if nondisabled," unless "the nature or severity of the disability is such that education in regular classes with the use of supplementary aids and services cannot be achieved satisfactorily" (p. 128). Courts have ruled favorably for inclusive education; for example, the 3rd Circuit Court, in *Oberti v. Board of Education* (1992/1993), ruled that schools cannot place a student outside of a general education classroom without providing supplementary aids and supports and making "sufficient effort" to include the student with nondisabled children.

The provisions of both the 2001 reauthorization of ESEA and IDEIA share many goals and areas of emphasis, addressing the nexus between general and special education, and in some ways move toward a more unified system of education. Both pieces of legislation emphasize reading achievement and the use of scientifically based instruction, materials, and interventions to ensure proficiency in basic skills for all students.

One of the major principles of IDEIA is the right to a "free appropriate public education" (FAPE). The first case before the Supreme Court challenging the law (then known as the Education of All Handicapped Children Act) was *Board of Education of the Hendrick Hudson Central School District v. Rowley* (1982), in which student Amy Rowley, who was deaf but able to read lips, was denied a sign language interpreter in school because she was doing very well in school even though she could only understand approximately half of what her teachers and classmates said. The Supreme Court decided that Congress, in passing the Act, did not intend to maximize the potential of students with disabilities, but rather to provide a "basic floor of opportunity" (p. 201) and instruction that would "enable the child to receive educational benefit" (p. 208). Although there has been no further FAPE challenge at the high court, the findings section of the reauthorized law (IDEIA) purports an extension of the basic floor of opportunity, in asserting that

almost 30 years of research and experience has demonstrated that the education of children with disabilities can be made more effective by . . . having high expectations for such children . . . and ensuring their access to the general education curriculum in the regular classroom, to the maximum extent possible, in order to . . . meet developmental goals and, to the maximum extent possible, the challenging expectations that have been established for all children; and . . . be prepared to lead productive and independent adult lives, to the maximum extent possible. (20 U.S.C. §1400(c)(5))

Clearly, Congress has raised the floor and has moved, through the partial conflation of IDEIA and ESEA, toward a more purposeful and meaningful way of looking at educational benefit and equality of educational opportunity.

Appropriate supports and accommodations are important to the education of students with disabilities and for English language learners. The *Oberti* case hinged on the provision of accommodations, supplementary aids, and services in the general education classroom. Like *Brown, Lau v. Nichols* (1974) was decided on the basis of the 14th Amendment, specifically, Title VI of the Civil Rights Act, prohibiting educational discrimination on the basis of, among others, national origin, where the Supreme Court found that the San Francisco school district did not provide appropriate accommodations to Chinese American students, thus denying them equal educational opportunity. *Lau* facilitated the growth of bilingual education programs from the 1970s through the 1990s, but the 2001 reauthorization of ESEA mandates that instruction for English language learners be grounded in "scientifically based research," and support for, and interest in, bilingual education programs has waned. Further evidence of the erosion of bilingual instruction can be found in *Horne v. Flores* (2009), in which the U.S. Supreme Court struck down a lower court ruling that Arizona violated the Equal Educational Opportunity Act clause mandating "appropriate action to overcome language barriers that impede equal participation" by students (20 U.S.C. §1703(f)) and remanded the case back to the lower court. The case was initiated in 1992, and the Supreme Court determined that during this time, Arizona moved from bilingual education to Structured English Immersion (SEI), noting that research and the Department of Education "support the view that SEI is significantly more effective than bilingual education" (p. 24). Hence, despite a continued achievement gap for Hispanic students in Arizona—a graduation rate of 64.7% in 2007 compared with a 73.4% total graduation rate (Arizona Department of Education, 2008)— the Supreme Court considers these students to have equality of educational opportunity.

SOCIAL JUSTICE, SCHOOL INCLUSION

"A policy frames the way we think and act" (Barton, 2004, p. 70); conversely, how we frame policy has a relationship to ways we enact those policies.

Social justice transcends law and the utilitarian ways in which schools classify students according to their abilities and then programmatically instruct them to achieve benchmarks and outcomes set out by policy. In this way students and schools are accountable to policy, instead of policy being accountable to students and schools. Carr (2007) asks, "What is the function of education in contemporary society?" (p. 7). In this era of accountability, when the focus of education seems to be passing standardized achievement tests, the purpose of education as set out by the *United Nations Universal Declaration of Human Rights* —"the full development of human personality and the sense of its dignity . . . [to] enable all persons to participate effectively in a free society, promote understanding, tolerance and friendship among all nations and all racial, ethnic or religious groups"—is increasingly diminished. Socially just schooling honors difference while "acknowledging our fundamental human equivalence" (Abu El-Haj & Rubin, 2009, p. 452).

CONCLUSION

This chapter has given a broad overview of policy that can be seen to have mapped a route for greater inclusion in school. However, the philosophical underpinning of the policy is based in social justice and equity that asks school leaders to take up the mantle of developing a socially just school. Socially just school leaders do not simply enter into a social contract with the intent of mutual reciprocity, or allocate resources based on cost-benefit, but work within the constructs of policy and systems to interrogate the structures that marginalize students and develop less oppressive structures that embed supports into the general education classroom that are "made available to support any or all students who need them, whenever they need them" (Ferri, 2009, p. 427).

REFERENCES

Abu El-Haj, T., & Rubin, B. (2009). Realizing the equity-minded aspirations of detracking and inclusion: Toward a capacity-oriented framework for teacher education. *Curriculum Inquiry, 39* (3), 435–463.

American Psychiatric Association Task Force on Nomenclatuer and Statistics. (1970). *Diagnostic and Statistical Manual of Mental Disorders-II* (DSM-II), Washington, DC: American Psychiatric Association.

Amnesty International. (n.d.). *Economic, social and cultural rights: Questions and answers.* Retrieved March 19, 2011, from http://www.amnestyusa.org/escr/files/escr_qa.pdf

Arizona Department of Education, Accountability Division, Research and Evaluation Section. (2008, November). *2007 four year grad rate for the state by ethnicity*. Retrieved March 19, 2011, from http://www.ade.state.az.us/Research-Policy/grad/2007/GradRate2007statebyethnicity2.pdf

Barton, L. (2004). The politics of special education: A necessary or irrelevant approach. In L. Ware (Ed.), *Ideology and the politics of (in) exclusion* (pp. 63–76). New York: Peter Lang.

Beattie v. Board of Education of Antigo, 172 N.W. 153 (Wisc. 1919).

Board of Education of the Hendrick Hudson Central School District v. Rowley, 458 U.S. 176 (1982).

Brown v. Board of Education, 347 U.S. 483 (1954)

Carr, P. (2007). Standards, accountability and democracy: Addressing inequities through a social justice accountability framework. *Democracy and Education, 17*(2), 7–16.

Chicago Municipal Code, § 36034 (repealed 1974).

Civil Rights Act, 42 U.S.C. § 2000.c et seq. (1964).

Education of All Handicapped Children Act (Pub. L. No. 94-142 (1975).

Elementary and Secondary Education Act (ESEA). Pub. L. No. 89-10, 79 Stat. 27, 20 U.S.C. § 236-41 (1965).

Equal Educational Opportunity Act of 1973. Pub. L. No. 93-380, § 204, 88 Stat. 484, 515, 20 U.S.C. § 1703 (1973).

Ferri, B. (2009). Doing a (dis)service: Reimagining special education from a disability studies perspective. In W. Ayers, T. Quinn, and D. Stovall (Eds.). *Handbook of social justice in education* (pp. 417–430). New York: Routledge.

Horne v. Flores, 129 S.Ct. 2579 (2009).

Immigration and Nationality Act. Pub. L. No. 89-236 , 79 Stat. 111 (1965).

Individuals with Disabilities Education Act, (IDEA). (2004). Pub. L. No. 108-446.

Kluger, R. (1975). *Simple justice: The history of Brown v. Board of Education and Black America's struggle for equality*. New York: Vintage.

Laird, J. Cataldi, E., KewalRamani, A., & Chapman, C. (2008). *Dropout and completion rates in the United States: 2006*. Washington, DC: National Center for Educational Statistics, U.S. Department of Education.

Lambda Legal. (2002). *Facts: Gay and Lesbian Youth in Schools*. Retrieved March 31, 2011, from http://www.lambdalegal.org/our-work/publications/facts-backgrounds/page-31991643.html

Lau v. Nichols, 414 U.S. 563 (1974).

Lawrence v. Texas, 539 U.S. 558 (2003).

Lynch, J. (2001). *Inclusion in education: The participation of disabled learners*. Paris: UNESCO.

Mills v. Board of Education of the District of Columbia, 348 F. Supp. 866 (D.C. 1972).

Muthukrishna, N. (2000). *Transforming the system: The development of sustainable inclusive education policy in practice in South Africa*. Retrieved March 31, 2011, from http://www.isec2000.org.uk/abstracts/keynotes/muthukrishna.htm

Naturalization Act of 1790 (1 Stat. 103).

No Child Left Behind Act of 2001. Pub. L. No. 1070-110, 115 *Stat.* 1425 (2002).

Oberti v. Board of Education, 789 F.Supp. 1322 (D.N.J. 1992).

Pennsylvania Association for Retarded Citizens (PARC) v. Commonwealth of Pennsylvania, 334 F. Supp. 1257 (E.D. Pa. 1971).

Plessy v. Ferguson, 163 U.S. 537 (1896).

Policy concerning homosexuality in the Armed Forces. 10 U.S.C. § 654

Schweik, S. (2007). Begging the question: Disability, mendicancy, speech, and the law. *Narrative, 15*(1), 58–70.

Spring, J. (1994). *Deculturalization and the struggle for equality: A brief history of the education of dominated cultures in the United States.* New York: McGraw-Hill.

Stillwell, R. (2010). *Public school graduates and dropouts from the common core of data: School Year 2007–08* (NCES, 2010-341). Washington, DC: National Center for Educational Statistics, Institute of Science, U.S. Department of Education. Retrieved from http://nces.ed.govpubsearch/pubsinfo.asp?pubid=2010341

Thomson, R. G. (1997). *Extraordinary bodies: Figuring physical disability in American culture and literature.* New York: Columbia University Press.

U.N. General Assembly. *Convention on the Elimination of All Forms of Discrimination Against Women* (CEAFDW), G.A. Res. 34/180, 34 U.N. GAOR Supp. (No. 46) at 193, U.N. Doc. A/34/46 (1981).

U.N. General Assembly. *Convention on the Rights of the Child* (CRC), G.A. Res. 44/25, annex, 44 U.N. GAOR Supp. (No. 49) at 167, U.N. Doc A/44/49 (1989/ in force 1990).

U.N. General Assembly. *International Convention on the Elimination of All Forms of Racial Discrimination* (ICERD), G.A. Res. 2106 (XX), Annex, 20 U.N. GAOR Supp. (No. 14) at 47, U.N. Doc. A/6014 (1965/in force 1969), 660 U.N.T.S. 195.

U.N. General Assembly. *International Convention on the Protection and Promotion of the Rights and Dignity of Persons with Disabilities* (CRPD), G.A. Res. 61/106, Annex I, U.N. GAOR, 61st Sess., Supp. No. 49, at 65, U.N. Doc. A/61/49 (2006).

U.N. General Assembly. *International Covenant on Civil and Political Rights* (ICCPR), G.A. Res. 2200A (XXI), 21 U.N. GAOR Supp. (No 16) at 52, U.N. Doc A/6316 (1966/in force 1976).

U.N. General Assembly. *International Covenant on Economic, Social and Cultural Rights* (ICESCR), G.A. Res. 2200A (XXI), 21 U.N.GAOR Supp. (No. 16) at 49, U.N. Doc. A/6316 (1966/in force 1976), 993 U.N.T.S. 3.

U.N. General Assembly. *Statement on Human Rights, Sexual Orientation and Gender Identity,* 18 December 2008. Retrieved June 30, 2011, from http://www.unhcr.org/refworld/docid/49997ae312.html

U.N. General Assembly. *Universal declaration of human rights* (UNDHR), G.A. Res. 217A (III), U.N. Doc. A/810 at 71 (1948).U.S. Const. amend XV (1870).

U.S. Const. amend XIX (1920).

U.S. Const. amend XXIV (1964).

U.S. Department of Education, Office of Special Education and Rehabilitative Services, Office of Special Education Programs. (2006). *26th Annual (2004) Report to Congress on the Implementation of the Individuals with Disabilities Education Act* (Vol. 1). Washington, DC: Author.

Verma, R. (2009, 11 May). *White House treaty priorities list.* Retrieved March 19, 2011, from http://www.globalsolutions.org/files/general/White_House_Priorities_List.pdf

Voting Rights Act of 1965 (42 U.S.C §1973)

Waterman, S. (2007). A complex path to Haudenosaunee degree completion. *Journal of American Indian Education, 46* (1), 20–40.

Wood, R. (2009, 18 March). *UN Statement on "Human Rights, Sexual Orientation, and Gender Identity* [Press release]. Washington, DC: Bureau of Public Affairs. Retrieved March 19, 2011, from http://www.state.gov/r/pa/prs/ps/2009/03/120509.htm

World Declaration on Education for All. (1990). Adopted by participants at the World Conference on Education for All, Jomtien, Thailand.

Yell, M. L. (2006) *The law and special education* (2nd ed.). Upper Saddle River, NJ: Pearson.

Part II

EXAMPLES AND STRATEGIES FOR INCLUSIVE PRACTICE

This Part presents examples of strategies and processes that can help a school leader promote successful inclusive practices. The examples come from the perspective of special education, literacy, and youth justice.

Special education, covered in Chapter 4, is where Phyllis Jones illustrates the powerful role of professional attitudes, knowledge, and skills in creating (or destroying) positive inclusive experiences for students and families. This chapter demonstrates the need for schools to create robust and accountable systems of support based upon individual strength, learning preference, and need—systems of support with high expectations for every student, accepting that not all students learn in the same way. More specifically, this chapter explores the contributions of well-differentiated teaching and learning to proactively respond to the best practices of Least Restrictive Environment (LRE), Response to Intervention (RTI), Schoolwide Positive Behavior Support (PBS), and well-differentiated teaching and learning.

The way a community defines literacy has the capacity to include or exclude certain members, according to Chapter 5. G. Pat Wilson demonstrates how literacy builds and binds a community system by contributing to its collective knowledge, understandings, and, therefore, its values. The extent of inclusiveness in the school community system is reflected in how literacy is defined: by instructional practices in place, by the literature, by the multimodality of text being read and composed. The level of inclusion is also reflected in the role that individuals (teachers, staff, children, parents, community members) and their respective ecologies play in building an inclusive literate community. Literacy is defined, and its role in an inclusionary community is explicated; the research-based components of literacy instruction in inclusionary communities are reviewed; and implications for leaders' support of literacy for systemically building and sustaining an inclusionary community are offered.

School leaders are encouraged to appreciate the role of literacy in relation to each individual's capacity to respond to, make sense of, and help build the world. Development of an appreciation of the role of literacy in a school is enhanced through an examination of how literacy is impacted by the larger sociopolitical/historical community, the local community, and the school community. Throughout the chapter, school leaders explore a comprehensive language arts program that promotes an underlying value of diversity within the school community and adopt a participatory stance where authority does not reside in texts alone, but in teachers and students as well.

Youth justice, explored in Chapter 6, brings a different and refreshing experience of working with young people who are at risk of or have actually dropped out of school or who have failed the formal system. Jenni Menon Mariano examines the conditions that must exist in order for us to develop an education system that realizes the ideals of inclusion in a way that is beneficial and effective for all learners. These conditions are societal and include the commitment of necessary resources to education on behalf of policy makers in government. They are psychosocial and include the cognitive, behavioral, and emotional development and learning of children and adults. Examining these latter variables is critical because no policy measure is adequate by itself as a measure to make inclusion fully realized: Hearts and worldviews must undergo a change. This point is illustrated via the example of desegregation of schools following *Brown v. Board of Education.*

CHAPTER 4

Differentiation: Positive Attitudes and Inclusive Practices for Students with Exceptional Needs

Phyllis Jones

Conrad is a 9-year-old boy with Down Syndrome. He has significant learning issues and is just beginning to read one or two words. He is the youngest of four boys. All the way through school, from pre-K through second grade, Conrad was included fully in both school and out-of-school activities. Second grade was possibly Conrad's best school placement experience. His teacher had a background in special education, which enabled her to create an environment where Conrad's needs were met, academically and socially. The class had a full-time paraprofessional who helped the teacher provide individual support and supervision. Conrad was a part of all school activities and was invited to birthday parties outside of school. Conrad's teacher fully believed that having Conrad in her class enhanced the learning of *all* students. She also understood that the lessons Conrad would teach her and the other children were priceless.

Conrad's mother wrote this brief vignette about successful inclusive experiences in elementary school. Throughout this chapter, Conrad's story will inform the discussion to illustrate the powerful role of professional attitudes, knowledge, and skills in creating (or destroying) positive inclusive experiences for students and families. The chapter shows how important it is for school leaders to create robust and accountable systems of support, which are based upon individual strength, learning preference, and need.

The systems of support they create should have high expectations for every student while at the same time accepting that not all students learn in the same way. The chapter focuses on teaching students with exceptionalities (labels of gifted and disability) but the processes that school leaders employ for this group of learners can also be applied to all learners in school.

Currently, learning support in American schools is mainly created around a categorical-based system (IDEA, 2004 & Section 504 that relate to educational and civil rights protection for children with disabilities). Even though Response to Intervention (RTI) is heralding a change in identifying children with specific learning disabilities, students earn their place in exceptional student education (ESE) through their performance on IQ tests or other standardized measures. Labels carry major implications for the students and their families both in and out of school. Many schools are structured according to labels of exceptionality and many times students are placed in classes with others who share the same label. Individual Education Plans (IEPs) spell out the specific goals and intervention strategies a team of professionals, including parents, have decided the student needs. Barton (2004) warns that forms of reference to special educational need (labels) are often synonymous with notions of failure. Indeed, many students who receive a label have to demonstrate some inability to do something; they are seen as unsuccessful and not reaching the "norm." School experiences are created around the information in the IEP, and IEP goals are tracked and evaluated according to adherence to policy (IDEA, 2004). This approach to systems of support and intervention, which is illustrative of historical practices, can be interpreted as leading to more segregated service delivery models (Barton, 2004; Byrom, 2004).

In second grade, Conrad's experience was the exception to traditional schooling for students with Down syndrome; he was successfully included in a meaningful way where his presence in the second-grade class was seen as a positive contribution. However, at the end of the academic year the situation for Conrad changed, as recounted by his mother here:

> When second grade was ending, we were faced with making the decision about Conrad's placement for the following year. The IEP team agreed that for the first time, inclusion might not be appropriate for Conrad. He was showing signs of being frustrated, wanting to do the worksheets, write the paragraphs, read the stories that the rest of his classmates were assigned. He was working on letter recognition and simple words, but watched his peers accomplishing much higher level tasks. This was becoming a problem that the IEP team felt would become an even greater gap in the older elementary grades. In order to meet Conrad's academic needs, and in order to avoid the frustration of his having different work from his peers, it was agreed that

Conrad would benefit from spending a greater amount of time in a self-contained environment. The suggestion was made to have his academics taught in a Varying Exceptionalities (VE) classroom, and then spend nonacademic times like lunch, recess, fine arts, PE, field trips, and the like with his grade-level peers. My greatest fear as a parent of a child with special needs is that the system will stop trying to teach my son. However, the school Conrad was attending had just lost the VE teacher and was in the hiring process. I was very worried. Another problem was finding a third-grade teacher who was willing to work to include Conrad in her class during the times Conrad would be mainstreamed. This proved to be very difficult, and Conrad's experience with his typically developing peers was drastically reduced in the third grade. Conrad began to copy behavior he saw in the VE classroom and his previous academic progress began to regress.

Conrad was "seen" to not fit into the third-grade general education classroom, and it was assumed that he required a learning environment that was different from his peers in the general education class. This is unfortunate and has potential lifelong repercussions for Conrad and his family. Conrad's story highlights some problematic issues related to professional attitudes toward difference in children and teacher understandings of how instruction can be differentiated to meet the learning strengths, needs, interests, and preferences of students who present as different. School leaders are in a prime position to influence teacher attitudes toward exceptionality by role modeling how valuable such learners are for the school community.

ATTITUDES TOWARD DIFFERENCE

In Conrad's situation, his IEP team believed that he had become too different to be included in general education; his learning needs had become too dissimilar from his typically developing peers. This conclusion reflects a particular attitude toward difference, disability, and inclusion. That is, students can only be included if they are close to "normal" (whatever "normal" is perceived to be), but will be excluded as soon as their behavior and responses move too far away from a view of normality, however it is perceived. In the United States, a psychological framework influences this view of normality where individual deficits are identified in order to develop individual solutions (Young & Mintz, 2008). This approach to difference applies to students across the wide continuum of learning diversity. For example, students who present as gifted and talented are given a label and often taught in separate contexts, which have far-reaching implications for the students. This approach to difference represents a medical and individual construct of disability that views disability as a problem to be solved (Brechin, 1999). Invariably, this construct has negative connotations for how students with exceptionalities are perceived (Kliewer & Bicklin, 1996). A social construct of disability does not see disability as a problem to be solved but instead embraces the role of context and environment in appreciating diversity in a community (Corker & Shakespeare, 2006). These two theoretical perspectives of disability lead to different ways of understanding and responding to students with disability labels. Social constructs of difference, diversity, and disability help us to appreciate the traditional organizational structures that have prevented students from accessing social and academic experiences (Young & Mintz, 2008). Indeed, in another school, in another district, or in another state, it is possible that Conrad would be placed in a general education classroom with carefully tailored instructional, social, and emotional support. In this different schooling scenario Conrad has not changed, but the school environment has evolved to welcome and include him meaningfully.

Nurturing Positive Attitudes

Teacher attitudes matter; they are inextricably related to notions of professional values, which have a major impact on how a teacher responds to students (MacArthur, 2004). However, school leaders have the potential to inform and shape how students with (or without) labels of exceptionality are viewed. They set the expectations as well as the tone of the learning community. They are also in a rare position to shape teachers' understandings of disability/exceptionality and to help teachers connect their understandings to their attitudes and classroom practice. In order to do this, school leaders must be willing to reflect upon their own understandings and attitudes toward exceptionality and difference, remembering that historical influences on schools have traditionally come from the medical model of disability. They can then facilitate a supportive but rigorous environment, encouraging teachers to question their own understandings and attitudes.

In Conrad's story, attitudes were influential in two ways. First, it was agreed by the IEP team that because Conrad was showing signs of frustration about not doing the "same" work as his peers, he would need another placement. The reality is that Conrad does require individualized interventions and may need different work than his peers, and this will become more marked as he becomes older and moves through school. This is a simple fact of Conrad's life. The message he and his classmates receive when he is moved to a more restrictive environment is that difference is not welcomed in their learning community. What does this communicate to Conrad and his peers about tolerance and acceptance of any form of difference? Alternatively, this could be an opportunity for Conrad to be supported in a personally meaningful way. He is going to be different from his peers and many times his schoolwork will be varied (but perhaps not all of the time). Conrad's social and emotional well-being is related to valuing who he is as a person. For Conrad to value his own difference it also needs to be valued by those around him. It is also important for Conrad to appreciate the similarities he shares with his peers, something that is difficult to achieve when Conrad's differences are always highlighted.

In Conrad's story, his mom was worried about finding a teacher who would be "willing" to include her son and she acknowledges that a positive attitude of the teacher is crucial to her son's successful inclusion. A school leader who is serious about impacting successful inclusive practices pays attention to offering professional learning opportunities for the school to understand different constructs of disability and how these impact attitudes and practices is crucial. One approach could be to invite adults with exceptionalities into the school to share their school experiences and perspectives of schooling. This offers teachers an opportunity to hear about the past school experiences of people with exceptionalities; the stories may not be pretty, and teachers can be sensitively guided to reflect on their own classrooms in the light of such stories. Many teachers do not realize that under current legislation, students should be considered for a Least Restrictive Environment in the first instance (IDEA, 2004). Indeed, school leaders themselves can benefit from a clear understanding of LRE and how it applies to all students with exceptionalities across the school.

Understanding Differentiation

Naturally, when Conrad is in any classroom, his meaningful participation in learning must be effectively managed. Teachers and school leaders can promote professional practices that effectively meet diverse learning profiles by building up differentiated teaching and learning practices across the school. *Differentiation* is a common term in every school, but it is important to be aware that in some schools and with some teachers the term *differentiation* may carry negative connotations. One strategy a school leader may choose to employ is a process that highlights similarities rather than differences. Figure 4.1 illustrates a student/class profile that a school leader can promote to support a move toward a more complete view of students with exceptionalities, which also highlights similarities across learners. A school leader can use this tool with individual teachers or grade-level teams to support a more positive view of the participation and contribution of a student who may present as very different.

For many teachers, differentiation may equate to students with exceptionalities being placed in their classroom with an expectation for them to differentiate teaching without the professional skills and support to do so. This occurs for students who are labeled as disabled or gifted. Differentia-

FIGURE 4.1. A Student/Class Learning Profile

Student name:	Class:
Preferred learning styles:	Peers who share these styles:
Student interests:	Peers who share these interests:
Proven successful teaching strategies for student:	Peers who respond well to these teaching strategies:
Student learning needs (from IEP):	Peers who share these learning needs:

tion may look very different for these two groups of learners. Students with intellectual disabilities may need differentiated instruction in order to support their engagement with key concepts of the task whereas students who are gifted need scaffolds to support their engagement with higher and more abstract concepts. Some teachers may equate differentiation to individualized instruction and believe they are expected to differentiate for the 30 students in their class.

Other teachers may believe that differentiation occurs in other settings (self-contained classrooms, resource room provision) and does not apply to their classroom. A school leader has the opportunity to frame the school's approach to differentiated teaching and learning and ensure there are shared understandings, expectations, and practices that are supported through targeted professional development and resources. Differentiation, tiered lessons, and collaborative practices can offer schools a powerful way to create successful learning environments. Tomlinson (2001) captures the nature of differentiation: "In a differentiated classroom, the teacher proactively plans and carries out varied approaches to content, process, and product in anticipation of, and response to, student differences in readiness, interest and learning needs" (p. 7). It sounds simple in text but can be very complex to ensure quality implementation in classrooms and requires vigilant attention by the whole school community. Differentiation as a concept has had a long and successful history in gifted education where teachers have been cognizant of engaging students in higher levels of conceptual skills by changing the content, process, or product of the task (O'Meara, 2010). Kaplan (2009) extends this concept to discuss the need to "layer" differentiated instruction for students who are gifted that has the content of the curriculum as a standard foundation for subsequent layers; the layering approach supports a depth of study that allows the "student's attention on increasingly more difficult, divergent, and abstract qualities of knowing a discipline or area of study" (p. 115). The process of layered differentiation is complex, and teachers would benefit from access to ongoing support to build up their capacity to plan and teach in this way.

Differentiation as a process is multifaceted and demands teachers be confident and competent working with varied instructional approaches. It is linked to the fundamental ideas set out in the Universal Design for Learning (UDL) approach, which admonishes traditional approaches of "one-size-fits-all" teaching and learning that leads to the creation of barriers to learning for many students. Supporters of UDL affirm: "Learners with disabilities are the most vulnerable to such barriers, but many students without disabilities also find that curricula are poorly designed to meet their learning needs" (National Center for Universal Design for Learning, 2011, para. 2).

UDL naturally applies to all students who have a varied learner profile, including students who are labeled as gifted. UDL asks schools to be proactive in paying attention to three principles that underpin well-differentiated pedagogy (Hall, Stangman, & Meyer, 2003):

- To provide multiple means of representation. This is the "what" of learning and appreciates that students differ in the ways they perceive and comprehend the information presented to them.
- To provide multiple means of expression. This is the "how" of learning and appreciates that students differ in the ways they navigate learning and are able to express what they know.
- To provide multiple means of engagement. This is the "why" of learning and appreciates that students can be engaged or motivated to learn in many different ways.

The process of assessment for learning is a crucial component of successful UDL and differentiated practices. Assessment for learning is quite simply data-driven instruction where teachers collect student performance data and analyze this data to inform future instructional planning. School leaders have an important role in facilitating the process of assessment for learning and ensuring the process includes all students across the spectrum of abilities; indeed, it has been shown that the most effective leaders facilitate ongoing data-driven instruction (Fenton & Murphy, 2010). This may mean providing ongoing professional development and creating time in the busy school day to talk about student progress.

The practicalities of including students who learn very differently into any class can be challenging, and Conrad's mom worried about this: "My greatest fear as a parent of a child with special needs is that the system will stop trying to teach my son." Often, students are placed in general education classrooms without adequate support and many do not have their individual needs met. This is unacceptable for both students and teachers, and school leaders must be constantly aware of such situations.

School leaders, as advocates for the most effective teaching and learning, can support teachers in employing strategies to ensure individual student needs are effectively met in LREs. This can be achieved by building systems of support (for teachers and students) in school that are accountable and explicitly valued. School leaders, working with knowledgeable special educators, have the decision-making authority to create a context and enact systemic change that can have a genuine impact on these processes. This may involve school leaders revisiting the way teams of professionals work across a school (Villa & Thousand, 2005). For example, a school leader may support a coteaching model where general and special educators share responsibility for all students in a class or a transdisciplinary team meeting structure where a wide range of professionals come together and share expertise to facilitate changes in the classroom environment to support more successful learning. In a more inclusive environment, other learning partners take on more responsibility for learning, including the students themselves. School leaders, who capitalize upon the contributions of students, parents, families, teaching assistants, curriculum experts, instructional technology experts, and others are in a stronger position to offer supported meaningful learning experiences.

EFFECTIVE PLANNING FOR DIFFERENTIATED INSTRUCTION

Differentiated teaching and learning also calls for different approaches to lesson and unit planning (Moll, 2005). Figure 4.2 illustrates the features of an effective differentiated lesson plan (or unit plan) in a format that school leaders can use to review teacher plans. SMART objectives play an important role in a well-differentiated plan; SMART stands for Specific, Measurable, Attainable, Realistic, and set within a Time frame (Bartle, 2010). One way SMART objectives can be used in a differentiated lesson plan is through tiered lesson planning. In the following example the teacher has three different objectives for three groups of learners in the class: on-level, below-level, and above-level students.

- Tier 1—on-level students will create a seven-sentence paragraph in 30 minutes using a dictionary.
- Tier 2—below-level students will create a three-sentence paragraph in 30 minutes with key words given.
- Tier 3—above-level students will create two paragraphs of seven sentences in 30 minutes using a dictionary.

FIGURE 4.2. Form for Evaluating a Differentiated Lesson Plan

Element of Differentiated Lesson Plan	Present (Yes or No)	Comment
Are curriculum standards included?		
Is information about learning context included?		
Are differentiated student groupings included?		
Are SMART objectives for the lesson included? (These may be varied for different student groups where appropriate and would include accommodations and modifications.)		
Are optimal teaching strategies included? (These may also include accommodations, modifications, Assistive Technology, and additional multisensory resources.)		
Is assignment of adult roles clarified?		
Is assessment of learning included that links back to SMART objectives?		

Greater differentiated learning is promoted through teacher planning that includes these characteristics; formats may change from year to year or subject to subject, but the elements should remain standard. School leaders, who set expectations for and support planning of this nature, offer a strong message about expectations that are also an integral part of the school accountability system. Sharing positive examples as models of effective planning across the school can help teachers who may need additional support.

Planning is the first step in achieving meaningful participation for all learners; however, the crucial part is how such planning is translated into practice. For some teachers, the learning objectives on an IEP may seem too different from the experiences they create in the classroom. This can lead to stress and frustration, and teachers may decide they do not want the students in their classroom at all. In these instances, school leaders can encourage the use of an *infused grid* (Beech, McKay, Barnitt, & Orlando, 2002). An *infused grid* is a planning document that sets out where students' IEP targets (or learning priorities) are going to be met throughout the day. It was initially developed for students with more complex needs but is an excellent tool for scheduling direct instruction. In an infused grid, teachers identify, across the school day, where the student is going to have a natural encounter with a situation that relates to a personal objective or learning priority, a situation where the student engages in activities related to the learning profile. School leaders need to help teachers make decisions about where direct and explicit instruction is going to take place throughout the day. Students with learning differences must have access to explicit and regular direct instruction (Beech et al., 2002). Figure 4.3 presents an example of an infused grid format, which maps out a student's individual IEP/learning priority goals across classroom/school/curricular experiences. Remember, this grid would only be used for students who have an IEP.

The infused grid creates an instructional map that is manageable and can be shared across professionals in the school. Completing the infused grid also helps support the development of more positive attitudes, as it demonstrates that students with labels of exceptionality do benefit from their time in the general education classroom. Figure 4.4 shows an example of an infused grid completed for a fifth-grade student. It could be used as an exemplar to show how opportunities in a LRE can provide valuable learning opportunities for students with IEPs where they are learning a modified curriculum. The tool is also valuable in helping teachers manage instructional time, as it explicitly asks teachers to identify opportunities for experience and also opportunities for explicit direct instruction.

In Conrad's story, the completion of an infused grid may have generated important information about meaningful instruction based upon his personalized learning profile. Effective professional development around differentiated instruction extends beyond merely understanding the nature of differentiation, to how teachers can meaningfully apply differentiated practices into their classroom (Heacox, 2002; Moll, 2005; Tilton, 2000). Small learning communities among teachers (and students) across grade levels can be very helpful in maintaining support and interest in teaching and learning practices that meet diverse learning needs. Sometimes, outside consultants can contribute fresh eyes, ears, and perspectives on practice; these consultants can be district based or federally supported state programs. For example, in Florida the federally funded Florida Inclusion Network (FIN) works with and in schools to build capacity in all adults to support meaningful engagement in learning by students. However, what is crucially important is that school leaders pay attention to differentiated teaching and learning in their walk-through and lesson observations. They need to know what to look for in a differentiated classroom. O'Meara (2010) presents a 10-step holistic process of differentiation that covers planning, assessment, instruction, and evaluation.

Two principles can be particularly helpful to school leaders in identifying differentiated classroom as they move through the school. These principles have been framed as questions:

FIGURE 4.3. Infused Grid for Scheduling IEP Instruction and Experiences

Student:		Grade:		
Priority Goals from IEP	Welcome/ Bell Work	Language Arts	Recess	Music
1.				
2.				
3.				
4.				

Note. Adapted from *Meaningful Participation: Planning Instruction for Students with Significant Disabilities*, by M. Beech, J. P. McKay, V. Barnitt, and C. Orlando, 2002. Tallahassee, FL: Florida Dept. of Education.

FIGURE 4.4. Infused Grid Completed for Sally's IEP Goals

Student: Sally		Grade: 5th		
Priority Goals from IEP	Welcome/ Bell Work	Language Arts	Math	Music
1. Sally will use her DynaVox to choose between two items.	DI	DI	E	E
2. Sally will sequence familiar symbol/words (5 in sequence).	E	DI	E	E
3. Sally will complete task with peer.	DI	E	E	E
4. Sally will complete 2 digit computations to 10.	E	E	DI	E

Note. E shows where Sally will have experience of and engage with her priority goals. DI shows where Sally will receive direct instruction on her priority goals

1. Are there varied strategies for instruction that support concrete, representational, and abstract student engagement?
2. Is there a range of instructional activities that includes individual, small-group, and whole-group instruction?

O'Meara (2010) warns that walk-throughs may miss much differentiated teaching and learning, and more sustained presence in classrooms by school leadership offers a better opportunity to evaluate the quality of differentiated practices.

Evidence-Based Practice

Evidence-based practices for all students in a school have become common and expected. Developing appreciation of the value of the power of instructional strategies has contributed much to the repertoire of evidence-based best practices in schools for all students (Marzano, 2007). In this developed appreciation, teachers pay attention to how they are communicating new content knowledge (visual, dramatic, verbal), how they are supporting student engagement in new content knowledge (graphic organizers, cues, questioning, collaborative grouping), and how they are enabling students to demonstrate their understanding (nonlinguistic representations). Many of the evidence-based practices used for all students benefit students with exceptionalities (e.g., RTI) and many evidence-based practices for students with exceptionalities benefit all students (e.g., PBS). Careful consideration of evidence-based practices is a way teacher leaders can support effective, sensitive, and differentiated teaching and learning. It is important to collect evaluative data of evidence-based practices to ensure that the intervention is indeed meeting the needs of the school.

Response to Intervention (RTI)

Response to Intervention is a strategy endorsed by the U.S. Department of Education that began life in the field of learning disabilities but is being interpreted as a more holistic schoolwide system of intervention and support for all learners (Brown & Doolittle, 2008). In RTI, the school builds a system of intervention based on student need in relation to instructional needs of all, some groups of, or individual students. When viewed as a whole-school response to diversity, RTI is a structure that helps create tiers of differentiated instruction. There are three tiers to RTI:

- Tier 1 relates to differentiated instructional strategies that all students in the class would benefit from.
- Tier 2 relates to differentiated instructional strategies that some students in the class would benefit from.
- Tier 3 relates to differentiated instructional strategies that are highly individualized. (Howard, 2009).

Response to Intervention supports the collation and analysis of the impact of the intervention. The schoolwide emphasis of RTI as a systemic response to student instructional needs promotes effective differentiated teaching and learning, and it influences the way teachers are able to respond to learners in the different tiers of learning support of RTI. Time spent on building school capacity in differentiation is time very well spent.

Positive Behavior Support (PBS)

Positive Behavior Support is a system of intervention that school leaders and teachers can adopt to support positive behavior across the school as a whole (Janney & Snell, 2000). A three-tiered model of support, PBS is similar to the RTI model:

- Tier 1 relates to the positive behavior of all students (primary).
- Tier 2 relates to the positive behavior of some groups of students (secondary).
- Tier 3 is highly focused individualized support (tertiary).

The process of developing PBS across the school is as important as the product. Through the process, adults across the whole school engage in consistent and sustained conversations about nature, expectations, and consequences of behavior. PBS has been associated with decreases in behavioral referrals, improved academic outcomes, and social interactions among students (Hunter & Chopra, 2001).

MONITORING SCHOOL-LEVEL PROGRESS

A school leader is naturally very concerned with the efficacy of school organization, interventions, and support and evaluation of school inclusion in a rigorous way. Effective evaluation focuses upon the process as well as the product of learning and, to mirror the complexity of the teaching and learning, evaluations are multifaceted. Clearly, school leaders and teachers can follow the progress of students with labels of exceptionality through AYP scores on state standardized tests. Other measures, such as behavior referrals, student performance, and surveys by teacher, parent, and student, can also generate important insights that may inform future planning. A few tools for collecting these data and using them for instructional decision making were shared earlier in the chapter. Many of these measures can be custom made by teachers working together and with parents and students within the school setting—cocreating a seamless system for supporting teaching and learning.

School leaders involved in supporting greater inclusive practices for all students across a school naturally have to pay attention to policies, practices, and associated developments at a systems level. Kozleski and Smith (n.d.) discusses leadership for greater inclusion as one that says, "all work should concentrate on improving the present situation and planning for improved futures, rather than accepting and acquiescing to the way things are" (p. 1). This asks school leaders to be cognizant of current policies, appreciating how such policies are actually translated into school practice, as well as to be visionary in their leadership in order to improve current policies and practices. School leaders need access to a holistic systems review tool that pays attention to teaching and learning that is inclusive for all students regardless of race, ethnicity, gender, sexual orientation, age, disability, or religion. There are a number of systemwide tools currently available that are potentially beneficial to the school leader. Best Practices for Inclusive Education (Barnitt, Ryndak, Benner, Hayes, & Weser, 2007) is an audit that is endorsed by the Florida Department of Education as an approved tool for reflecting upon current practices and future action planning for greater inclusive practices at the district, school, and classroom level. The Index for Inclusion (Booth & Ainscow, 2002) is a tool developed in the United Kingdom that emanates from the Center for Studies on Inclusive Education and is used in an international context (Deppeler & Harvey, 2004) to support the evaluation of how inclusive schools are for all students. An overview of both of these tools will help to determine some best principles and practices in developing a systemswide audit that school leaders can use for all learners in their school.

Best Practices for Inclusive Education (BPIE)

Best Practices for Inclusive Education was developed in Florida as a collaborative project between the Florida Department of Education, University of Florida, Indian River County School District, and Florida Inclusion Network. FIN is a statewide project that is intended to support the development of greater inclusive practices in schools across Florida by offering technical assistance and professional learning at the district, school, and classroom level. The BPIE instrument is a result of extensive collaborative research around best practices that are currently supporting effective inclusive practices. There are three dimensions that are central to the BPIE tool:

- Values and climate of the district, school, or classroom
- Access to general education
- Policies and support (leadership, program development and evaluation, and instructional support and pedagogy)

In each of these dimensions, indicators of best practices for inclusive education have been developed. A multiprofessional BPIE team is established that represents the whole school community. The team meets for a series of meetings convened and managed by an outside facilitator. The team discusses the discrete indicators and ranks their school's performance in relation to these indicators. The meetings are planned so that data from the district, school, or classroom is available to support evaluations by the team (e.g., the mission statement).

A core principle of the BPIE is the quest to make judgments through consensus; this entails facilitated conversations between BPIE team members who rank indicators differently. At the end of the ranking process, the team creates an action plan for the next year that demonstrates a proactive development toward greater inclusive practices. The BPIE team meets at the end of the next year to review progress and tweak the action plan. Some central characteristics of the BPIE audit process that can help a school leader promote a systems-level review for greater inclusive practices for all students regardless of race, ethnicity, gender, sexual orientation, age, disability, or religion are:

- Developing a set of research-based best practice indicators related to inclusive schooling for all students
- Creating a multiprofessional review team that is committed to greater inclusive schooling and is representative of the school demographics
- Sharing ownership of the evaluation and action planning process
- Providing an outside facilitator to manage the review process
- Creating opportunities for consensus building across the team in their decision making
- Developing an action planning process that influences future inclusive policies and practices

The Index for Inclusion

The Index for Inclusion takes a broad, community-based view of school inclusion and, as such, adopts a social model of disability (Carson, 2009). A model of disability that accepts the synergy between the environment and individual is a determining factor of disability. The Index for Inclusion has a set of principles that guides the audit and is intended to influence future practices of inclusive schooling (Booth & Ainscow, 2002). The principles are based upon the following requirements for a school community:

- Value all students and staff equally
- Increase the participation of students in, and reduce their exclusion from, the cultures, curricula, and communities of their local school
- Restructure the school's cultures, policies, and practices so that it is able to respond to the diversity of students in the locality
- Reduce the barriers to learning and participation for all students, not only those with impairments or those who are categorized as "having special educational needs"
- Learn from the attempts of others to overcome barriers to the access and participation of particular students to make changes for the benefit of students more widely

- View the differences between students as resources to support learning rather than as problems to be overcome
- Acknowledge the right of students to an education in their locality
- Improve the school for staff as well as for students
- Emphasize the role of the school in building community and developing values, as well as in increasing achievement
- Foster mutually sustaining relationships between schools and communities
- Recognize that inclusion in education is one aspect of inclusion in society

The Index for Inclusion is a tool intended for school self-evaluation of inclusion based upon a reflection of school culture, policies, and practices as they relate to the explicit principles of the Index. Again, there are dimensions and indicators that give detailed and specific guidance to the review team about desired practices for greater inclusion. Inherent in the process of the Index for Inclusion is shared ownership across the school community of future developments for greater inclusive policies and practices.

Any schoolwide intervention strategy takes sustained and proactive leadership. The examples of evidence-based processes discussed here offer the potential to create schools that are more supportive to individual student difference. Collaborative practices between teachers, parents, other professionals, and the students themselves also help create environments where meaningful learning and teaching take place. School leaders can be flexible and creative in the systems of support that are developed. The move to a more differentiated way of teaching and learning that supports greater inclusion also requires attending to the emotional and intellectual health of teachers in the school. Working in inclusive contexts is highly rewarding but can also be stressful and physically and intellectually demanding. Therefore, it is important for school leaders to create a context of mutual support and nurturing for the well-being of the children, teachers, and other adults in the school (Hargreaves, 2004). The impact of these kinds of robust environments is mighty.

CONCLUSION

This chapter has explored some of the attitudes, knowledge, and practices that school leaders can support in order to promote differentiated teaching and learning in a school that is moving toward greater inclusion. Differentiation is a major component of meaningful inclusive practice, and school leaders must pay attention to the quality of differentiated teaching and learning that occurs for all learners. School leaders who build accountability systems that focus upon planning, implementation, and impact of differentiated practices are supporting the whole school to become more inclusive. The staff can together build the capacity of the school to be proactive and positive in responding to student differences.

REFERENCES

Barnitt, V., Ryndak, D. L., Benner, S., Hayes, E., & Weser, S. (2007). *Best practices in inclusive education: An assessment and planning tool for systemic change.* Tallahassee, FL: Florida Inclusion Network.

Bartle, P. (2010). *SMART objectives community empowerment.* Retrieved August 25, 2010, from http://www.scn.org/cmp/modules/pd-smar.htm

Barton, L. (2004). The politics of special education: A necessary or irrelevant approach. In L. Ware (Ed.), *Ideology and the politics of (in) exclusion* (pp. 63–76). New York: Peter Lang.

Beech, M., McKay, J. P., Barnitt, V., & Orlando, C. (2002). *Meaningful participation: Planning instruction for students with significant disabilities.* Tallahassee: Florida Department of Education.

Booth, T. & Ainscow, M. (2002). *Index for inclusion (Revised).* Bristol, UK: Center for Studies on Inclusive Education.

Brechin, A. (1999). Understandings of learning disability. In J. Swain & S. French (Eds.), *Therapy and learning difficulties: Advocacy, participation and partnership* (pp. 58–71). Oxford: Butterworth.

Brown, J., & Doolittle, J. (2008). A cultural, linguistic and ecological framework for Response to Intervention with English language learners. *Teaching Exceptional Children, 40*(5), 66–73.

Byrom, B. (2004). A pupil and a patient. In S. Danforth & S. Taff (Eds.), *Crucial readings in special education* (pp. 25–37). Ohio: Pearson.

Carson, G. (2009). *The social model of disability.* Glasgow, Scotland, UK: Scottish Accessible Information Forum.

Corker, M., & Shakespeare, T. (2006). *Disability/postmodernity: Embodying disability theory.* Cornwall, UK: MPG Books.

Deppeler, J., & Harvey, D. (2004). Validating the British Index for Inclusion for the Australian context: Stage one. *International Journal of Inclusive Education 8*(2), 155–184.

Fenton, B., & Murphy, M. (2010). New leaders for new schools: Data driven instruction. *ASCD Express.* Retrieved November 14, 2010 from http://www.ascd.org/ascd-express/vol5/508-fenton.aspx

Hall, T., Stangman, N., & Meyer, A. (2003). Differentiated instruction and implications for UDL implementation. *National Center on Accessible Instructional Materials.* Retrieved March 24, 2011, from http://aim.cast.org/learn/historyarchive/backgroundpapers/differentiated_instruction_udl

Hargreaves, D. (2004). Inclusive and exclusive educational change: Emotional responses of teachers and implications for leadership. *School Leadership and Management, 20*(3), 280–309.

Heacox, D. (2002). *Differentiated instruction in the regular classroom.* Minneapolis, MN: Free Spirit.

Howard, M. (2009). *RTI from all sides.* Portsmouth, NH: Heinemann.

Hunter, L., & Chopra, V. (2001). Two proactive primary prevention program models that work in schools. *Emotional and Behavioral Disorders in Youth, 71(1),* 57–58.

Individuals with Disabilities Education Act, Pub. L 101-476, 104 Stat. 1142.

Janney, R., & Snell, M.,(2000). *Behavioral support.* Baltimore: Brookes.

Kaplan, S. (2009). Layering differentiated curricula. In F. A. Karnes & S. M. Bean (Eds.), *Methods and materials for teaching the gifted* (3rd ed., pp. 107–136). Waco, TX: Prufrock.

Kliewer, C., & Bicklin, D. (1996). Labeling: Who wants to be called retarded? In W. Stainback & S. Stainback (Eds.), *Controversial issues confronting special education: Divergent perspectives* (pp. 83–95). Boston: Allyn & Bacon.

Kozleski, E., & Smith, A. (n.d.). Note from the director. *National Institute for Urban School Improvement.* Retrieved March 24, 2011, from http://www.urban-schools.org/about_us/note_from_director.html

MacArthur, J. (2004). *The book on leadership.* Nashville, TN: Thomas Nelson Inc.

Marzano, R. J. (2007). *The art and science of teaching.* Alexandria, VA: Association for Supervision & Curriculum Development.

Moll, A. (2005). *Differentiated instruction guide for inclusive teaching.* Port Chester, NY: Dude.

National Center for Universal Design for Learning. (2011, February 1). *Three principles.* Retrieved March 24, 2011, from http://www.udlcenter.org/aboutudl/whatisudl/3principles

O'Meara, J. (2010). *Beyond differentiated instruction.* Thousand Oaks, CA: Corwin Press.

Section 504 of the Rehabilitation Act of 1973, as amended, 29 U.S.C. § 794 (Section 504). Retrieved April 20, 2011, from http://www2.ed.gov/about/offices/list/ocr/504faq.html

Tilton, L. (2000). *Inclusion: A fresh look.* Shorewood, MN: Covington Cove Publications.

Tomlinson, C. A. (2001). *How to differentiate instruction in mixed ability classrooms* (2nd ed.). Alexandria, VA: Association for Supervision & Curriculum Development.

Villa, R., & Thousand, J. (2005). *Creating an inclusive school* (2nd ed.). Alexandria, VA: Association for Supervision & Curriculum Development.

Young, K., & Mintz, K. E. (2008). A comparison: Difference, dependency, and stigmatization in special education and disability studies. In S. Gabel & S. Danforth (Eds.), *Disability and the politics of education: An international reader* (pp. 499–517). Oxford, UK: Peter Lang.

CHAPTER 5

Developing Literacy, Developing Community

G. Pat Wilson

Debbie Reese (2009b) read and responded to a news article about a teacher in Arizona who read the *Little House* series (Laura Ingalls Wilder) daily for the last 32 years to her students. The book to which she refers is *The Little House on the Prairie* (1935, 2004):

> [The teacher] adopts different voices as she reads to the children. . . . I wonder how she reads, "The only good Indian is a dead Indian" (the phrase appears in the book four times)? I wonder how many Native kids she's read to in those 32 years? How many kids, in these 32 years, heard her say, "The only good Indian is a dead Indian." I wonder how the Native kids felt hearing that, and, I wonder what effect it had on the non-Native kids?

Debbie Reese's reflections, as a children's literature scholar who is also tribally enrolled at Nambe Pueblo and as a mother, illustrate a premise of this chapter. Literacy builds and binds a community system by contributing to its collective knowledge, understandings, and therefore its values. However, the literacy building practices of a community can inadvertently exclude members. It takes purpose and planning to be an inclusive, literate community. Consideration of the following questions is necessary:

1. How is literacy defined? What defines a literate person in an inclusive community?
2. Who is represented (and how) in the literature available to the community?
3. What instructional practices build an inclusive literate community? Through these practices, who has the opportunity to become more literate?

4. What principles support building literacy for an inclusionary community while incorporating multiple ecologies converging within the school?

These questions address how literacy is defined, the literature and instructional practices used to build literacy, and the involvement of the individuals who comprise the school as well as the local and broader sociocultural communities. All of these parts are connected and that which affects one affects the others, even if subtly. How a school defines literacy influences what literature is supported, what educational practices are promoted, and whether each member is positioned as an active participant or as a fringe participant. This is not a hierarchical relationship; the influences do not flow in one direction. For example, what the members see as literate influences the community's definition of literacy and what books will be promoted in the school. Below I discuss each question individually.

DEFINING AN INCLUSIVE AND LITERATE COMMUNITY

Although many have come to use the term *literacy* as a synonym for *reading*, it encompasses a broader meaning. Literacy is more than the language arts of reading, writing, speaking, listening, and viewing. These are the tools through which literacy is built. Marie Clay (1995) studied, through close observation, young children's development in reading and writing. She described the process as one of becoming literate through the construction of inner control. Clay says, "The young learner creates a network of competencies which power subsequent independent literacy learning" (p. 1). The skills children acquire are applied as they seek knowledge and understanding of the world and of themselves. Their social and cultural environment influences what they seek to learn about. Comber and Cormack (1997) explain that many theories of reading are based on laboratory tests, analysis of readers' answers to questions, think alouds, and interviews. Through these practices, researchers sought information about the processes undertaken by a reader and what conditions supported them. These studies were inadequate for the complexities involved in literacy acquisition and so research turned toward "how literacy was used in different settings and how it was taught, learned and practiced in different communities" (Comber & Cormack, 1997, p. 22).

> Literacy viewpoints across these different communities influence reading acquisition, including the goals and intentions of those learning to read and those providing instruction.

Reading had also been seen as a problem-solving process, where the individual reader uses strategies to figure out the text (Calais, 2009). However, this model did not offer enough insight into a comprehensive analysis of literacy acquisition. For example, to determine what the rebus "10SNE1" means, a reader draws on knowledge of numbers, letter names and sounds, and the communicative purpose of language. The reader tries various combinations until reaching one that makes sense, such as "tennis anyone." However, literacy requires problem solving and more. Literacy includes knowing ways to generate understandings, such as through analysis and new, unforeseeable connections. All this is within the framework of what the community deems literate. *Literate competence* is defined based upon "culturally preferred ways of talking, listening, and behaving" (Comber & Cormack, 1997, p. 22).

Shirley Brice Heath's (1994) landmark ethnographic study of three communities illustrates Comber and Cormack's premise that literacy is culturally defined and has implications when building an inclusive community. The three communities of Heath's study were only a few miles apart geographically and fed the same school. Each community's social use of language differed, that is, their narrative styles differed. She found four different discourse forms. *Recounts* were similar to the narrative discourse found in schools: The speaker voluntarily or in response to a question recounts an event and is expected to adhere to facts. *Accounts* are volunteered by speakers and invite use of the imagination or of evaluative statements: Accounts are based on actual events, with some elaboration. *Eventcasts* are running narratives either during an event or just after. *Stories*, the fourth narrative discourse, are more than accounts and are goal directed to lead the listener through events of a story, with twists and exaggerations. Successful communication in each narrative is based on tacit rules that are followed by the community. Children learn these rules, and bring them to school, where their mode of talk might not parallel the mainstream. Whereas children may be viewed as competent in their home community, they may be viewed as incompetent in another community, including school, as uncovered by Shirley Brice Heath in her study of three communities (Heath, 1983). Since literacy is a socioculturally based concept tied to notions of what being literate means, defining it in a school community needs careful consideration.

Heath (1994) notes that literacy contributes to each individual's capacity to respond to, make sense of, and help build the world. Too narrow a concept of literacy leads to a limited capacity to understand and influence the world. The notion of literacy is embedded with the values and constructs of the school community, which in turn is influenced by factors such as government (e.g., departments of education), teacher education programs, community organizations and their leaders (such as businesses and church organizations), school leaders, individual families, media images, books, and news sources. Some factors have a more immediate influence on the school, but all are forces in how literacy and being a literate person is defined. The way in which a community defines literacy has the capacity to include or exclude. In an inclusive school, literacy can be instrumental in supporting notions of belonging, respect, and value.

The implications are twofold. The educational community will influence the larger community definition of literacy; however, schools can find themselves acting in an exclusionary manner by not honoring the many forms of literacy of their represented communities. If literacy contributes to each person's capacity to respond, make sense of, and help build the world, and schools set a goal to expand the world of each child, the children should be literate in their own community and in others outside the local environment. In order for students to have true choice about where and how they want to live, they need to be literate in the various social worlds in which they exist.

When students are not prepared as literate persons in the broader world, their choices are limited, which restricts the nature of the world where they can be successful. A relatively simple example resides in the consideration of regional dialects. Lucy Lauren Razor (2009), a graduate student in education, drew on her experience with the effect of having a distinct dialect having been raised in Appalachia when she wrote, "At first glance it may seem that a child from the hills and hollows of Appalachia has nothing in common with a child from our country's inner-cities. . . . Nonetheless, a common thread runs through their lives. They both speak low-status English dialects" (p. 1). Goodman and Buck (1997) explain the disadvantage of low-status dialects:

> The only special disadvantage which speakers of low-status dialects suffer in learning to read is one imposed by teachers and schools. Rejection of their dialects and educators' confusion of linguistic difference with linguistic deficiency interferes with the natural process by which reading is acquired and undermines the linguistic self-confidence of divergent speakers. (p. 455)

In other words, it is not the dialect that interferes with reading acquisition; it is the attitude of the educators. Part of the solution is in how schools respect dialectical differences and teach their students how to code-switch between dialects, or as described by Wheeler and Swords (2004), how they teach by "contrasting" versus "correcting." These authors noted that "a correctionist . . . would explain what we do and do not say" (p. 474), but one could teach the contrasts between the two forms, thus displaying the vernacular and the standard English form for comparison and discussion, with explicit emphasis that code switching runs in both directions. One is not "wrong" and the other "right." As Razor (2009) notes, "teachers must give students knowledge of and context for both of their languages so they can then take ownership over the words they speak, read, and write" (p. 7).

Determining what being literate means in the school community requires consideration of the nature of that community—locally, nationally, and globally. The students are part of the same set of communities, and if they learn to use the tools to navigate these communities, they will be in a better position to make decisions about their lives. An inclusive literacy building community fosters each student's identity and sense of agency such that they have a place in the world and are able to respond to, make sense of, and build the world, as noted earlier by Heath (1994). Literature is one factor that shapes identity, and certain forms of instruction promote children's agency, that is, their understanding of their power to set goals, evaluate, and learn intentionally.

LITERATURE IN THE COMMUNITY: AN INCLUSIVE IDENTITY

The literature found in the community makes a statement about who belongs and who does not, and thus the literature that is available to readers is significant. As Debbie Reese (2009b) suggests in her reflection on how Indians are portrayed in the book *Little House on the Prairie* (see above), the literature read in a classroom has significant impact on children's understanding of themselves and others. An inclusive community is fostered when literature in the classroom is as widely diverse as its members, such that readers recognize, for example, their own and others' religion, race, gender, class, family structure, sexual identity, and ability. Representation (and misrepresentation) through literature provides a fulcrum in the role literature plays in inclusionary practices. The manner of portrayal "affects readers' perceptions of themselves and the world around them. Underrepresentation or misrepresentation can lead to false assumptions and the perpetuation of stereotypes that reiterate the very misconceptions such literature attempts to subvert" (Crisp & Wilson, 2009, p. 2). The attempts found in literature to represent diversity in order to expand children's worldview is not always successful. Reese (2009a) points out that the Plains Indians are misrepresented in *Little House on the Prairie* when depicted as inept hunters, unsophisticated in their understanding of the world. History documents the fallacy in such descriptions, yet when these descriptions are the experiences children have relative to American Indians, they become the images children draw from to visualize the Native people of North America (Reese, 2009a).

Similarly, a common theme in literature is that people with disabilities often "save the day" but die or are institutionalized by the end of the story

(White, 2009). In accurate portrayals, literature is inclusive; in inaccurate portrayals, it excludes.

As the incidences of representation are less for some groups than for others, representation from various sources is needed, for "one text cannot carry the burden of representing a diverse population" (Crisp & Knezek, 2010, p. 79). Experience, through reading and discussing a wide array of literature, helps children form a deeper, more sophisticated understanding of people and concepts. Relying on the stories in commercially produced reading programs is not enough. These programs, with their anthologies, are still a single source with materials preselected by the publishers, thereby meeting criteria set by the publishers. Nancy Jordan (2005) analyzed the texts of two popular reading programs, Reading Mastery II (Engelmann & Bruner, 1995) and *Collections for Young Scholars* (SRA/McGraw-Hill, 1995). The stories in the *Reading Mastery* anthologies were written by two to four program authors (Wilson, Wiltz, & Lang, 2005), while the Open Court publishers used published literature by an array of authors. In her analysis of volume 2, book 2, of the *Collections for Young Scholars,* Jordan (2005) found that although the "pictures, the topics, the events in the texts appear to represent the lives and experiences of many different groups of people . . . these stories are mainly authored by White writers, both males and females" (p. 212). Jordan also studied the themes embedded in the stories that, when taken together, transmit specific messages. She found that the Reading Mastery anthology, *Storybook II*, pitched a message that learning to read made one a good person and a nice person, and that being good resulted in a nice home, car, cash, and a dog. In the Open Court anthology Jordan analyzed, the persistent message was that being virtuous and honest was better than being rich, and being poor and giving made one happy because it was better than being rich and greedy. Any single source of literature will reflect the values or goals of that source. Utilizing multiple sources provides readers the opportunity to gather information from divergent sources, and if read in an atmosphere of discussion and evaluation or pleasure, supports readers' construction of a deeper understanding of themselves, the world, and their ability to shape both.

Learners need the opportunity afforded by literature to build understandings of themselves and their world, that is, to build their identity of who they are within the world. "Within a literate culture, personal and collective identities are caught up in ongoing practices of reading and interpretation. Such cultural interpretation practices . . . are integral to the ways in which literate subjects learn about themselves, about others, and about their shared worlds" (Davis, Sumara, & Luce-Kapler, 2000, pp. 233–234). Literature supports an inclusionary community through its capacity to help individuals understand themselves and others; however, how the literature is used in school and how instruction is conceived heavily influence whether learners recognize their own abilities.

INSTRUCTION IN THE COMMUNITY:
SUPPORTING THE LEARNER AS A CAPABLE PERSON

Inclusion through literacy-building instruction is a decision, a deliberate act. Part of that decision is to recognize students' agency in the learning process as goal-oriented, intentional learners. Instructional practices that involve learners provide experiences that help them grow in their understanding of their abilities as well as teach the skills and strategies that the learner uses in becoming literate (Clay, 1995). An apprenticeship model guides educators in developing and maintaining participatory practices in which learners' agency is recognized and incorporated into the learning system. Barbara Rogoff (1990), who studies child development from a sociocultural perspective, defines the learning process in the following terms:

> [Children are] apprentices in thinking, active in their efforts to learn from observing and participating with peers and more skilled members of their society, developing skills to handle culturally defined problems with available tools, and building from these givens to construct new solutions within the context of sociocultural activity. (p. 7)

This positions children as thinkers who intentionally seek information and learning, who are guided by peers and adults within a sociocultural environment. This premise is operationalized through Wade and Moje's (2000) participatory models of instruction, as opposed to transmission models. Alexander and Fox (2004) refer to this as engaged learning, which is characterized by a change in perception of text from printed material to inclusion of media read in nonlinear fashion (e.g., hypermedia, Internet sites). Further, engaged learning shifts perceptions of readers from users of strategies by which information is gleaned to intentional learners with interests, "goals, self-efficacy beliefs, as well as . . . self-regulation and active participation in reading" (Alexander & Fox, 2004, p. 51). A participatory, engaged learning approach differs from a transmission-oriented approach toward teaching; this does not promote the agency of learner, for "if reading is presented as a set of skills to be used to extract meaning from texts, the learner must be positioned as a non-participant, a more-or-less-passive receiver of truths that have already been established" (Davis, Sumara, & Luce-Kapler, 2000, p. 234). The role of the learner and perceptions about how learning occurs in an apprenticeship model support inclusion, based on understanding that every child learns by taking an active interest in learning, though a child's particular goal at a particular time might not match that of her teacher or parent. Nevertheless, it is through participating in a social environment where literacy is core that children become aware of and act on what they see and hear, with the guidance of others in the social environment.

Some commercial reading programs focus on teaching skills and do so effectively, but are not effective in building agency. For example, the aforementioned Reading Mastery Program (Engelmann & Bruner, 1995) bases instruction on behaviorist principles and being "simple and effective" (Dudley-Marling & Paugh, 2005, p. 159); however, the program does not foster children's sense of their own ability to problem solve, such as when something they read (e.g., a word) does not make sense to them. In a study of second graders in an urban metropolitan school, researchers found the children "depended almost exclusively upon teacher directions and being told whether what they read was right or wrong. If a teacher seemed to accept their reading, then the children thought the reading was fine" (Wiltz & Wilson, 2006). The program fosters dependency on teachers because teachers are directed to interrupt if a mistake is made and take immediate corrective action instead of helping children identify when their reading does not make sense (Wilson et al., 2005; Wiltz & Wilson, 2006).

Teachers' orientation toward learning and learners matters. It matters that they view learners as competent, albeit perhaps novice learners in a given area. Educators should position students as capable and focus on ability, that is, "elicit stories of the competent aspects of their students' lives" (Wansart, 1995, p. 166). In order to recognize a student's ability, teachers analyze what it is that the child understands about a given concept or skill, determining his assumptions and any misconceptions. From this foundation, they can build upon what the child knows and understands, and teachers can then build the child's experiences and/or engage in explicit instruction.

With the emphasis on ability comes the expectation of participation. Some instructional components to an effective language arts program that reflect inclusionary and participatory principles include literature circles and book clubs; independent reading and read alouds; writers' workshop and independent composing and communicating; guided reading, readers' workshop, and retrospective miscue analysis. Each has built-in, differentiated instruction, makes use of flexible grouping (versus tracking), and allows the teacher to expand or compact instruction to match children's instructional needs against what they have already learned. Each respects the agency of the learner, builds experience in developing and using tools of literacy, strengthens skills, and is part of a comprehensive language arts program. Further, each can be used across curriculum content areas, thus broadening students' understanding of themselves and the world.

Reading, Thinking, Learning

Book clubs or literature circles, independent reading, and read alouds are three components of a strong literacy program that involve learners in thinking about literature and the ideas therein, though each has its own set of benefits. Literature circles and book clubs involve small groups of readers in the discussion of books, books that are interesting and complex enough to provoke thinking and talk. Often each member has a role, which helps that member engage in discussion. Typically, there is a discussion director or question seeker, a passage master (who finds passages of interest to discuss), a word finder (who finds several unfamiliar, unclear, or fascinating words), an illustrator, and a text connector (who makes connections between this text and others). Literature circles have evolved from the reciprocal teaching strategy (Palincsar & Brown, 1984), which has been well researched and found effective in improving reading achievement (National Reading Panel, 2000). Students develop their own voice and a sense of their own position relative to others through literature circles and book clubs, and they are engaged in reading an array of literature.

During independent reading, students read books of their choice, and share something of their reading with others. Choice promotes agency, recognizing that readers have reasons behind their decisions about what to read. Sometimes it is to learn more about a topic, or sometimes because particular authors or genres are enjoyed. Sometimes children choose a book because it will teach them something about reading (Hansen, 1996/2001). Choice is part of literacy building, and "in classrooms in which students always have at least one book of their choice going, and in which they frequently and regularly share them, they know who they are as readers" (Hansen, 1996/2001, p. 12); hence their identity as a reader evolves, while their experience grows.

Read alouds can be powerful and should not be limited to early elementary grades or to language arts instruction. Through these, teachers can build students' knowledge base and provide access to literature and text more complex than students can read independently. Teachers can share enjoyment of books for the sake of reading. They can, through open-ended questions, promote discussions and the sharing of different points of view or interpretations.

Each of these three components to a comprehensive language arts program is ready-built for differentiated instruction. The literature can be varied to match individual skills of independent readers and their interests. The cooperative learning strategies of literature circles support learners. Ways of sharing responses to the readings can vary to include verbal, written, sketched, or dramatized responses to literature, employing each student's strengths. In each type of response, students are engaged in full literacy building acts, but supported in accordance with individual needs.

Composing, Learning, Communicating

Writers' workshop and independent writing time offer learners an apprenticeship in writing, complete with models, guidance, and independent writing. During writers' workshop, instruction is provided in writing (modeling, guided practice) while independent writing provides young authors time to write on the topics of their choice and in the mode they desire (e.g., story, flyer, book jacket, novel, news report). Through both, they build experience. In order to develop as writers, students need time to write, and need responses to their writing through structures such as author's chair, peer conferences, and conferences with their teacher. An environment in which children share their writing and ideas, creates an community wherein the members know each other. Structures, such as routines, procedures, and rules help children proceed independently. Choice, tied with self-evaluation, strengthens authors' recognition of their agency and power (Graves, 1994; Hansen, 1996/2001). These two components can provide these benefits. Writing is more than stringing words together in an organized fashion. The process of writing requires consideration of ideas, determination of importance to a perceived audience, and the planning of how to communicate these ideas. Although writing with words is a core component, the concept of writing can be expanded, with an emphasis on composing (thinking) and communicating through other mediums beyond writing.

Words are held in high esteem within most definitions of literacy and what it means to be a literate person. Students' ability to articulate, to write a clear and well-composed paper, and to understand an author's encoded message, are not only valued but usually necessary for success in the world. Students learn to think through words, often talking aloud to brainstorm ideas or writing in order to think through an idea. Yet, non-word-based text (drawings, paintings, musical renderings, and performances) also offer mediums through which to think. Language is not a strength for everyone for a variety of reasons, including having a language disability, learning English as a new language, preferring a mode other than language, or because a student's language abilities are still emerging. Students still have ideas to be represented, developed, and communicated through other means. In written language, words represent or symbolize ideas, and grammar indicates relationships between the ideas. Similarly, sketches, color, and gesture can also represent ideas and show relationships between them. A child can use movement to show the effect of wind on a leaf falling from a tree, or the emotion of a character frightened by a monster in the closet, or show how two characters feel about each other through tableaux. Graphic organizers also convey relationships between ideas. There is room to use other mediums in school and the benefits are worthwhile.

The use of two or more sign systems, such as language and sketching, as a means to think about an idea, is called *transmediation*. Transmediation "increases students' opportunities to engage in generative and reflective thinking because learners must invent a connection between the two sign systems, as the connection does not exist a priori" (Siegel, 1995, p. 460). Two strategies, sketch to stretch and tableaux, show how transmediation can be used in literacy instruction intended to be more inclusive of learning strengths, needs, and preferences.

In sketch to stretch, children are asked to draw what a certain story means to them (Harste, 2000). To accomplish this, they must think about what the text means and then determine a way to represent these ideas in another sign system, which requires metaphorical thinking. Sketch to stretch is more powerful in a social setting where the sketches (and story) are discussed (Harste, 2000).

Tableaux are a theatre convention wherein participants create a still, silent "frozen" scene (a tableau) using expression, gesture, posture, and positioning relative to others in order to communicate an idea. Tableaux encourage children's ability to reason while providing support and minimizing reliance on language (Wilson, 2003). They can be used to represent a scene or concept, and thereby show children's understanding of that scene or concept. Emotions of characters, their relationship to each other, as well as action can be represented through tableaux. For example, to show sadness, children might make themselves look small and listless, and to show anger, large and rigid. Gathering close can represent friendship, while turning backs shows displeasure.

Use of tableaux and sketch to stretch does not require much in the way of materials. Children need to be given a few minutes to think about what they want to show in their sketch or tableau, then time to figure out how they will show it. After creating it, they need to share—put into words—what they showed. In this manner, children work with words, images, and words again, thus enacting the process of transmediation. The sketches and tableaux can act as bridges to support language and reasoning by helping children think through an idea, then describe that idea in words. Efforts to remediate literacy in some students often result in students' time being "spent on developing basic skills rather than on activities that call for reasoning . . . we stunt children's reasoning by not allowing them time to think about ideas or providing support for them to work through complex scenarios. We inadvertently reduce opportunities for children to develop their capacity to reason" (Wilson, 2003, p. 375). In creating an inclusive literacy environment, the use of transmediation and mediums other than words support children's literacy growth and capacity to communicate.

TEACHING THE TOOLS FOR BUILDING LITERACY

There are components to effective literacy instruction that promote participation by each member of the classroom community. Guided reading, readers' workshop, and retrospective miscue analysis offer ways to teach children the tools they must use to become literate. Guided reading (Fountas & Pinnell, 1996), particularly effective with novice readers, provides a place for explicit instruction within small groups. With its close monitoring of each reader's development, and because guided reading is an adaptation of reading recovery, it can also be used to structure one-on-one instruction. Children learn to use cuing systems (graphophonic or alphabetic cues, meaning-based cues, and grammar cues) in context.

In guided reading, books are chosen by the teacher with careful attention to ease in reading and usefulness in teaching the skills and strategies the child needs. One of the principles of guided reading is teaching children to talk about how they read and about the strategies they use, so that they understand the processes involved in reading. This principle continues into readers' workshop, which is focused on comprehension building strategies such as connecting the current text to other texts read previously, how to use the senses to create images of what is read, and how to summarize in order to pull information together (Harvey & Goudvis, 2007; Keene & Zimmermann, 2007). Readers' workshop is a forum for a wide range of instruction in reading, conducive to small-group and large-group instruction.

Retrospective miscue analysis (RMA), usually seen with third graders and older, is a strategy found successful with students receiving special education services (Moore & Gilles, 2005). In RMA, students study and discuss their own reading within a social (small-group) setting. They learn which of their strategies are effective and which are not, and often uncover assumptions that are detrimental to reading for meaning. For example, many less-than-proficient readers think reading fast and without any errors is the goal. They do not realize that the text should make sense and that they should use their knowledge to figure out what the author is saying, especially since taking the time to figure something out can interrupt their speed. RMA engages the student in learning about themselves as readers. The teacher's role includes analysis of the miscues to determine where readers are effective and efficient, and where they are not.

In any strategy adopted for literacy instruction, the key is to identify to what degree the instruction supports children's agency and identity, and then identify how the strategy provides the experience needed in developing literacy. A comprehensive language arts program can promote an underlying value of literate diversity within the school community, with a participatory stance wherein authority does not reside in texts (alone), but in teachers and students as well.

GUIDING PRINCIPLES TO SUPPORT LITERACY, INCLUSIONARY COMMUNITY, AND MULTIPLE ECOLOGIES

The overarching principles that direct composing and foster guiding an inclusive, literate community of diverse but united people can include the elements that Don Graves (1994) and Jane Hansen (1996/2001) have noted as vital to writers' growth: community, choice, time, structure, response, and self-evaluation. First, the community itself has an identity in how it defines literacy and people who are literate. There needs to be unity in goals and beliefs about participatory instruction to support learner agency, while maintaining a respect for differences. The structures (ways of doing business, the routines of instruction, the literature, and other resources) need to work with, not undermine, these goals for literacy. Each member within the school society needs response from others in the community in order to help self-evaluate their actions, whether they are in the form of teaching or learning. This can be formalized using an apprenticeship model, but can also be fostered informally through time for teachers and staff to talk and plan how they want to meet the goals of inclusion and literacy building. Finally, choice is necessary. Each member of the school group has decisions to make about how he can use his abilities to contribute to the literacy of the community. Each needs support in realizing his choices through plans and follow-through actions on goals.

There is also incorporation of the ecologies each teacher or staff person brings to consider, because these tie to their knowledge, abilities, experience, and connectedness to communities inside and outside the school. For example, librarians/media center specialists are knowledgeable about literature and informational text. They act as a conduit between readers and literature, answering children's questions and guiding them to sources of information on their queries (Jenkins, 2008). Similarly, they are a resource to teachers, but they can also be a conduit between the media center and the larger community through programs for families and ties to the public libraries. Hosting adult education classes as well as community events centered on literacy fosters a broader membership in the school community. Since public libraries also offer such programs, the libraries can form partnerships. There are also community service organizations that support literacy and benefit from partnerships with schools, such as Big Brothers Big Sisters' Reading Bigs program wherein volunteers work with children (Larkin & Wilson, 2009).

The questions one can ask in assessing the status of inclusion include:

- Does the literature in this school represent the diversity of its members and of the world at large? Does the literature avoid stereotypes? Are there people knowledgeable about literature and open to questions by readers who assist readers in finding texts?

- In terms of literacy, are the values of the community reflected in what is valued by the school? How does the school contribute to the values of the community?
- What are the assets each member of this community brings? How does each member contribute to the literacy of the community?
- Does instruction in the language arts start with the abilities and understandings of the children? Is the focus of instruction the continual building and extending of knowledge, skills, and the capacity to reason?
- In what ways is this school a center of literacy in the local community?

Creating an inclusionary, literate educational community is a decision. Literacy can be used as a uniting thread that builds the community through common goals, with recognition (and celebration) that each of its members brings different abilities toward meeting those goals. That which is true for supporting the inclusion of all children through support of their agency, identity, and growth in becoming literate is true for the adults in the school community as well. Each holds authority; authority does not just reside in the curriculum or in the texts being read. Each is both learner and teacher. Each has a voice and abilities that are part of the makeup of the community. Each is part of the community, and so needs the community to support the development of identity as a literate person who is a member of multiple communities. Taken together, the separate elements—the members with their abilities, agency, and identities; the manner of instruction in which they participate as teacher and learner; and the array of literature and other materials read and discussed—can form a dynamic, inclusive social system: an inclusive and literate community that is able to respond to, make sense of, and build the world.

REFERENCES

Alexander, P. A., & Fox, E. (2004). Historical perspective on reading research and practice. In B. R. Ruddell & N. Unrau (Eds.), *Theoretical models and processes of reading* (5th ed.). Newark, DE: International Reading Association.

Calais, G. J. (2009). The vee diagram as a problem solving strategy: Content area reading/writing implications. *National Forum Teacher Education Journal, 19* (3), 1–8.

Clay, M. M. (1995). *Becoming literate: The construction of inner control.* Portsmouth, NH: Heinemann Education.

Comber, B., & Cormack, P. (1997). Looking beyond "skills" and "processes": Literacy as social and cultural practices in classrooms. *Reading, 31*(3), 22–29.

Crisp, T., & Knezek, S. (2010). "I just don't see myself here": Challenging conversations about LGBTQ adolescent literature. *English Journal, 99*(3), 76–79.

Crisp, T., & Wilson, G. P. (2009). *Representations of diversity.* Paper presented at the Children's Literature Symposium, University of South Florida, Sarasota-Manatee.

Davis, B., Sumara, D., & Luce-Kapler, R. (2000). *Engaging minds: Learning and teaching in a complex world.* Mahwah, NJ: Erlbaum.

Dudley-Marling, C., & Paugh, P. (2005). The rich get richer; the poor get direct instruction. In B. Altwerger (Ed.), Reading for profit: How the bottom line leaves kids behind (pp. 156–171). Portsmouth, NH: Heinemann. Engelmann, S., & Bruner, E. (1995). Reading mastery II: Direct instruction—storybook 2. Columbus, OH: SRA Macmillan/McGraw-Hill.

Fountas, I., & Pinnell, G. S. (1996). *Guided reading: Good first teaching for all children.* Portsmouth, NH: Heinemann.

Goodman, K. S., & Buck, C. (1997). Dialect barriers to reading comprehension revisited. The Reading Teacher, 50(6), 454-459.

Graves, D. H. (1994). *A fresh look at writing.* Portsmouth, NH: Heinemann.

Hansen, J. (2001). *When writers read* (2nd ed.). Portsmouth, NH: Heinemann. (Original work published 1996)

Harste, J. C. (2000). Six points of departure. In B. Berghoff, K. A. Egawa, J. C. Harste, & B. T. Hoonan (Eds.), *Beyond reading and writing: Inquiry, curriculum, and multiple ways of knowing* (pp. 1–16). Urbana, IL: National Council of Teachers of English.

Harvey, S., & Goudvis, A. (2007). *Strategies that work: Teaching comprehension to enhance understanding* (2nd ed.). Portland, ME: Stenhouse.

Heath, S. B. (1983). *Ways with words: Language, life, and work in communities and classrooms.* Cambridge, UK: Cambridge University Press.

Heath, S. B. (1994). Separating "things of the imagination" from life: Learning to read and write. In W. H. Teale & E. Sulzby (Eds.), *Emergent literacy: Writing and reading* (pp. 156–171). Norwood, NJ: Ablex.

Jenkins, C. (2008, December). *Of theories, tape recorders, and texts: Untangling methods in the interdisciplinary study of children's literature.* Paper presented at the National Reading Conference, Orlando, FL.

Jordan, N. (2005). Basal readers and reading as socialization: What are children learning? *Language Arts, 82*(3), 204–213.

Keene, E. O., & Zimmermann, S. (2007). *Mosaic of thought: Teaching comprehension in a reader's workshop* (2nd ed.). Portsmouth, NH: Heinemann.

Larkin, E., & Wilson, G. P. (2009). Reading Bigs: An intergenerational literacy mentoring program. In J. C. Richards & C. A. Lassonde (Eds.), *Evidence-based quality literacy tutoring programs: What works and why* (pp. 21–33). Newark, DE: International Reading Association.

Moore, R. A., & Gilles, C. (2005). *Reading conversations: Retrospective miscue analysis with struggling readers 4–12.* Portsmouth, NH: Heinemann.

National Reading Panel. (2000). *Teaching children to read, an evidence-based assessment of the scientific research literature on reading and its implications for reading instruction.* National Institute of Child Health and Human Development, National Institutes of Health. Available at http://www.nichd.nih.gov/publications/nrp/report.cfm

Osborn, S. (1995). *Reading Mastery series guide*. Worthington, OH: SRA Macmillan/McGraw-Hill.

Palincsar, A. S., & Brown, A. L. (1984). Reciprocal teaching of comprehension-fostering and comprehension-monitoring activities. *Cognition and Instruction, 1*(2), 117–175.

Razor, L. L. (2009). Dialect and disadvantage: How speaking non-standard English influences academic success. Unpublished Paper. University of South Florida Sarasota-Manatee.

Reese, D. (2009a, February 21). *Keynote: Representations of Diversity*. Paper presented at the Children's Literature Symposium, University of South Florida, Sarasota-Manatee.

Reese, D. (2009b). Little House on the Praire (in Arizona), *American Indians in Children's Literature*. Retrieved April 21, 2011, from http://americanindiansinchildrensliterature.blogspot.com/2009/03/this-just-in-little-house-on-prairie-in.html

Rogoff, B. (1990). *Apprenticeship in thinking*. New York: Oxford University Press.

Siegel, M. G. (1995). More than words: The generative power of transmediation for learning. *Canadian Journal of Education, 20*(4), 455–475.

SRA/McGraw-Hill. (1995). *Open Court: Collections for young scholars* (Vol. 2). Chicago: SRA Macmillan/McGraw-Hill.

Wade, S. E., & Moje, E. B. (2000). The role of text in classroom learning. In M. L. Kamil, P. B. Mosenthal, P. D. Pearson, & R. Barr (Eds.), *Handbook of reading research* (Vol. 3, pp. 609–627). Mahwah, NJ: Erlbaum.

Wansart, W. L. (1995). Teaching as a way of knowing: Observing and responding to students' abilities. *Remedial and Special Education, 16*(3), 166–177.

Wheeler, R. S., & Swords, R. (2004). Codeswitching: Tools of language and culture transform the dialectally diverse classroom. *Language Arts, 81*(6), 470–480.

White, J. (2009). *Constructions of disability in children's and adolescent media*. Paper presented at the Children's Literature Symposium, University of South Florida, Sarasota-Manatee.

Wilder, L. I. (1935, 2004). *Little house on the prairie*. New York: HarperCollins.

Wilson, G. P. (2003). Supporting young children's thinking through tableau. *Language Arts, 80*(5), 46–54.

Wilson, G. P., Wiltz, N., & Lang, D. (2005). The impact of Reading Mastery on children's reading strategies. In B. Altwerger (Ed.), *Reading for profit: The commercialization of reading instruction*. Portsmouth, NH: Heinemann.

Wiltz, N., & Wilson, G. P. (2006). An inquiry into children's reading in one urban school using SRA Reading Mastery. *Journal of Literacy Research, 34*(4), 493–528.

CHAPTER 6

Getting at the Heart of Inclusion Through Reflective Teaching: A Positive Youth Development Perspective

Jenni Menon Mariano

It's important to give money to poverty because the whole world isn't like this, where you can go to school and live a nice, regular life. There are people in the world that hardly go to elementary school, and it's just terrible. . . . To be a good person you need to do something that you think where your limits end. You need to try to stand out and to do something for another person. Like, do something else to help somebody else, just little or small, just to help out. . . . I'm just going to go beyond my limits and see where I end up.

It's like, how should I put this? Just one second. I'm looking for an analogy. It's like a candy bowl, like at those hotels. It's right over there, actually. When you walk in, you can take one and leave some for the people behind you to benefit. Or you can just take them all. To everything there's a consequence. But by taking them all and eating them all, then you might get very sick. —Jason, 12 years old

As educators know from experience, children and youth often say remarkable and insightful things. This truth is highlighted in the interview conducted with 12-year-old Jason, quoted above, in the lobby of a hotel in a west coast U.S. city. Jason had been invited by a nonprofit organization to give a speech about the work he was doing to improve the living conditions of schoolchildren in developing countries. Jason's discourse introduces a real-life model of what it means for young people to behave, think, and feel

81

inclusively. One of the most interesting things about Jason's thinking is his profound understanding, especially profound for a 12-year-old, of what it means to be good and generous. For Jason, being generous means to push the boundaries of self and "go beyond" one's limits to make a difference in the world. This chapter focuses on the lessons school leaders can learn from a positive youth development (PYD) perspective to aid them in creating more inclusive communities in K–12 schools. It calls for school leaders to reflect upon three main PYD beliefs: adopting a strength-based approach to all students in school; integrating inclusive ideas into school culture and curriculum; and supporting responsive, deliberate, and unambiguous teaching of the strengths of inclusion in the classroom. Jason was chosen for the interview because he had demonstrated an active commitment to others over an extended period, so his ideals were not limited to wishes alone. According to both Jason and his mother, he became seriously concerned at age 6 about issues of water quality and supply in developing countries through a teacher's class presentation. With the support of Jason's parents and others, this concern developed into an active program of fund-raising for water and sanitation projects in 16 countries.

Jason's case, although relevant to many of our most pressing issues in youth development, is also relevant to the issue of inclusion. In this sense, *inclusiveness* refers to a quality of the mind and heart—a psychological way of being—by which the individual commits to the progress of others. *Empathy* (Hoffman, 2000), *compassion* (i.e., Glaser, 2005; Warren, in press), *altruism* (Post, 2003), *moral commitment* (Colby & Damon, 1992), *noble purpose* (Damon, Menon, & Bronk, 2003), and *generosity* (Lerner, Roeser, & Phelps, 2008) are only some of the overlapping terms used by human development scholars to capture the experience of youth like Jason. Whatever name is given to the phenomena, however, it is clear that these qualities are useful for cultivating inclusive cultures in our classrooms and schools.

An important aim for educators is to understand what processes can foster these strengths in children. This chapter explores the development of these strengths and offers recommendations for fostering the strengths in young people. Specifically, the philosophical approach and resulting contribution of the positive youth development approach is discussed as one model for fostering these strengths. As a synonym for the study of human virtue, strength, optimal well-being, and the processes and institutions that support healthy development, PYD is a philosophical approach to education that illuminates aspects of prosocial action in young people, as well as effective practices to promote it in school contexts. By many of the definitions discussed in the introduction to this book, inclusion is about prosocial action and sentiment as applied to the classroom.

This chapter also addresses the contribution that key PYD ideas can make to teachers' reflective practice in working toward greater inclusive teaching and learning. Teaching for inclusive ways of being in our students constantly requires educators to examine some of the most basic assumptions about children's development inherent in our cultural and scientific history. Three broad reflections are offered for school leaders, based on key social science literature applicable to PYD. The reflections are offered as practical and philosophical perspectives for school leaders to consider. Though not exhaustive by any means, they are offered as starting points for the application of a PYD approach to inclusive teaching in the K–12 context. As Jason's case so nicely illustrates, *inclusion* as discussed here is about what emerges in the mind and the heart first, and then is subsequently expressed in practice. The discussion of PYD begins with considering the necessary prerequisites in the minds and hearts of educators (teachers, teacher leaders, other adults and professionals working in the school) and with venturing into applications that could happen in classroom practice and educational programming to make inclusion a reality.

REFLECTION 1: ADOPT A STRENGTHS PERSPECTIVE ON CHILDREN'S DEVELOPMENT

Though the traditional approaches in social science focusing on young people's problems are useful, developing a more extensive, applied science of the pathways by which youth thrive is imperative (Keyes, 2002; Larson, 2000; Peterson, 2006). Peterson and Seligman (2004) make a valuable point by indicating a need to "reclaim the study" of things like "character and virtue" as "legitimate topics of psychological inquiry and informed societal discourse" (p. 3). In another work, Peterson (2006) offers that "human goodness and excellence"—the very building blocks of real inclusive practice—"are as authentic" to human experience "as disease, disorder, and distress" (p. 5). Fortunately, educators are in a good position to "reclaim" the study of inclusion-oriented strengths as "legitimate topics" in the classroom too.

One way that school leaders can approach this goal is by adopting a *strengths perspective* on child development. Certainly, compared with many other professions, educators cannot be charged with neglecting children's strengths. Many individuals aspire to teach in the first place because they have high esteem for children's capacities. Yet, even those of us with the most confidence in the brighter side of children's natures will benefit from reflective practice. Furthermore, this perspective needs to be placed within a broader cultural and historical context. Surprisingly, cases like Jason's are only recently of interest among social scientists. They represent a relatively new trend toward studying positive internal conditions as they emerge in young people, and how they can be fostered. A case in point is that in the

1960s, a dominant interest of social science was in the causes and sources of nonconforming or *noninclusive* ways of being, like violence, or the diffusion of ethical responsibility when people are in group situations. The study of prosocial behaviors attained a focus as a by-product of these other interests (Darley & Latané, 1968; Yarrow, Scott, & Waxler, 1973). Currently, however, there is much support for adopting a strengths perspective. A series of compelling arguments offered by Jeffrey Arnett (2007) draws on examples pertaining to adolescents and *emerging adults*, a recently defined period of development referring to 18- to 25-year-olds. Arnett warns that by virtue of our history, educators are exposed to faulty deficit "myths" about the younger generations that may inadvertently trickle down into school practice and suggests that many of these myths are not simply "incomplete," but are prevailing notions that need to be debunked. Highly applicable to our discussion of fostering inclusive ways of being, for instance, is the misperception that most adolescents are "hyperemotional, and at war with their parents and the world" (Arnett, 2007, p. 23). From the lens of practice, adoption of this first myth implies that adolescents are incapable of taking on the qualities of cooperativeness necessary for inclusive ways of being. Another incomplete, prevailing notion is that adolescents and young adults are naturally selfish (p. 25). Both extreme positions are faulty because they fail to take into account a range of developmental and historical factors and the broader ecological system in which young people reside.

Let us look at both ideas: that young people are innately driven by ego and inherently uncooperative. A common story line is that young people today care much less about prosocial matters, like civic engagement, than earlier generations and are getting progressively worse. However, from a historical perspective, it seems that youth civic engagement may be not declining at all, but rather that the ways in which youth engage civically has evolved. Young people of the present generation "are more likely than ever to engage in volunteer work" (Arnett, 2007, p. 26). An international study (Torney-Purta, 2002; Torney-Purta, Lehmann, Oswald, & Schulz, 2001) conducted across 28 countries suggests that today's young people's idea of engaged citizenship extends beyond conventional notions of "civics" as political participation, and includes activities that are of benefit to the broader community (Torney-Purta, 2002, p. 206). In one instance, 80% of 14-year-olds surveyed in the United States thought it was important or very important that adults participate in helping out their community or other social causes, such as promoting human rights or protecting the environment (Baldi, Perie, Skidmore, Greenberg, & Hahn, 2001; Torney-Purta, 2002). Fifty percent reported membership in volunteer organizations (Torney-Purta, 2002).

Contrary to some common views, this evidence shows how adolescents express concern over issues pertaining to some aspect of the whole of humanity (Warren, 2011), rather than just their own personal concerns. Granted, these concerns may be more central in the lives of some adolescents, winning their time and energy, while other adolescents may just show lip service. But these findings clearly show that the propensity for unselfish action thrives at this stage of life.

The intention to contribute to the world beyond the self may be more common in adolescence than some may think and could surely be further developed given proper attention by educators. The previously mentioned Stanford University study (Bronk, 2005; Damon, 2008) reports that 270 sixth, ninth, and twelfth graders, as well as college students, were interviewed and surveyed about their purposes in life. The results suggest a progressive increase in intentions to make some sort of social contribution during this age period. Findings indicated that 28% of the sixth graders expressed intentions to make a prosocial difference to people, ideas, or some domain of experience (i.e., work, school, family, social causes, and so on). These percentages increased during adolescence so that by college almost 50% of the young people indicated this intention (Moran, 2009). In addition, by twelfth grade and college even more of those adolescents said that they were actually acting on their prosocial intentions in a systematic way (Moran, 2009). This finding about adolescents supports school leaders in providing opportunities for garnishing these intentions to build an inclusive context in school.

Four more studies in the PYD tradition also offer encouraging evidence that youth entertain lofty moral ideals about what it means to be a thriving, caring, and contributing human being. In the first study Amy Alberts and her colleagues (2006) asked 691 parents/guardians and early adolescents to define the notion of youth "thriving." The proportion of adolescents who mentioned characteristics relating to inclusive-oriented and general moral and civic behavior differed significantly from the proportion of those qualities mentioned by the adults. For example, 48.8% of youth mentioned character as central to thriving, whereas only 14.1% of the adults did so; "caring" was mentioned by 21.9% of youth and 14.1% of adults, while "contribution" was reported by 42% of adolescents and only 13.6% of adults. Even more notable is the fact that when parents did mention contribution as a salient facet of youth thriving, they emphasized contribution to self while youth focused on contribution to the community.

In another study Pamela King and her colleagues (2005) also examined adolescents' views of what it means to "thrive" and found that many included inclusion-oriented qualities such as accepting diversity, being respectful, being kind, being considerate, caring for others, being empathic, and making positive contributions to others.

In a third investigation Flanagan and Faison (2001) asked adolescents to identify the characteristics of a "good citizen." Though many adolescents described passive or "lowest common denominator qualities," such as "someone who stayed out of trouble, didn't lie, cheat, or steal," many others described proactive people who "helped others" and "contributed to the community" (p. 11).

Similar results arose from a fourth study in which a small cross-national sample of sixth and ninth graders was asked to describe "the good life" and "the good person." Broad categories for characterizing a good person such as "helping others" and "giving of oneself" were identified by at least as many youth as the categories of "achieving personal goals" and "making oneself happy" were. And, notably, the category of "staying out of trouble" was reported less frequently. Similarly, "treats other well" and "helps others" were also the most commonly mentioned category descriptors attached to someone leading a good life (Bronk, 2008, pp. 721–722).

Taken together, this body of work underscores the presence of higher order ideals on the part of many young people about who they wish to become. It attests that prosocial ways of being are a part of young people's concerns. Prosocial purpose is emerging as a developmental trend that naturally correlates with age during adolescence. Further, some studies suggest that people who are more purposefully caring have stronger and warmer relationships with mentors (Bronk, 2005, p. 391; Hart, Yates, Fegley, & Wilson 1995 p. 338), and they glean more opportunities from their environments to form and test their prosocial commitments (Hart, Yates, Fegley, & Wilson 1995, p. 338). What impact can deliberate and systematic efforts in these directions have on youngsters' "purposeful" prosocial development, and on their "thriving" in general?

The misunderstanding of adolescents as fundamentally selfish beings may be grounded in a faulty notion in Western culture pitting prosocial action and intentions as antithetical to self-serving motives. Consider the following indictment, based on an incomplete interpretation of developmental theory. During the period of adolescence, when individuals first consider who they want to become and who they are, their cognitive and physical capacities are changing and developing rapidly (Erikson, 1968). Such rapid development necessitates an investment in self-consciousness and self-focusing that gives rise to a level of self-absorption that precludes acting in the interests of anyone but oneself. This argument draws upon developmental theory to present a deceptive picture, and the dualistic view of self-absorption as opposite of prosocial behaviors is misleading.

Two additional reports from the Stanford Youth Purpose study (Mariano & Michalowski, 2009; Yeager & Bundick, 2009) found that adolescents actually report multiple motives for their intentions and life goals. Prosocial inclinations do not preclude those that are directed toward the development of self. Moreover, new understandings of self-development recast many aspects of adolescents' egocentrism as foundational to the prosocial abilities associated with inclusive ways of being. For instance, compared with younger children and adults, adolescents may have the tendency to believe that they are the focus of everyone else's attention and concern—a phenomenon known as "imaginary audience" (Elkind & Bowen, 1979). They may develop an overexaggerated opinion of their own importance, feeling that they are special and unique—a cognitive distortion called the "personal fable" (Berk, 2009, p. 252). But these tendencies are at least partly an indication of advances in perspective taking because they signal a heightened concern with what others may think (Berk, 2009, p. 252; see also Vartanian & Powlishta, 1996). Youth with perspective-taking skills are more likely to show empathy and sympathy toward others, as well as handle difficult social situations with more maturity (Fitzgerald & White, 2003). When youth are asked to take on the perspective of another person, such as through role-playing activities, they are more likely to be accepting of others whom they see as different from themselves, and they may show more prosocial behaviors (Chalmers & Townshend, 1990). Thus prosocial and self-focused behaviors can coexist and are not necessary mutually exclusive of each other.

Actually, research on the psychology of moral commitment shows that individuals who act in the interests of others see their actions also as serving their own self-interest (e.g., see Colby & Damon, 1992; Snyder & Omoto, 1992). Similar evidence shows that concern for other people is not incompatible with caring for others either within or outside of one's own immediate environment (Baltes, Lindenberger, & Staudinger, 2006; Cialdini, Brown, Lewis, Luce, & Neuberg, 1997). Acting in the interests of other people can make young people feel good about themselves and support their self-esteem. Plus, when young people view themselves in a positive light, as moral and noble people, then acting in noble ways promotes their own psychological integrity because their personal and moral goals align. Young people who showed commitment to improving their communities actually had a strong sense of who they were as people and their prosocial activities had strong personal salience (Hart, Yates, Fegley, & Wilson, 1995).

The idea of adolescents as a group that is uniquely selfish and uncooperative is incomplete for another reason. No phenomenon can be separated from the context in which it is embedded. Therefore, adolescents' "rebelliousness" must be placed within a larger ecological systems context if we are to understand it properly—a problem that the PYD approach addresses. Bioecological models of human development (Bronfennbrenner & Morris, 1998) recognize that children and youth are nested within structures including home, school, and neighborhood, and each of these layers impacts that young person's development and behavior. Further, bidirectional influences occur, so that adolescents and adults mutually influence each other's development. As children enter adolescence it is not uncommon for them to distance themselves psychologically from their parents as they strive for independence (Berk, 2009, p. 205; Gure, Ucanok, & Sayil, 2006), and families may experience a rise in parent-child conflict during this time. However, Steinberg and Silk (2002) observe that children's puberty may also coincide with their parents hitting middle age. As parents realize that their children will soon leave home, they may push for more family togetherness, and this imbalance can also contribute to perceptions of a rise in conflict. The reality is, however, that by the end of late adolescence, continuing conflict of this type is not the trend (Berk, 2009, p. 205). In spite of this potential conflict, most teenagers continue to value family as central in their lives and as a strong source of emotional support. Their prosocial commitment to family endures throughout adolescence.

REFLECTION 2: INTEGRATE INCLUSIVE IDEAS INTO THE SCHOOL CULTURE AND CURRICULUM

Understanding the research-based realities of adolescent development, we can be confident as educators that adolescents will respond to our efforts to promote the emergence of inclusive behavior in the classroom if our approaches are informed and systematic. Educators should be assured that adopting a strengths perspective on young people's capabilities is not just a sentimental notion. It is grounded in theory and research.

Adopting a perspective focused on student strengths, as described in developmental theory, can easily be translated into educational approaches and programs. No doubt, elementary and middle school teachers will already be practicing some viable techniques. A common practice, for instance, is the behaviorist technique of rewarding students through recognition for good behavior, or by bringing attention to behaviors where they are lacking. Placing stars in front of students' names in a public space is a popular practice that comes to mind (though one that may be frequently used for rewarding academic success, rather than exemplary inclusive behavior).

However, school leaders can assist teachers to expand this type of practice by utilizing social and evaluation programs that more deeply integrate inclusive practices into the school context. Even more broadly, educational leaders will do well to promote a school culture in which students are not only expected to excel academically, but where they are also expected to excel in personal skills. "Character education" is a term that is often used to describe this expanded type of approach. Yet, character education can refer to a wide variety of approaches and programs that may include anything from fostering thoughtful inquiry on moral issues to the consideration of personal virtues (McKenzie, 2004). Choosing from this wide repertoire of existing approaches may be overwhelming to educators; one strategy is to choose programs that incorporate principles of inclusive ways of being. Schools can endeavor to move away from using programs that place a strict focus on addressing specific problem behaviors, such as cheating, merely tolerating others who we see as different, or bullying, to explore how they might promote the upper limits of inclusive behaviors in their students. Though they have their own merit, a singular focus on teaching children and youth to avoid problem behaviors will be less useful than those that present a more proactive vision of what children and adolescents can accomplish.

Flanagan and Faison (2001) suggest attention would be better spent on applying a "civic" standard to character education in schools. To apply such a civic standard they note that two questions school leaders should address are: "(a) to what extent is an orientation to the well-being of others and the common good thematic in the program, and (b) to what extent are participants encouraged to think critically about and be actively engaged in concerns of their community?" (p. 11). They argue that other reflective and prosocial skills are not often a part of character education approaches. Flanagan and Faison's standard can be taken even further to reflect an "inclusion" approach that incorporates ideas about the positive capacities of young people.

Character education programs that prescribe a set of virtues to students do exist. However, they have been widely criticized if they are absent of thoughtful reflection or practical direction. When they are delivered in the context of critical thinking and action that is useful to the students is involved, however, they can be highly effective for promoting inclusion (Flanagan & Faison, 2001). An example of such a program occurred with hundreds of teachers in a postwar Eastern European country where statewide interethnic violence had been rampant (International Education for Peace Institute, 2006, http://www.efpinternational.org). In this project, teachers integrated social and personal peace-building principles, such as the concept of unity in diversity, gender equality, and the concept of the fundamental equality and oneness of all people, into the school subjects of elementary, middle school, and high school classrooms. Students then used school assignments and artistic presentations to share their understandings with peers across ethnic communities. Students held cross-community dialogues in which they created vision and mission statements and plans around affecting moral leadership in their country. In addition, they attended interactive study groups and lectures in which they were asked to critically consider real-world applications of peace-enhancing principles at various social levels, including their personal lives, family, school, country, and the world. In this project some teachers designed their history lessons so as to introduce interpretations of civilizations as reflecting varied expressions of unity and diversity. A distinguishing feature of the program described here is the creative license given to teachers to apply general principles relating to inclusion into their areas of expertise. In recent years multiple other programs in schools across the United States have been recognized for their whole-school and whole-community approach to promoting positive youth development (see Character Education Partnership, 2010). Although the term "inclusion" was not used specifically, it was a theme that applies to this project and the cultural context. The activities were effective because students critically applied their learning in the real world.

Although the postwar project described was not based on empirical research per se, a few research-based models depicting children's strengths have been developed since then. Peterson and Seligman's (2004) model defines and discusses six sets of "character strengths and virtues" with useful real-life examples. The strengths of "humanity" (i.e., kindness, compassion, and care) and of "justice" (i.e., citizenship, fairness, and social responsibility) lend themselves well to inclusion-oriented strengths and could be used to guide development of these skills and attitudes as well as to monitor school, classroom, and students' progress. The model offers behavioral and attitudinal standards with illustrative examples of well-developed strengths in each of the six areas.

The apparent advantages of the strength approach are multiple. It is grounded in research, but is inevitably designed by those who use it, typically school leaders, guidance staff, and teachers. It initially allows flexibility and originality in creating examples, activities, and assessments while simultaneously building each educator's own skill base. This approach could be implemented on a smaller level than in the Eastern European example, but it is easy to imagine how this type of assessment might take on greater proportions, given the needs and inclination of specific schools. School leaders, working with staff and teachers, can develop schoolwide standards, expectations, and activities that are age appropriate, designating enhanced levels of exemplary attitudes and behaviors as students grow. Schools could follow their students longitudinally, developing unique assessments for their particular emphases, eventually gathering uniform information from classrooms to form a school database.

One limitation of Peterson and Seligman's (2004) model, however, is the apparent focus on adults in a good deal of their examples of strengths. This is not an inherent weakness of their work by any means, but requires school leaders and teachers to interpret for younger role models in the K–12 context.

Two other prominent models that deal with children and youth also offer guidance in developing these kinds of programs in schools. First, Search

Institute's Developmental Assets model (Benson, 2006) offers a framework of 40 characteristics ("assets") that support thriving in a child's life. A number of these assets are inclusion-oriented personal strengths like "caring" and "equality and social justice" (p. 33). A second model offered by Richard Lerner and his colleagues (2005) is an empirically derived list of five components of positive youth development. These five "C's" are building blocks of positive development. They include "competence" in various areas, like "positive social connections" and "self-confidence," but they also include the inclusion-oriented strengths of "caring and compassion" and "character." Additionally, they hypothesize that when some combination of these five characteristics is present in a young person's life, a sixth "C," "contribution," may emerge.

The strength of these two models is that they offer an ecological perspective on children's strengths. In other words, they explicitly recognize that the child is affected by several developmental contexts and influences over time (i.e., family, extended family, school, societal values), and in turn the child can act upon those settings and experiences (Bronfenbrenner & Evans, 2000). Relationships are therefore bidirectional, so that children's strengths shape the classroom environment and the environment shapes their strengths. Accordingly, teachers might devise evaluations that assess inclusive strengths of individual students and also of the classroom culture. The Search Institute model (Benson, 2006), for instance, offers a number of other personal, familial, and larger societal assets that teachers can develop and monitor in conjunction with inclusion-oriented strengths.

REFLECTION 3: RESPONSIVE, DELIBERATE, AND UNAMBIGUOUS TEACHING FOR INCLUSION

Up to this point, this chapter has discussed the psychological stance that educators can adopt when teaching for inclusion. As noted, critical assessment of existing dominant worldviews about children's abilities and natures is a foundational step toward teaching for inclusion. Also, teachers can effectively exercise creative license in teaching and assessment of inclusive ways of being. A third critical element, however, calls for use of specified and high-quality instruction that works in concert with responsiveness. Research shows that warmth without skillful instruction is less than optimal to achieve educators' intended aims, even in the area of teaching for inclusion-oriented strengths. Support for this idea comes from one study conducted by Margaret Burchinal and her colleagues (2008) that evaluated 240 randomly selected prekindergarten programs. They studied classroom quality and academic achievement for more than 700 children in both the prekindergarten and kindergarten year and found that sensitive and instructional quality in prekindergarten predicted social skills through the end of kindergarten.

These specific combinations of responsiveness and instruction will also be more likely to work than other approaches when teaching for inclusion. Most teachers will discover what works and what does not through their own experimentation, but evidence shows that being deliberate and unambiguous in communicating ideals of inclusion are necessary ingredients for successful practice. Evidence also shows that students will benefit from attending schools that provide active, focused, and deliberate curricular instruction in inclusion. Consider, too, that parent and peer attitudes may not always be the main influence on children's attitudes pertaining to inclusion. In their research, Aboud and Doyle (1996) found racial attitudes of elementary school students were not necessarily shared by either parents or friends; rather, the larger community context, as demonstrated through social institutions, may affect children's attitudes most. Children gather implicit messages from their environments, so the absence of deliberate, explicit, and clear communication of information may actually act to the detriment of inclusive strengths. As one expert notes, under those circumstances "children may fill in the gaps with messages they learn from the media, or elsewhere" (Berk, 2009, p. 471).

Recognition of the powerful role schools play in shaping students' attitudes can make the teaching of inclusion seem like a daunting task. How can schools counteract the multiple negative messages in media, culture, and society at large? Educators can be encouraged by the fact that children are highly influenced by symbols and by the conduct of authority figures in schools. As the context in which they spend a good number of their waking hours, therefore, school is an opportune place in which to influence children's attitudes. A forceful piece of evidence comes from a study conducted in 2001 by Bigler, Brown, and Markell. More justly replicating the "blue-eyed, brown-eyed" study of the 1970s, students (7–12 years old) at a summer school program were made to wear either yellow or blue shirts; posters were hung in the classroom that assigned high status to one of the two groups. In one assignment teachers organized students according to these social groupings, thereby recognizing differential status between the groups. Attitude measures given to these students showed that they developed prejudice against low-status group members. In a second situation, however, when teachers ignored the status hierarchy, no prejudicial attitudes emerged.

Another study illustrates "deliberate" and "unambiguous" teaching for inclusion-oriented strengths. This research points to very specific types of modeling behavior that school leaders can nurture and teachers can utilize. Yarrow, Scott, and Waxler (1973) evaluated preschoolers' sympathetic sentiment and action by exposing them to theoretical and real situations that called for helpfulness. In one case, the children were asked to respond to pictures of people and animals in distress. The children who had observed their teacher modeling empathic responses to similar pictures 2 days earlier said they would offer help significantly more frequently than did the children who had not seen this modeling. The helpful children made sympathetic comments like "I'd get him a band aid" or "I'd pick up her packages" (p. 250).

In a second situation in this same study, the preschoolers were observed for actual caring behavior through exposure to staged scenarios. For example, in a house adjacent to the preschool, a mother invited the child to play with her infant. In the course of the visit, the mother "accidentally" drops various objects and the preschooler is given the opportunity to pick them up for her (Yarrow et al., 1973, p. 248). In this case, children who had observed their teachers model care in both theoretical (pictures or play dioramas) and behavioral interactions were the ones who showed the greatest prosocial behavior. Interestingly, children who had been exposed to a nurturant teacher—one who initiated friendly interaction with the children, was sympathetic and protective, praised the children, and expressed confidence in their abilities (Yarrow et al., 1973, p. 245)—showed statistically significant strengths in this area more than others. In contrast, those children with the same training, but from teachers who maintained a reserved attitude and were critical or nonattentive, showed fewer or nonsignificant marked strengths. Thus findings indicated that educators must embrace the importance of deliberate, extensive, and ongoing modeling. Further, such modeling must be accompanied by responsiveness and a genuinely supportive attitude on the part of the instructor.

Metaphors about the nature of the child, gleaned from developmental and learning theory, also illustrate the point that children show empathy and prosocial behaviors and attitudes at an early age and these patterns continue through adolescence and beyond. Growth models of the child's development and the role of the adults in fostering it emerge in sociocultural theory. In Vygotsky's scheme, interaction with knowledgeable adults powerfully shapes children's progress. As adults "scaffold" children's learning in specific skills within a "zone of proximal development" the child picks up new competencies (Berk, 2009). For many inclusion-oriented strengths, however, the metaphor is more one of enhancement than of origination. In a variety of cases, children come into the world already possessing the roots of inclusion-oriented moral strengths like empathy, self-control, and fairness (for variants of this argument, see Damon, 1998; Wilson, 1993). Most scholars agree that empathy, for instance, is a natural building block of later moral sentiment, and is an action that is present at birth. Empathic tendencies are present in hospital nurseries when newborns show signs of distress at other infants' crying (Hoffman, 2000). Moreover, children are not passive recipients of values, but "advance themselves" as they try out a variety of skills (Berk, 2009, p. 267). More recent "developmental systems" theories advocate this idea as well, showing how organisms are able to change themselves by their own activities (Thelen & Smith, 1998).

CONCLUSION

Although many of the studies cited in this chapter focus on classroom-level research, the findings clearly show the value of reinforcing attitudes and behaviors by creating a schoolwide culture of inclusion with high expectations and standards. Undoubtedly, building a culture consistent across classrooms, grades, and teachers would enhance the influence of collective modeling of deliberate, responsive, and unambiguous adults on students. This chapter presented a set of initial recommendations to address this question from a PYD perspective. The recommendations are by no means exhaustive, but they highlight two essential points. First, advances in developmental theory accentuate children's potential to think, feel, and act in inclusive ways in real-life settings. The opening comments by Jason attest to this potential, as does a growing body of research. Second, school leaders, staff, and teachers are in a favorable position to influence children's attitudes and behavior toward inclusion. Because they stand at the interface between developmental research and practice, teachers can offer deliberate, specific, and creative instruction in inclusion. Jason's case also exemplifies this point. Though Jason was self-directed, motivated, and possessed the strength of empathy as a 6-year-old, the adults in his life played a critical role in helping him bring this strength into the realm of sustained action. His teacher's classroom presentation inspired him and supported his action in a specific direction. Teachers and other adults were alert to Jason's concerns and responded through ongoing encouragement and practical help. They helped him raise money, for instance, and gather other concerned citizens around this effort. Jason's case, as well as developmental theory, therefore, outlines a developmental pattern that supports inclusion. Within this pattern, educators contributed, providing bridges between children's strengths and the realization of those strengths. Getting at the heart of inclusion challenges educators to consider their own worldviews and the psychological and developmental workings of the young people they serve.

REFERENCES

Aboud, F. E., & Doyle, A. (1996). Parental and peer influences on children's racial attitudes. *International Journal of Intercultural Relations, 20*(3/4), 371–383.

Alberts, A. E., Christianson, E. D., Chase, P., Naudeau, S. Phelps, E & Lerner, R. M. (2006). Qualitative and quantitative assessment of thriving and contribution in early adolescence: Findings from the 4-H study of positive youth development. *Journal of Youth Development: Bridging Research & Practice, 1*(2). Retrieved from http://www.nae4ha.org/directory/jyd/index.html

Arnett, J. J. (2007). Suffering, selfish, slackers? Myths and reality about emerging adults. *Journal of Youth and Adolescence, 36,* 23–29.

Baldi, S., Perie, M., Skidmore, D., Greenberg, E., & Hahn, C. (2001). *What democracy means to ninth-graders: U.S. results from the international IEA Civic Education Study* (NCES 2001-096). Washington, DC: U.S. Department of Education, National Center for Education Statistics.

Baltes, P. B., Lindenberger, U., & Staudinger, U. M. (2006). Life span theory in developmental psychology. In R. M. Lerner & W. Damon (Eds.), *Handbook of child psychology: Vol. 1. Theoretical models of human development* (6th ed., pp. 569–664). Hoboken, NJ: Wiley.

Benson, P. L. (2006). *All kids are our kids: What communities must do to raise caring and responsible children and adolescents* (2nd ed.). San Francisco: Jossey-Bass.

Berk, L. E. (2009). *Child development* (8th ed.). Boston: Pearson.

Bigler, R. S., Brown, C. S., & Markell, M. (2001). When groups are not created equal: Effects of group status on the formation of intergroup attitudes in children. *Child Development, 66,* 1072–1087.

Bronfenbrenner, U., & Evans, G. W. (2000). Developmental science in the 21st century: Emerging theoretical models, research designs, and empirical findings. *Social Development, 9,* 115–125.

Bronfenbrenner, U., & Morris, P.A. (1998). The ecology of developmental processes. In R. M. Lerner (Ed.), *Handbook of child psychology: Vol. 1. Theoretical models of human development* (5th ed., pp. 535–584). New York: Wiley.

Bronk, K. C. (2005). Portraits of purpose: A study examining the ways a sense of purpose contributes to positive youth development. *Dissertation Abstracts International. Humanities and Social Sciences,* AAT 3187267.

Bronk, K. C. (2008). Humility among adolescent purpose exemplars. *Journal of Research in Character Education, 6*(1), 35–51.

Burchinal, M., Howes, C., Pianta, R., Bryant, D., Early, D., Clifford, R., & Barbarin, O. (2008). Predicting child outcomes at the end of kindergarten from the quality of pre-kindergarten teacher-child interactions and instruction. *Applied Developmental Science, 12*(3), 140–153.

Chalmers, J. B., & Townshend, M. A. R. (1990). The effects of training in social perspective taking on socially maladjusted girls. *Child Development, 61,* 178–190.

Character Education Partnership. (2010). 2010 National schools of character: Award-winning practices. Retrieved November 30, 2010, from http://www.character.org

Cialdini, R. B., Brown, S. L., Lewis, B. P., Luce, C., & Neuberg, S. L. (1997). Reinterpreting the empathy-altruism relationship: When one into one equals oneness. *Journal of Personality and Social Psychology, 73*(3), 481–494.

Colby, A., & Damon, W. (1992). *Some do care: Contemporary lives of moral commitment.* New York: Free Press.

Damon, W. (1998). *The moral child: Nurturing children's natural moral growth.* New York: Free Press.

Damon, W. (2008). *The path to purpose: Helping our children find their calling in life.* New York: Free Press.

Damon, W., Menon, J., & Bronk, K. C. (2003). The development of purpose in adolescence. *Applied Developmental Science, 7*(3), 119–128.

Darley, J. M., & Latané, B. (1968). Bystander intervention in emergencies: Diffusion of responsibility. *Journal of Personality and Social Psychology, 8,* 377–383.

Elkind, D., & Bowen, R. (1979). Imaginary audience behavior in children and adolescents. *Developmental Psychology, 15,* 33–44.

Erikson, E. H. (1968). *Identity: youth and crisis.* New York: Norton.

Fitzgerald, D. P., & White, K. J. (2003). Linking children's social worlds: Perspective-taking in parent-child and peer contexts. *Social Behavior and Personality, 31,* 509–522.

Flanagan, C. A., & Faison, N. (2001). Youth civic development: Implications of research for social policy and programs. *Social Policy Report* (Society for Research on Adolescence), *15*(1), 3–18.

Glaser, A. (2005). *A call to compassion: Bringing Buddhist practices of the heart into the soul of psychology.* Berwick, ME: Nicolas-Hays.

Gure, A., Ucanok, Z., & Sayil, M. (2006). The associations among perceived pubertal timing, parental relations, and self-perception in Turkish adolescents. *Journal of Youth and Adolescence, 35,* 541–550.

Hall, G. S. (1904). *Adolescence: Its psychology and its relations to physiology, anthropology, sociology, sex, crime, religion, and education.* Englewood Cliffs, NJ: Prentice-Hall.

Hart, D., Yates, M., Fegley, S., & Wilson, G. (1995). Moral commitment in inner-city adolescents. In M. Killen & D. Hart (Eds.), *Morality in everyday life: Developmental perspectives* (pp. 317–341). Cambridge, UK: Cambridge University Press,.

Hoffman, M. (2000). *Empathy and moral development.* Cambridge, UK: Cambridge University Press.

Keyes, C. L. M. (2002). The mental health continuum: From languishing to flourishing in life. *Journal of Health and Behavior Research, 43,* 207–222.

King, P. E., Dowling, E. M., Mueller, R., White, K., Schultz, W., Osborn, P., et. al. (2005). Thriving in adolescence. The voices of youth-serving practitioners, parents, and early and late adolescents. *Journal of Early Adolescence, 25,* (1), 94–112.

Larson, R. (2000, January). Towards a psychology of positive youth development. *American Psychologist, 55*(1), 170–183.

Lerner, R., Lerner, J. V., Almerigi, J. V., & Theokas, C. (2005). Positive youth development, participation in community youth development programs, and community contributions of 5th grade adolescents: Findings from the first wave of the 4-H Study of Positive Youth Development. *Journal of Early Adolescence, 25*(1), 17–71.

Lerner, R. M., Roeser, R. W., & Phelps, E. (2008). Positive development, spirituality, and generosity in youth: An introduction to the issues. In R. M. Lerner, R. W. Roeser, and E. Phelps (Eds.), *Positive youth development and spirituality: From theory to research* (pp. 210–230). West Conshohocken, PA: Templeton Foundation Press.

Mariano, J. M., & Michalowski, J. (2009). Is there a language of youth purpose? References to positive states and coping styles by adolescents with different kinds of purpose. *Journal of Research in Character Education, 7*(1), 1–24.

McKenzie, M. (2004). Seeing the spectrum: North American approaches to emotional, social, and moral education. *The Educational Forum, 69*, 79–90.

Moran, S. (2009). Purpose: Giftedness in intrapersonal intelligence. *High Ability Studies, 20*(2), 143–159.

Peterson, C. (2006). *A primer in positive psychology.* Oxford: Oxford University Press.

Peterson, C., & Seligman, M. E. P. (2004). *Character strengths and virtues: A handbook and classification.* Oxford: Oxford University Press.

Post, S. G. (2003). *Unlimited love: Altruism, compassion, and service.* West Conshohocken, PA: Templeton Foundation Press.

Snyder, M., & Omoto, A. M. (1992). Who helps and why?: The psychology of AIDS volunteerism. In S. Spacapan & S. Oskamp (Eds.), *Helping and being helped: Naturalistic studies* (pp. 213–239). Newbury Park, CA: Sage.

Steinberg, L. D., & Silk, J. S. (2002). Parenting adolescents. In M. H. Bornstein (Ed.), *Handbook of parenting: Vol. 1. Children and parenting* (2nd ed., pp. 103–134). Mahwah, NJ: Erlbaum.

Thelen, E., & Smith, L. B. (1998). Dynamic systems theories. In W. Damon & R. M. Lerner (Eds.), *Handbook of child psychology: Vol. 1. Theoretical models of human development* (5th ed., pp. 563–633). Hoboken, NJ: Wiley.

Torney-Purta, J. (2002). The school's role in developing civic engagement: A study of adolescents in twenty-eight countries. *Applied Developmental Science, 6*(4), 203–212.

Torney-Purta, J., Lehmann, R., Oswald, H., & Schulz, W. (2001). *Citizenship and education in twenty eight countries: The civic knowledge and engagement of adolescents.* Amsterdam: IEA (International Association for the Evaluation of Educational Achievement).

Vartanian, L. R., & Powlishta, K. K. (1996). A longitudinal examination of the social-cognitive foundations of adolescent egocentricism. *Journal of Early Adolescence, 16*, 157–178.

Warren, A. E. A. (2011). Strengthening human potential for great love: Compassion through elaborative development. In A. E. A. Warren, R. M. Lerner, & E. Phelps (Eds.), *Thriving and spirituality among youth: Research perspectives and future possibilities.* Hoboken, NJ: Wiley.

Wilson, J. Q. (1993). *The moral sense.* New York: Free Press.

Yarrow, M. R., Scott, P. M., & Waxler, C. Z. (1973). Learning concern for others. *Developmental Psychology, 8*, 240–260.

Yeager, D. S., & Bundick, M. J. (2009). The role of purposeful work goals in promoting meaning in life and in schoolwork during adolescence. *Journal of Adolescent Research, 24*(4), 423–452.

Part III

PERSPECTIVES ON INCLUSIVE PRACTICES

This Part offers a multiperspective view of inclusive practices through the lenses of students who are racially and ethnically diverse, students who have refugee status, students who are English language learners, students who are lesbian, gay, bisexual, transgender, and queer/questioning (LGBTQ), and examines gender and poverty issues in student learning.

Key research on the races, ethnicities, and cultures represented in today's classrooms is presented in the following chapters. In Chapter 7 Marie Byrd Blake discusses research on races, ethnicities, and cultures represented in today's classrooms. The chapter summarizes studies of schools that show the changes required in schools and curriculum to ensure the academic achievement of students of all races, ethnicities, and cultures. Examples of what works are included to ensure that all students make adequate academic progress. Implications for leadership in schools to foster academic achievement of all students are discussed, as well as the procedures required in teacher preparation to develop and assess culturally responsive education. Culturally congruent critical pedagogy is also explained as a fundamental component of the education of students from diverse races, ethnicities, and cultures. Despite continued attention, differences continue to prevail among Hispanic, Black, American Indian/Alaska Native, Asian, Native Hawaiian or Other Pacific Islander, and White students. Lessons from the area of English language learning support the creation of a school community that nurtures feelings of belonging among different groups of language learners in a school. Effective programs for welcoming multiple languages in schools are presented in Chapter 8. Here Rebecca Burns shares effective programs for welcoming multiple languages in schools. The diversity of students who are English language learners is poorly reflected in a diversity of programs. Most U.S. schools offer no bilingual education, relying instead on decreasing amounts of pull-out English instruction. States vary in training requirements for teachers who work with English language learners; the number of teachers with appropriate training lags far behind the number of positions. Classroom educators work around imposed restrictions to meet the needs of learners, but political extremism surrounding the education of English language learners reinforces the marginalization of these students. The chapter explores many important questions: What counts as a language? How language proficient does one have to be to count as a speaker? Shall we include major English dialect groups? A history of these developments and protected access is shared, along with a lesson in ownership and authorship of school data and policies. In such programs, language awareness is one tool for identifying bias and barriers and for constructing an inviting curriculum.

Refugee youth are often confused with immigrant youth, yet there are huge differences between refugees and other immigrants; Chapter 9 discusses this distinction. J. Lynn McBrien highlights important characteristics of refugee youth, describes the issues surrounding this group in schools, and outlines the policies and practices of inclusion related to refugee youth. Refugee youth are often confused with immigrant youth, yet there are huge differences between refugees and other immigrants. Political refugees do not cross borders in search of economic, educational, or social gains, but rather for fear of their lives, with many families having experienced one or more traumatic experiences. The chapter describes what schools can do to support the academic success of refugee youth and increase family understanding about academic expectations through networks between refugee agencies and their liaisons. School leaders aware of the impact of commonplace events in school—for example, bells to announce class changes or fire drills, which may trigger traumatic memories of bomb blasts—are in a much stronger position to be able to support the creation of a sensitive environment conducive to learning. Following the terrorist attack on the United States, many refugees, especially Muslims, experienced heightened instances of discrimination in schools. The chapter describes research on best practices, which shows that when given support, refugee youth can overcome discrimination in order to achieve academically and attain competent levels of acculturation.

An exploration of ways in which lesbian, gay, bisexual, transgender, and queer/questioning (LGBTQ) young people and families are marginalized in schools and underrepresented in classrooms and curriculum is explored in Chapter 10. Tom Crisp explores ways in which young people who are LGBTQ and their families are marginalized in schools and underrepresented in classrooms and curriculum. A synthesis of research findings initiates an examination of how American classrooms habitually reflect on and reinforce heteronormativity. Focusing on physical components of schools (i.e., locker rooms, restrooms) and classrooms (i.e., literature used, textbooks, posters) as well as attitudes, perspectives, and language, this chapter makes explicit the ways heterosexuality is constructed as a "normal" way of being. This chapter examines (mis)conceptions, key concepts, and theoretical as well as pedagogical approaches to inclusive classrooms that work to disrupt heteronormativity and confront homophobia. The chapter also outlines specific ways that teachers and curriculum leaders can make classrooms more inclusive of LGBTQ students and their families. Creating effective communities of learning for students who are LGBTQ is a politically charged issue but one that is central to how a school creates a community of learning for all students.

The latter part of this section focuses upon issues of gender and poverty. Major themes in perceptions of gender in schools form the backdrop of the perspective and contribution of gender issues to understanding effective inclusive practices. Changes in trends related to gendered stereotypes, selection, behavior, and educational outcomes, as well as the practice of single-sex classrooms, programs, and schools, are presented in Chapter 11. Here Janice R. Fauske begins with explanations of gender as being different from sex (male or female), with two cases for illustration. This chapter then outlines four major themes in perceptions of gender in schools: (1) trends related to gender stereotypes, selection, behavior, and educational outcomes; (2) single-sex classrooms, programs, and schools, citing research and implications for student learning; (3) school, district, state, and national trends and policies as well legal and social implications; and (4) creating a safe and inviting space for multiple gendered ecologies to intersect and thrive. Conceptualizations of poverty and economic disadvantage as they pertain to the experience of children in schools are offered in Chapter 12. Judy F. Carr examines existing conceptualizations of poverty and economic disadvantage as they pertain to the experience of children in schools. Key concepts from the work of Ruby Payne (2005) are summarized, and a critique of Payne's work is offered in order to provide a structure from which school leaders, both teachers and administrators, may confront inequalities that may be based on socioeconomic differences among students in their schools. The unequivocal conviction is established that students who are socioeconomically disadvantaged can learn at high levels and schools as systems can help these students do so, no matter how severe their economic disadvantage may be. Tools and strategies to assist school leaders in reflecting on their own belief systems about children and families in poverty are included.

CHAPTER 7

Ethnicity, Race, and Culture: A Case for Cultural Competence

Marie Byrd-Blake

She remembers the first day of kindergarten vividly. The bus dropped her off at a building that was larger than any she'd ever seen. When she was ushered into the classroom, she looked around and didn't see anyone with her skin color or hair that looked like hers. When the teacher spoke, her language and vocabulary were similar to what she'd heard on television, but it was not the language she'd become fluent in. Wanting to disappear, she didn't utter a word because she didn't know how to speak this new form of English. No one looked like her or sounded like her. The picture on the cover of the book the teacher read to the class was of children with blond and brown straight hair, nice clothes with pretty colors, and pale skin with rosy cheeks. The children in the book were playing games she had never played.

The teacher asked her name, but she dared not respond; she didn't want the others to laugh at how she spoke. On the playground, she sat alone on a swing as some of the other children pointed at her and said things. All throughout the day, her feelings of inadequacy caused her to remain silent and not utter a word. Her only thought was to go back home where everyone looked and sounded like her, where all was familiar, and where she felt accepted. At school, she quickly learned that being different equated to not being accepted. Thus began the burdensome need she acquired of having to prove her worth when she was at school or in a situation where the majority race was greater.

The needs of the changing demographic population in the United States have long surpassed the focus and response of the educational and political community. Today's educators are focused on the accountability of schools as a result of national standardized testing policies and mandated state and local academic standards. Such accountability policies and standardized testing mandates will not reach success until the diversity in today's schools is taken into account through a focus on educator cultural competence and instructing students through culturally inclusive instructional strategies. Significant achievement gaps in student performance continue to exist between racial/ethnic subgroups (Planty et al., 2009). These data have identified a national predicament in American schools that warrants attention. The academic achievement of students from minority races, ethnicities, or cultures continues to hinder the overall American national achievement.

The statistics are alarming. Although almost half (44% in 2006) of the students enrolled in U.S. public and private schools are identified as being of a racial/ethnic minority or nonwhite, over 80% of the teachers who instruct them identified themselves as White (NCES, 2008). The U.S. Census Bureau (2010) has estimated that ethnic minorities will encompass over 50% of the United States by the year 2050. As a result, public school teachers will continue to interact regularly with a culturally pluralistic population. Seidl (2007) explains the interaction between cultures in this way:

> For many middle-class White people, relationships with people of color often occur within a context where there are few people of color in number and, thus, White people may experience no discernible alternative cultural presence. . . . though many prospective teachers of color may have experienced diverse cultural contexts, most have been educated within public school systems where they experienced a Eurocentric approach to education and have been provided with few opportunities to consider culturally relevant practices. (p. 168)

This Eurocentric approach to education for all races and/or ethnicities stemmed from the need to equalize educational opportunities before and during the civil rights movement. Today, however, the focus is not necessarily to equalize the educational opportunities of all students, but to ensure that students of varying races/ethnicities are taught using the most effective strategies and practices in order to meet their diverse educational needs in the classroom. Having had an education that focused on more traditional methods, teachers of American schools who identify themselves as White and those who identify themselves as a racial/ethnic minority are in need of professional development to increase further their abilities to utilize adaptive and authentic teaching strategies to meet diverse learning needs and styles.

This chapter offers suggestions regarding what must change in schools to ensure the academic achievement of students of all races, ethnicities, and cultures; effective teaching practices that emphasize strategies to ensure that all students make annual adequate academic progress; and implications for leadership in schools to foster academic achievement of all students.

LANGUAGE AND LABELS

The American Psychological Association's (2002) definitions serve as the standard to categorize and classify race, ethnicity, and culture. *Race* is the category to which others assign individuals on the basis of physical characteristics, such as skin color or hair type, and the generalizations and stereotypes made as a result. *Ethnicity* is the acceptance of the group mores and practices of one's culture of origin and the concomitant sense of belonging. *Culture* is defined as the belief systems and value orientations that influence customs, norms, practices, and social institutions. The federal Office of Management and Budget (OMB) and Office of Information and Regulatory Affairs (1995, http://www.whitehouse.gov/omb/fedreg/race-ethnicity.html) classify race and ethnicity in the following way:

> Race—American Indian or Alaska Native, Asian, Black or African American, Native, Hawaiian or Other Pacific Islander, White Ethnicity.
>
> Ethnicity—Hispanic or Latino or Not Hispanic or Latino.

CULTURAL COMPETENCE

Cultural competence is a term that originated in the health care industry to address patient/family-centered care with an understanding of the social and cultural influences that affect the quality of medical services and treatment (AAMC, 2005; Byrd-Blake & Olivieri, 2009). The most commonly cited explanation of cultural competence has appeared in literature from the National Center for Cultural Competence (NCCC) at Georgetown University Child Development Center. The goal of the center is to increase the capacity of health care programs to incorporate cultural competence. NCCC describes cultural competence as having the capacity to (1) value diversity; (2) conduct self-assessment; (3) manage the dynamics of difference; (4) acquire and institutionalize cultural knowledge; and (5) adapt to diversity and the cultural contexts of the communities served (NCCC, 2008).

The National Association of School Psychologists (NASP) addressed cultural competence in its mission to enhance the learning of all children and youth. It defined a culturally competent school as "one that honors, respects, and values diversity in theory and in practice and where teaching and learning are made relevant and meaningful to students of various cultures" (Klotz, 2006, p. 11). The National Association of State Boards of Education (1994) strongly recommended policies regarding cultural relevance or competence should be linked with teacher training and in-service professional development programs so that teachers are able to meet the needs of a diverse student body (NASBE, 1994).

HOW THINGS STAND

An assessment report by the National Center for Education Statistics noted the educational progress and challenges that racial and ethnic minorities face in the United States (KewalRamani, Gilbertson, Fox, & Provasnik, 2007). The report indicated that academic achievement differences continue to exist among Hispanic, Black, American Indian/Alaska Native, Asian, Native Hawaiian or Other Pacific Islander, and White students. The National Assessment of Educational Progress reported that White students continue to outperform Black and Hispanic students in both reading and mathematics (Campbell, Hombo, & Mazzeo, 2000, p. 45). A report by Veronica Terriquez and colleagues (2009) published by the Civil Rights Project predicted that if the current trends in education continue, the educational achievement gap between advantaged White and disadvantaged minority students will not close by 2014, the year mandated by the No Child Left Behind Act (NCLB, 2002) to ensure that all students are able to read and do mathematics at grade level or above.

In its attempt to address the need for cultural competence for teacher educators, the Office of Academic Affairs of the Oregon University System conducted a survey in 2001 of the teacher certification requirements in 24 states to determine their cultural competence requirements for teacher licensure to advise and inform the Oregon legislature's consideration of a State Senate bill addressing cultural competence. The survey revealed several interesting facts:

- Sixteen states did not have any certification requirements for cultural competence for teachers.
- Fifteen states had generic requirements; those incorporated cultural competence into a general statement of standards.
- Six states had coursework requirements for teachers.
- Three states stated that their certification requirement followed the National Council for Accreditation of Teacher Education (NCATE) 2000 standards.

- Seven states had specific cultural competence requirements: Alabama, Alaska, California, Indiana, Iowa, Minnesota, and New Mexico. (Oregon University System, 2001)

Clearly, standards and expectations for cultural competence in teacher certification are uneven across the states.

WHAT MUST CHANGE?

Teachers in America's schools are not prepared to address the racial, ethnic, and cultural differences among the students they teach. In a recent survey of first-year teachers from across the country, conducted by the National Comprehensive Center for Teacher Quality, participants were asked which improvements they recommended for the teaching profession. Preparing teachers to teach in diverse classrooms ranked in the top two recommendations for the improvement of the teaching profession (Rochkind, Ott, Immerwahr, Doble, & Johnson, 2007). As reported by Darling-Hammond, Wise, and Klein (1997), teachers must be prepared to address the substantial diversity in experiences children bring with them to school.

How do teacher candidates and practicing teachers develop the ability to work productively with diverse populations? An isolated course on multiculturalism or a single professional development session will not meet this urgent need. Broad and universal methodologies of culturally competent instruction that allow them to focus on their local school populations, however, facilitate the personalization of abstract concepts and theories related to teaching diverse students. Such methodologies will allow the teachers and leaders to engage in the process of improving the academic achievement of racial and ethnically diverse populations through pedagogical strategies that are inclusive in their practices. Thus the immediate change needed is to prepare preservice teachers appropriately and provide professional development for employed teachers to become culturally competent to teach the 44% of the student population who are categorized as nonwhite.

Culturally congruent pedagogy is fundamental to the education of students from diverse races, ethnicities, and cultures, since it is based on the experiences and perspectives of the learners rather than on an imposed culture (Nieto, 1999). Developmentally and culturally appropriate practices (DCAP) enhance the learning of diverse students, lead to improved student achievement, and eventually narrow the achievement gap. These strategies align with best practices for inclusion across the board. It has been revealed that to implement DCAP successfully, teachers should be exposed to professional development opportunities that both reflect and promote culturally congruent pedagogy and that are process-oriented (Jensen & Kiley, 2005). Edgar, Patton, and Day-Vines (2002) support this developmental process for teachers:

> Developing cultural competence is a process, a way of being that one cannot turn on and off like an appliance. . . . we must recognize that cultural competency is not some artifact we pull out of a closet or cupboard at random, but rather that it is a quality that when applied with a sense of respect, integrity, and concern for justice and equity permeates all aspects of our being. (p. 231)

Research-Based Best Practices for Educating Students of Diverse Races/Ethnicities

Preparing educators for instructing students from diverse backgrounds is a process involving long-term professional development and a commitment to lifelong learning. Far too often, "culturally relevant teaching may often be misunderstood as the need to replicate the styles and behaviors of exemplary teachers of color or may be reduced to creating activities on what often amounts to stereotypical, trivialized, or overgeneralized beliefs on culture" (Seidl, 2007, p. 168). This approach is limiting and mostly ineffective.

Byrd-Blake and Olivieri (2009) describe a comprehensive model for preparing public school teachers to become culturally competent to teach in high-poverty, high-risk, and culturally diverse schools. The premise of the model is based upon the assumption that cultural competence involves the professional and personal growth of teachers of students in diverse, high-risk, and high-poverty schools in multidimensional ways. Central to the work of Byrd-Blake and Olivieri is a conceptualization of a cultural competent teacher. Such teachers are self-reflective in relation to their own cultural background, appreciative of the historical impact of race and class, understanding about the dynamics of difference, and appreciative of the impact of teacher expectations. Such teachers apply positive behavior management, involve parents, collaborate with colleagues, pay attention to their own stress management and professionalism, advocate for a culturally representative literacy program, and encourage all students to be curious and critical investigators.

This model challenges the inclination of defining a highly qualified teacher solely as one who has met individual state certification requirements. Byrd-Blake and Olivieri (2009) propose a new definition of a highly qualified teacher who is inclusive of the educational needs of students from racially and ethnically diverse families and communities. It may encompass preservice teacher preparation or the continuing professional development of practicing teachers. These redefined expectations for teachers have deep implications for schools and their leaders.

Culturally Responsive Instructional Practices

Culturally responsive teaching involves the authentic delivery of instruction. Gay (2002) has engaged in extensive study of the practice of culturally responsive teaching. At the classroom level she suggests that altering the instructional strategies to match the individual learning styles of students embodies culturally responsive teaching. Both Borich (2007) and Gay (2002) discuss diversifying or differentiating instruction to meet various learning styles including the following:

- cooperative group learning
- peer coaching, motion and movement
- variability in tasks and formats
- drama
- problem-solving activities
- project-based instruction
- advance organizers
- frequent use of examples and nonexamples
- use of questioning to guide search and discovery
- use of student ideas and experiences
- overall conveyance of a sense of nurturance and understanding

These strategies can frame professional development, instructional planning, and dialogue about teaching and learning schoolwide, across teachers and grades.

Integrating instruction across the curriculum enhances a teacher's ability to engage in culturally responsive instruction and encourages students of diverse backgrounds to make connections among subjects, rather than learning isolated concepts that reinforce the models of segregation and isolation of learning. Mueller (1999) explains the necessity of teachers planning culturally responsive units of instruction that integrate concepts across a student's academic experience:

> The world these students interpret is not limited to the school environment; it consists of everything they encounter in their lifelong learning experiences, including creative writing, dance/movement/physical education, drama/theater, foreign language, geography, history, language arts, literature, mathematics, music, science, social studies, and the visual arts. The students' world also includes their families, friends, neighborhoods, daily life experiences, and travel experiences. (p. 158)

Building Relationships. One key theme in culturally responsive instruction is building relevant relationships with students. It involves becoming aware of the students' backgrounds and personal lives and utilizing this knowledge to systematically infuse information throughout the learning experience (Villegas & Lucas, 2002). Making the curriculum relevant to the lives of diverse students outside of the school is vital to their active engagement. Building relationships with students of diverse races and ethnicities based on trust and mutual respect gives diverse students the confidence to share details of their lives that may not align with the majority culture. Once the relationships are formed, students from diverse backgrounds are encouraged to make connections between their home lives and that of the school and classroom. This approach to instructing students with diverse learning needs encourages them to embrace and build upon prior knowledge gained outside the classroom, rather than distancing themselves from it because it doesn't parallel the views and ways of thinking of the majority. The end result is to empower children, who along with their parents may have felt disempowered in the educational system. Empowerment of children regardless of their race or ethnicity to fully embrace the educational opportunities provided is one of the greatest gifts an education can give.

Actively Engaging Students in the Learning Process. A second key theme in culturally responsive instruction is actively engaging students in the learning process. This active engagement takes place throughout an instructional day, whether during direct instructional strategies where the teacher is the focus of attention (such as direct instruction) or during indirect instructional strategies where learning is student centered (such as cooperative learning activities). The seminal work of Bruner (1966) implied that learning is an active process where the students constantly make connections between new ideas and past knowledge.

To engage students actively in the constructivist process, teachers must initially stimulate students' metacognitive skills. This entails activating students' prior knowledge on the topic and building awareness of what they have learned after the lesson concludes. *Metacognition* can be defined as an appreciation of what an individual already knows, an awareness of the learning task and the knowledge and skills required, followed by cognitive dissonance where connections are made when prior knowledge is applied to new situations (Savery & Duffy, 1995; Taylor, 1999).

Embracing metacognition is essential in a constructivist classroom. In this environment, students of diverse backgrounds are engaged in "richly textured contexts, reflective of the natural environment. . . . Learners have opportunities to actively construct, refine, and take ownership of what they see and the meanings they derive from it" (Borich, 2007, p. 23). Taking ownership of the new knowledge is contrary to a one-size-fits-all way of teaching seen in rationalization of the desegregation of schools. Teaching in such a manner overlooks the vast and rich experiences individual students from diverse backgrounds bring to the classroom. Rather than teaching all students in an undifferentiated approach, constructivism individualizes instruction in a personal and meaningful manner. Brooks and Brooks (1993) suggested several strategies for teachers using the Constructivist Learning Theory. Among the recommended constructivist approaches are encouraging student autonomy and initiative, using student responses when determining instructional strategies and activities during teachable moments, inquiring about students' prior experiences about a concept before introducing the topic, encouraging communication, asking thoughtful and open-ended questions to encourage critical thinking and inquiry, placing students in situations that challenge their previous concepts, and providing time for students to construct their own meaning when learning something new. Through the use of metacognitive strategies in a constructivist learning environment, students who are not of the majority are actively engaged and included in the instructional process.

Affective Teaching. A third theme in culturally responsive instruction is developing a positive teacher affect with students of diverse races and ethnicities, promoting student active engagement in the learning process and renewed student motivation. Positive teacher affect can be characterized as the teacher praising the child, showing affection toward the child, or giving positive reinforcement to a child such as a pat on the back or a compliment (Stuhlman & Pianta, 2002). Teachers who are excited about teaching and allow their facial expressions, voice inflections, gestures, and movements to reflect this enthusiasm exhibit positive teacher affect (Borich, 2007). Studies have shown that positive teacher affect and trust impact student efficacy and, in turn, student efficacy positively influences students' academic achievement in class (Karp, 2010).

In their seminal work, *Pygmalion in the Classroom* (Rosenthal & Jacobson, 1968), a Harvard researcher and an elementary school principal manipulated the expectations of the school's teachers and led them to believe that 20% of their students were expected to "flourish academically and intellectually during the school year using the results of a fictional "Harvard Test of Inflected Acquisition." At the end of the year the teachers described the fictionally designated "bloomers" in their classrooms as having a greater chance of being more successful in later life, being happier, more curious, more interesting, more appealing, better adjusted, and more affectionate than the other students not designated by the fictional test as "bloomers." Thus the term *Pygmalion effect* was coined after Pygmalion from mythology. As with the mythological Pygmalion, the effect is closely associated with the self-fulfilling prophecy where teacher expectations of student performance play a large role in the actual achievement level of the students.

Mausehund, Timm, and King (1995) addressed the role of the Pygmalion effect in diversity training. They indicate that nonverbal behaviors can either improve or detract from the encouraging environment needed for effective communication. When the leader and other group members use nonverbal signals effectively to communicate positive effort, all participants sense a more trusting environment in which they can openly take part and participate. The same holds true for the educational classroom where the positive teacher affect is critical to the motivation of children from diverse races and ethnicities. Students in a classroom where their race or ethnicity is in the minority or does not match that of the teacher sometimes will distance themselves from the educational process in order to protect their sense of worth. Negative teacher affect usually results in a lack of student motivation and student apathy in class for any child, but especially for a student of diverse background. The role of the teacher in establishing a safe, secure, and nurturing learning environment in the classroom is particularly significant for students who have diverse learning needs. Affirming verbal and nonverbal body language can communicate to students that the teacher has their best interests in mind.

SCHOOL SITE LEADERSHIP IMPLICATIONS

The key themes shape the school environment and suggest several important considerations and strategies for school leaders. McLeskey and Waldron (2000) recognized the importance of school leadership behaviors when facilitating change in schools. They advocate the following behaviors: promoting and modeling support for the change, providing support for program development and implementation, ensuring teachers are in control of the changes, ensuring local school faculty are in support of the changes, ensuring the change is tailored to the needs of the local setting, encouraging risk taking and giving support if efforts do not succeed, supporting those involved in developing and implementing change, and encouraging ongoing evaluation and improvement. Kent (2004) agrees that professional development for school leaders plays an essential role in any school reform effort.

School leaders can proactively encourage the need for change among teachers and staff to embrace the notion that diversity of the student body is valuable to academic achievement and school prosperity. Realizing that culturally responsive teaching does not occur in isolation, but through ongoing collaboration and communication, serves as the foundation for facilitating such change. Developing a culturally responsive learning community requires the school leader to share decision making to facilitate the development of a collaborative culturally responsive culture. Suggested practices to achieve this end include modeling culturally competent thought, dialogue, and actions during interactions with the teachers, staff, student body, and the school community.

The proactive school leader facilitates the process of teachers and staff becoming advocates for cultural competence and culturally responsive instruction rather than obstructors of progress. Directly involving teachers and staff in the foundational development of the cultural competence platform, practicing clear and concise communication throughout the change process, and celebrating each accomplishment toward achieving target goals, will greatly contribute to the active involvement and support of teachers and staff.

School leaders are also responsible for making certain the changes for cultural competence in the school are reflective of the local community. An ideal prototype for cultural competence does not exist. School leadership should facilitate the process of analyzing the norms, social practices, and belief systems of the individual school community. This includes, but is not limited to, conducting ethnographic studies of the local community and operating a school with porous walls that welcomes ideas and insights of the community where it is housed. A school leader supports the translation of an abstract concept to the practical context of the school and classroom.

Engaging in the cyclical process of developing the cultural competence platform includes goal setting, strategic implementation, and ongoing assessment as key elements to change. Developing school processes that address, celebrate, and embrace racial, ethnic, and cultural differences among the students, and utilizing the knowledge to enhance academic achievement and school improvement is a never-ending process. The student, teacher, and staff populations may change each year; therefore, the cyclical process must continue.

CONCLUSION

Although schools have an extensive history of failing to connect with the socio-political and cultural worlds of students of color and of poor students, exemplary teachers of these children weave together curriculum from the content of their children's lives. (Seidl, 2007, p. 168)

Culturally competent instruction is synonymous with research-based best practice such as differentiating instruction to meet the individual learning needs of students and actively engaging students in the learning process through strategies that correlate with the constructivist philosophy of teaching and learning. However, culturally competent instruction goes further, to emphasize the importance of valuing the lived experiences of students from diverse races and ethnicities and integrating those experiences into the curriculum and school life. The goal is that students do not solely learn the preferences and principles from the dominant culture utilizing strategies that are preferred by the dominant culture in its effort to create a somewhat monoculture society, but are allowed to contribute actively to their learning environment through the sharing of prior knowledge and divergent experiences.

Culturally competent teachers and leaders avoid the stereotypes and overgeneralizations that some professional development programs promote, but actively seek to understand the community norms, values, and principles where they teach through exploration, inquiry, and genuine curiosity so that they may adapt their instructional techniques to meet the needs of the students.

Finally, culturally competent teachers and leaders are able to exude and transmit a genuine sense of compassion to students of diverse races and ethnicities through a warm and encouraging demeanor that allows the students to realize that they have high expectations for them and care about their academic achievement as well as overall well-being. As the opening vignette demonstrated, being in an environment with unfamiliar culture and norms and where your culture and norms are not evident is challenging and sometimes overwhelming, especially for young people. Creating a school and classroom environment that acknowledges, honors, respects, and celebrates differences with care and compassion is the foundation for the academic performance of students from diverse races, cultures, and ethnicities.

> She remembers the first day of kindergarten vividly. Her new teacher had actually called her mother the week before to introduce herself and encouraged her mom to visit the school prior to the opening day. Therefore, when the bus dropped her off at the school, she was nervous, anticipating the day her new teacher had described to her mom on the phone. When she was ushered into the classroom, she looked around and didn't see anyone with her skin color or hair that looked like hers. However, the warm smile and embrace of her new teacher gave her great comfort.
>
> On the walls she saw pictures of children of different colors and shades of brown and texture of hair. Even hearing the different language and vocabulary she was not capable of speaking didn't concern her because when the teacher asked her to share something special

about herself, the teacher seemed really interested in what she had to say! Her teacher said she did a great job of sharing and told the class that we all come from homes where people might speak differently and do things that are different. The picture on the cover of the book the teacher read to the class was of children who looked like her new classmates with rosy white skin and straight hair and of those who look like her with brown skin and curly hair in ponytails. The children in the book were playing games she had never played and also games she was familiar with.

On the playground the teacher led the class in a group game where everyone got a chance to play. She began to like her new friends and school. Throughout the day her feelings of importance were affirmed by her teacher. She did not want to go home at the end of the day. Thereafter, she learned that new way of speaking the teacher taught her, but she found out that it was okay to continue to speak in her other language at home. Her teacher said so!

REFERENCES

American Psychological Association. (2002, August). *Guidelines on multicultural education, training, research, practice, and organizational change for psychologists*. Washington, DC: American Psychological Association. Retrieved March 31, 2011, from http://www.apa.org/pi/oema/resources/policy/multicultural-guidelines.aspx

Association of American Medical Colleges (AAMC). (2005). *Cultural competence education for medical students*. Retrieved March 31, 2011, from: https://www.aamc.org/download/54338/data/culturalcomped.pdf

Borich, G. D. (2007). *Effective teaching methods: Research-based practice* (6th ed.). Upper Saddle River, NJ: Pearson. Education, Inc.

Brooks, J., & Brooks, M. (1993). *In search of understanding: The case for constructivist classrooms*. Alexandria, VA: Association for Supervision and Curriculum Development.

Bruner, J. (1966). *Toward a theory of instruction*. Cambridge, MA: Harvard University Press.

Byrd-Blake, M., & Olivieri, B. S. (2009). Operation 2014: Developing culturally competent teachers for a diverse society. *Florida Association of Teacher Educators Journal, 1*(9), 1–23.

Campbell, J. R., Hombo, C. M., & Mazzeo, J. C. (2000). *NAEP 1999 trends in academic progress: Three decades of student performance* (NCES 2000-469). Washington DC: Government Printing Office. Retrieved March 31, 2011, from Education Resources Information Center (ERIC) http://eric.ed.gov:80/ERIC-WebPortal/search/detailmini.jsp?_nfpb=true&_&ERICExtSearch_SearchValue_0=ED441875&ERICExtSearch_SearchType_0=no&accno=ED441875

Darling-Hammond, L., Wise, A. E., & Klein, S. P. (1997). *A license to teach: Building a profession for 21st century schooling*. Boulder, CO: Westview.

Edgar, E., Patton, J. M., & Day-Vines, N. (2002). Democratic dispositions and cultural competence: Ingredients for school success. *Remedial and Special Education, 23*(4), 231–241.

Gay, G. (2002). Preparing for culturally responsive teaching. *Journal of Teacher Education, 53*(2), 106–116.

Jensen, R. A., & Kiley, T. J. (2005). *Teaching, leading, and learning in pre-K–8 settings: Strategies for success*. Boston: Houghton Mifflin.

Karp, J. M. (2010). *Teacher expectations and the mediation effects of trust on eighth grade adolescent academic self-efficacy and achievement*. AAT 3405781. Retrieved March 31, 2011, from http://proquest.umi.com/pqdlink?did=20306803 61&Fmt=7&clientI d=79356&RQT=309&VName=PQD

Kent, A. M. (2004). Improving teacher quality through professional development. *Education, 124*(3), 427–435.

KewalRamani, A., Gilbertson, L., Fox, M., & Provasnik, S. (2007). *Status and trends in the education of racial and ethnic minorities* (NCES 2007-039). Washington, DC: National Center for Education Statistics.

Klotz, M. B. (2006, March). Culturally competent schools: Guidelines for secondary school principals. *Principal Leadership, 4*(5), 9–13.

Mausehund, J. A., Timm, S. A., & King, A. S. (1995). Diversity training: Effects of an intervention treatment on nonverbal awareness. *Business Communication Quarterly, 58*(1), 27.

McLeskey, J., & Waldron, N. L. (2000). *Inclusive education in action: Making differences ordinary*. Alexandria, VA: Association for Supervision and Curriculum Development.

Mueller, A. (1999). Celebrating our differences through multicultural activities: The collaboration and integration of music across the disciplines. In E. R. Hollins & E. I. Oliver (Eds.), *Pathways to success in school: Culturally responsive teaching* (pp. 1–7). Mawah, NJ: Erlbaum.

National Association of School Psychologists (NASP). (2007). *NASP's Committment to Culturally Competent Practice*. Retrieved March 31, 2011, from http://www.nasponline.org/resources/culturalcompetence/mission.aspx

National Association of State Boards of Education (NASBE). (1994). *Policy update: Cultural competence and public education* 2(13). Retrieved March 31, 2011, from http://nasbe.org/Educational_Issues/Briefs/Policy_Updates/Diversity/cultural.pdf

National Center for Cultural Competence. (NCCC). (2008). *Foundations of cultural and linguistic competence*. Washington, DC: Georgetown University Center for Child and Human Development. Retrieved March 31, 2011, from http://www11.georgetown.edu/research/gucchd/nccc/foundations/index.html

National Center for Education Statistics (NCES). (2007). *Condition of education; Contexts of elementary & secondary ed teachers & staff; Indicator 33; Table 33-1C: Number and percentage distribution of full-time teachers, by school level, school type, and selected characteristics: School years 1993–94, 1999–2000, and 2003–04*. Retrieved March 31, 2011, from http://nces.ed.gov/programs/

coe/2007/section4/table.asp?tableID=721

National Center for Education Statistics (NCES). (2008). *Digest of education statistics: Table 41. Percentage distribution of enrollment in public elementary and secondary schools, by race/ethnicity and state or jurisdiction: Fall 1996 and fall 2006.* Retrieved March 31, 2011, from http://nces.ed.gov/programs/digest/d08/tables/dt08_041.asp

National Council for Accreditation of Teacher Education (NCATE). (2008). *Professional standards for the accreditation of teacher preparation institutions.* Retrieved March 31, 2011, from http://www.ncate.org/LinkClick.aspx?fileticket=nX43fwKc4Ak%3D&tabid=669

Nieto, S. (1999). *Affirming diversity: The sociopolitical context of multicultural education* (3rd ed.). New York: Addison Wesley.

Office of Management and Budget (OMB). Office of Information and Regulatory Affairs. (1995). *Standards for the classification of federal data on race and ethnicity.* Retrieved March 31, 2011, from http://www.whitehouse.gov/omb/fedreg/race-ethnicity.html

Oregon University System, Office of Academic Affairs. (2001). *Cultural competence for teachers: A report on approaches in other states.* Eugene, OR: Author. Retrieved March 31, 2011, from http://www.luzsocialservices.org/ccc/symposium/approaches.htm

Planty, M., Hussar, W., Snyder, T., Kena, G., KewalRamani, A., Kemp, J., Bianco, K., & Dinkes, R. (2009). *The condition of education 2009* (NCES 2009-081). Washington, DC: National Center for Education Statistics.

Rochkind, J., Ott, A., Immerwahr, J., Doble, J., & Johnson, J. (2007). *Lessons learned: New teachers talk about their jobs, challenges and long range plans: Issue #1. They're not little kids anymore: The special challenges of new teachers in high schools and middle schools.* Report from the National Comprehensive Center for Teacher Quality and Public Agenda. Retrieved March 31, 2011, from http://www.publicagenda.org/reports/lessons-learned-new-teachers-talk-about-their-jobs-challenges-and-long-range-plans-issue-no-1

Rosenthal, R., & Jacobson, L. (1968). *Pygmalion in the classroom: Teacher expectation and pupils' intellectual development.* New York: Holt, Reinhart and Winston.

Savery, J. R., & Duffy, T. M. (1995). Problem-based learning: An instructional model and its constructivist framework. *Educational Technology, 35*(5), 31–38.

Seidl, B. (2007). Working with communities to explore and personalize culturally relevant pedagogies: Push, double images, and raced talk. *Journal of Teacher Education, 58*(2), 168–183.

Snyder, T. D., Tan, A. G., & Hoffman, C. M. (2006). *Digest of education statistics, 2005* (NCES 2006-030). U.S. Department of Education, National Center for Education Statistics. Washington, DC: U.S. Government Printing Office.

Strizek, G. A., Pittsonberger, J. L., Riordan, K. E., Lyter, D. M., & Orlofsky, G. F. (2006/2007). *Characteristics of schools, districts, teachers, principals, and school libraries in the United States: 2003–04: Schools and staffing survey* (NCES 2006-313 Revised). U.S. Department of Education, National Center for Education Statistics. Washington, DC: U.S. Government Printing Office.

Stuhlman, M. W., & Pianta, R. C. (2002). Teachers' narratives about their relationships with children: Associations with behavior in classrooms. *School Psychology Review, 31*(2), 148.

Taylor, S. (1999). Better learning through better thinking: Developing students' metacognitive abilities. *Journal of College Reading and Learning, 30*(1), 34ff.

Terriquez, V., Flashman, J., Schuler-Brown, S., & Orfield, G, (2009). *Expanding student opportunities: Prime 6 program review, Clark County School District, Las Vegas, Nevada.* Los Angeles, CA: Civil Rights Project/Proyecto Derechos Civiles. Retrieved March 31, 2011, from http://civilrightsproject.ucla.edu/ research/k-12-education/integration-and-diversity/expanding-student-opportunities-prime-6-program-review-clark-county-school-district-las-vegas-nevada/ terriquez-expanding-student-opportunities-2009

U. S. Census Bureau (2010). *State and county quick facts.* Retrieved March 31, 2011, from http://quickfacts.census.gov/qfd/states/00000.html

U.S. Department of Education (2002). *Building on results: A blueprint for strengthening.* Available at http://www2.ed.gov/policy/elsec/leg/nclb/buildingonresults. pdf

Villegas, A. M., & Lucas, T. (2002). Preparing culturally responsive teachers: Rethinking the curriculum. *Journal of Teacher Education, 53*(1), 20–32.

CHAPTER 8

Creating a Context of Belonging for English Language Learners

Rebecca Burns

> When I am in a class full of people who speak only English, I feel out of my element. It is frustrating because some teachers expect others and me, who aren't perfect in English, to know everything. If I spoke, wrote, and understood English well, my grades would be so much higher. It makes me so nervous and upset when I see my report card. I feel I should be doing better. Sometimes I feel like I am not good. It makes me feel like I can't make it far in life. —Sandra M. (College Board, 2006, p. 13)

Sandra has been immersed in English language education since the second grade, at least 8 years, and she is saying that she feels unable to succeed academically, in spite of her progression to high school, because of her lack of proficiency in English. Sandra's words reflect a struggle and sadness about her daily life in school, reflecting how she feels out of place in school and that she does not belong to her school community. Sandra is like many students in schools today. As of 2007, 20% of school-age children in the United States speak a language other than English at home. Eleven percent of all school-age children in the United States are designated as limited in English proficiency (LEP) with a greater proportion, 14%, in elementary schools where 72% of all public elementary schools report enrollment of limited English proficient speakers (Keigher & Gruber, 2009).

There is no simple recipe for academic success for students learning English. School leaders who want to create communities of belonging for students who are English language learners participate in ongoing reflection and development. The variables of individual learners have a profound impact on language learning outcomes: age of first exposure to English, literacy and academic experience acquired in the home language, talent for linguistic expression, linguistic and cultural identity, and family ties to non-English-speaking countries and communities. The community presence of people who speak languages other than English can be a politically charged issue. Public schools, governed by political bodies, are affected by community sentiments that are related to school practices, and communities often hold complex feelings and ideas about immigration, culture, and linguistic diversity. In this political context school leaders are challenged to create inclusive school settings that foster high academic achievement for all students within the political climate of their community.

This chapter explores issues related to the inclusion of students who are English learners, and illustrates how a school leader can pay attention and build opportunities to create communities of belonging for students like Sandra in their school and classrooms. The chapter begins with the legal history of the educational rights of students learning English in U.S. schools, which form the foundation of current policies and practices that can support or negate notions of belonging. This offers school leaders a historical perspective on the journey American schools have taken and the need to support current policy initiatives, for example, the requirements of the No Child Left Behind Act of 2001. A tool is offered to help school leaders evaluate professional learning opportunities in bilingual and bidialectical issues in reading and literacy. The next section presents a discussion of current models of education for students who are English language learners. The final section of the chapter presents specific practices that a school leader can employ to create contexts of belonging for students who are English learners in any classroom, school, or district. A tool is introduced that school leaders can use across the school to better appreciate the practices of the current program to create a community that supports belonging for students and families for whom English is a second language.

THE LEGAL JOURNEY OF STUDENTS LEARNING ENGLISH IN U.S. SCHOOLS

The United States has always been a multilingual nation. At the time of the first explorers, hundreds of American Indian languages were in use in North America. Settlers brought the languages of Europe, Africa, South America, and Asia to the New World. Spain claimed vast portions of the Western Hemisphere and maintained Spanish-speaking missionaries and government officials throughout the western half of North and

South America and the North American southwest. England promoted settlement of its colonies along the eastern seaboard; France promoted settlement of areas north of the English colonies and west of the Appalachian Mountains; and the early New Netherland colony of the Hudson River–New York Bay area was populated by speakers of Dutch, German, Swedish, Norwegian, Yiddish, Ladino, and many others (New Netherland, n.d.). The American colonies also had significant numbers of West African language speakers from their beginnings, having brought many of this population as indentured servants and slaves to build the New World as early as 1619 in the Jamestown Colony.

The forces that pushed English into prominence in the history of the American colonies are largely political. With the financial backing and the printing industry of England, the English colonies organized neighboring colonies to unite in order to resist domination from French armed forces. The momentum of English as the language of political unity in the colonies continued in the drafting of the Declaration of Independence and continues to this day, as English is used alongside other languages throughout regions of the United States. This section introduces school leaders to pertinent legal issues related to:

- Teaching foreign languages in American schools
- Segregation and ability grouping
- Equal access to meaningful education
- Appropriate action to provide meaningful instruction to all students
- Required standards and assessment of students learning English

This overview explains the current policies and practices inherent in No Child Left Behind, or NCLB (2002), and offers a tool to reflect on current practices and policies in schools that support a community of belonging for students and families for whom English is a second language.

Teaching Foreign Language in American Schools

The first U.S. Supreme Court ruling to address language and education was in 1923: *Meyer v. Nebraska.* In this case, Meyer had been found guilty of violating a Nebraska state law prohibiting the teaching of any foreign language to children younger than eighth grade when he taught his Lutheran pupil to read the Bible in German in a small, rural school. The high court ruled that such a prohibition by the state was unconstitutional as it deprived the teacher as well as the parents of liberty without due process of rights guaranteed by the 14th Amendment.

Segregation and Ability Grouping

The Nebraska prohibition on teaching foreign languages echoed a general anti-German and antiforeign sentiment that was widespread in the United States after World War I. Over the next 30 years Congress passed laws to restrict severely the numbers and the countries of origin of immigrants entering the United States. Racial segregation was part of American life during this time, and education practices reflected the ghettoization of minorities—schools that had large populations of minority students were grossly neglected, as were the students. Schools that had significant populations of mainstream students would often assign minority students to segregated classes. In 1947 a U.S. Court of Appeals upheld a ruling, based on the 14th Amendment, in the case of *Mendez v. Westminster* that required four California school districts to end the segregation of Spanish-speaking students. Later that year the California legislature repealed its school segregation laws under the governorship of Earl Warren, who went on to write the 1954 Supreme Court ruling in *Brown v. Board of Education*. These decisions illustrate how the courts have moved toward more inclusive learning opportunities for students learning English. Subsequent court decisions have further explicated the rights of students and the responsibilities of school districts.

Equal Access to Meaningful Education

Brown v. Board of Education set the stage for antidiscrimination, equal opportunity legislation. The Civil Rights Act of 1964 required all federally funded programs, such as education, to be equally accessible to all. Under Title VI of this act, discrimination lawsuits were made possible by demonstrating that groups defined by the law as protected categories (race, color, religion, sex, and national origin) were denied equal access to the basic rights afforded to all persons. The Education Office of Civil Rights issued a memorandum 6 years later that identified the responsibility of school districts to take affirmative steps to support English acquisition for students who would otherwise be unable to access the educational program offered by the district. The inability to speak and understand English was interpreted to be an artifact of national origin (42 U.S.C. § 2000(d)).

This interpretation of Title VI was tested in 1974, when students of Chinese ancestry were represented in a claim against the San Francisco school board that was eventually heard in the Supreme Court as *Lau v. Nichols*. The court found that the Chinese-speaking students in the San Francisco school system were being discriminated against because of national origin, due to the district's language policy, which did not systematically afford

English language instruction to its population of students who were learning English. The majority opinion stated, "There is no equality of treatment merely by providing students with the same facilities, textbooks, teachers, and curriculum; for students who do not understand English are effectively foreclosed from any meaningful education." This landmark case adds a key element to inclusive education practices, that of meaningful inclusion.

In meaningful inclusion, students receive instruction and resources in order to learn, and not simply to be present, in the classroom. Clearly, meaningful inclusive experiences are another key feature of supporting a community of belonging, where all students receive what they need to learn successfully.

Appropriate Action to Provide Meaningful Instruction to All Students

Shortly after the *Lau* decision, the U.S. Congress passed the Equal Educational Opportunities Act of 1974, which specifically stated that states failing to overcome language barriers that impede access to education were in violation of the law (20 U.S.C. §1203(f)). In 1995, the Education Office of Civil Rights issued a memorandum, based on the *Lau* decision, outlining the necessary components of a school district's compliance plan for the education of students learning English (Brisk, 1998):

1. Identification of English learners
2. Assessment of learners' English proficiency
3. English language instruction provided by qualified teachers

These criteria, often referred to as the Lau Remedies, were the basis of much legal activity over the next 5 years as the Education Office of Civil Rights conducted compliance reviews and negotiated settlement plans with school districts. The specifics of the legal definition of "appropriate action" to provide a "meaningful education" for English learners during these years were wide ranging; many judges determined that the appropriate, necessary remedy to afford equal participation in educational programs was to provide bilingual education (the use of students' home language as the medium of instruction until English proficiency was adequate for academic success in mainstream classes).

In 1981 the Fifth Circuit Court of Appeals wrote its decision in the case of *Castaneda v. Pickard* and established the three criteria used today for evaluating whether or not school districts have taken appropriate actions to comply with the law. The court found that the Raymondville School District of Texas had violated the Equal Education Opportunity Act in its policy of creating segregated classrooms for Spanish-speaking students. The court was careful not to prescribe any particular model of English language education, but determined that any program that met the following three criteria would meet the state and local obligations to take "appropriate action" to assist English learners:

a. Districts must provide an instructional program based on sound educational theory.
b. Districts must allocate resources, including personnel, to effectively implement the program.
c. Districts must evaluate program effectiveness and make improvements accordingly.

The following year, the Supreme Court heard a case that tested the obligation of public schools to provide education to students who could not document their legal status as residents in the United States. In *Plyler v. Doe* (1982) the court ruled that undocumented aliens were deemed persons, and were thus protected under the Equal Protection Clause of the 14th Amendment. Specifically, public schools may not deny undocumented immigrant students their right of access to public schools on the basis of their legal status.

One other case involving language and education is of particular interest because the students involved were native speakers of English. In the case of *Martin Luther King Junior Elementary School Children v. Ann Arbor School District* (1979), the U.S. District Court judge found:

a. A language barrier existed between the students and their teachers because of the failure of the teachers to take into account the home language or dialect of their students in teaching them to read standard English.
b. The dialect spoken by the students is a version of English called Black English and is related to race.
c. The language barrier impeded the children's equal participation in the school's educational program.
d. The school district is obligated to take appropriate action to overcome the language barrier.

The remedy was a training plan that would achieve four goals:

1. Help teachers understand and appreciate the characteristics of Black English
2. Help teachers identify speakers of Black English and determine if students have bidialectal proficiency in standard English

3. Help teachers strategically differentiate between reading errors and Black English pronunciation
4. Help teachers stay abreast of current research on Black English and its application to the teaching of reading standard English

The legacy of this case is the detailing of specific *teaching competencies* that are necessary for effective instruction of students with significant dialect differences. These same language-based competencies have been reapplied to court-mandated professional development programs to remedy violations of English learners' equal access to education. Figure 8.1 offers school leaders a protocol to use when selecting professional development programs for improving instruction and learning for students who are linguistically diverse. The tool provides a way to ensure that the four core language awareness and teaching competencies are the focus of a training program before approval.

REQUIRED STANDARDS AND ASSESSMENT OF STUDENTS LEARNING ENGLISH

The Elementary and Secondary Education Act of 1965 provided federal funding for states to implement educational programs that conformed to the policies and regulations of the legislation. Reauthorized in 2002 as No Child Left Behind (NCLB), this legislation guides public education policy at the state level. The law (and funding) is laid out under separate "Titles." Title I is named Improving the Academic Achievement of the Disadvantaged, of which Part C covers Migrant and Bilingual Education. Title III, named Language Instruction for Limited English Proficient and Immigrant Students, outlines seven components for English language learner students. One requires that they develop English proficiency (based on state expectations) and meet the academic content and achievement standards set for all students; two components outline parent notification and involvement requirements; the remaining four components describe the testing and reporting requirements of school districts (20 U.S.C.§ 6826). Each state has developed its own plan for meeting these federal requirements. Federal laws firmly establish the responsibility of school districts to show that students who are learning English make academic gains that are consistent with the district's expectations for all students. The specifics of identification, model of instruction, standards of language proficiency, teacher certification, and exit criteria are left to each state to design. School leaders need to understand the policies and resources, and they need to understand appropriate actions their states have implemented to comply with the legal requirements

FIGURE 8.1. Evaluation of Professional Development for Improving Instruction for Linguistically Diverse Students

Knowledge and Skill Objective	Staff Development Activity 1	Staff Development Activity 2
Does the activity help teachers explore the linguistic characteristics of dialects of English and languages other than English?		
Does the activity help teachers identify student proficiency in code switching between Academic English and the home language or variety of English?		
Does the activity help teachers make distinctions between reading errors and dialectal and second language pronunciations?		
Does the activity help teachers practice the most current and evidence-based recommendations for teaching linguistically diverse learners?		

for educating English language learners. Reports submitted by each state, outlining the state's plan for the education of students learning English, are available on the National Clearinghouse For English Language Acquisition (NCELA) Web site. In addition to the state documentation available on public Web sites, school leaders will then want to understand how their school's program for students learning English is being implemented. Figure 8.2 provides a comprehensive set of questions to guide such an inquiry. The review team should include key stakeholders, including teachers and parents.

Once the questions in Figure 8.2 have been answered, a school leader can move to Figure 8.3 to create meaningful plans for future development. Use this tool to prioritize three areas of strength and three areas for development in each of the three major program areas. The final column will help with monitoring of the action required for the proposed area for development.

MODELS OF ENGLISH LANGUAGE PROGRAMS

As mentioned above, federal legislation has never specified any model of English language instruction; it has only required that the models chosen by states and districts be effective. Past federal funding initiatives, however,

FIGURE 8.2. Review of School English Language Program

Review Indicator	Supporting Documentation/Examples of Practice
How do we systematically identify students who use a language other than English at the time of enrollment? Who collects this information?	
How do we assess a student's developmentally appropriate proficiency (listening, speaking, reading, and writing) in English?	
How do we take into account a student's home language development and prior academic experience?	
How have we improved our identification and assessment procedures in the past?	
What improvements are currently needed to improve our identification and assessment procedures?	
What kind(s) of English language program(s) do we provide? Who will know this?	
How is the soundness of our program judged by experts in the field—critics as well as advocates?	
Do our teachers have the state-required qualifications to teach learners of English in the model of instruction we have chosen?	
Does every learner of English have a qualified teacher throughout the day, every day?	
How do we know when a student is ready to exit the English language program?	
How are students in the English language program given full access to all school activities and programs? (e.g., Exceptional Student Services including Gifted and Talented, Accelerated or Advanced Placement programs, extra-curricular activities)	
How are learners of English being graded in their subject area coursework?	
How are learners of English being assessed in English language acquisition?	
How are learners of English accommodated in mandated standardized testing?	
How are parents of learners of English involved in their children's education in our school?	
Who reviews our English language program and promotes improvements?	
How often is our program reviewed?	
What improvements have we made to date?	
What do we consider "success" in our English language program?	
What do our students, their families, and our communities consider "success" for English learning in our school? How can we find out?	

FIGURE 8.3. Action Planning to Create Communities of Belonging for Students
Who Are English Language Learners

Members of the Program Review Team:

Program Indicator	Areas of Strength	Areas for Development	Action Required/ Date of Delivery
Identification and Assessment			
English Language Program & Its Implementation			
Evaluation			

have promoted different models of instruction. When the Bilingual Education Act of 1968 and Equal Education Opportunities Act of 1974 provided
supplemental funding for programs supporting English learners, bilingual
education programs were strongly encouraged. The prevailing instructional
model at that time was *transitional bilingual education,* which used home
language instruction to support English language learners for the shortest
time possible (typically 3 years or less) before students were transitioned
into mainstream English instruction. Another model option was a *maintenance bilingual education program,* in which students learned subject content material primarily in the home language and were immersed in English
in art, music, and physical education. Students gradually transitioned to
more content area instruction in English and less home language instruction, but home language was not eliminated.

Implementing any form of bilingual education requires same-age groups
of same-language speakers to form the instructional groups for the model.
Across the nation, 75% of students learning English in school speak Spanish at home (Aud et al., 2010), and most bilingual education programs in
the United States have been, and continue to be, Spanish-English programs.
The remaining 25% of ELLs speak one or more of hundreds of different
languages and are distributed in communities in which they may be isolated
in a very small language groups. For many students learning English, a bilingual education program has not been available.

Figure 8.4 presents the key terminology and concepts that are used to
describe English learners, English language learning, and methods and models of instruction for English learners.

FIGURE 8.4. Glossary of Common Terms, Abbreviations, and Acronyms Used in English Language Education

Terms Referring to Students

LEP	Limited English Proficient Used in legal contexts to define the population of English learners in schools affected by legislation.
ELL	English Language Learner Used in instructional contexts as a conscious replacement of LEP, which is seen as negatively focused on limitations.
Bilingual	The ability to use two (or more) languages. "Balanced bilingual" refers to a person who has native-like proficiency in both languages—a fairly rare achievement.
Biliterate	The ability to read and write in two (or more) languages.
Bidialectal	The ability to use two (or more) contrasting dialects of the same language.
Dual Language Learner	Refers to young children who are developing language skills in two languages. This is the terminology adopted by Head Start in recent rule changes requiring Head Start programs to provide meaningful home language experiences, in addition to English, for all children whose parents use a language other than English in the home (see http://eclkc.ohs.acf.hhs.gov/hslc/Dual%20Language%20Learners).
Native Speaker	A person who has acquired a language from very early in life.
Language Proficiency	A level of language skill (listening, speaking, reading, writing) that is measured and defined by formal or informal means. The first level is "no language proficiency," which describes a person who cannot understand the majority of what is being said. This level is often accompanied by an unwillingness to speak and lasts for several months or until the learner has acquired a basic working vocabulary. The next levels are degrees of "limited" language proficiency up to "proficient." Students who meet the district definition of "proficient" (based primarily on test scores) are exited from English language services.
Language Dominance	Refers to a bilingual person's greater facility in one of the two languages: "English-dominant bilingual" and "Spanish-dominant bilingual." Most bilinguals are dominant in one language, although dominance may be context dependent (more fluent in one language in social settings; more fluent in the other language in academic settings). Language dominance may change over time due to language experience and opportunity.
Language Acquisition	The subconscious brain mapping of language that develops through the use of language in all forms of natural communication.
Language Learning	The conscious, directed practice of activities to explore and rehearse language forms.

FIGURE 8.4. Glossary of Common Terms, Abbreviations, and Acronyms Used in
English Language Education, Continued

Terms Referring to Models of Instruction	
ESL	English as a Second Language Refers to the teaching and learning of English for nonnative speakers who reside in an English-speaking country.
EFL	English as a Foreign Language Refers to the teaching and learning of English for nonnative speakers who reside in non-English-speaking countries.
ESOL	English for Speakers of Other Languages Refers to the pedagogy (teaching and learning) of English for nonnative speakers, at home or abroad.
TESOL	Teaching English for Speakers of Other Languages Refers to the instructional practices and the profession of teaching English to nonnative speakers, at home or abroad.
Academic Language	The style or register of language used in academic subject reading, writing, and speaking. Its characteristics include a high percentage of low-frequency vocabulary words and complex sentence and discourse patterns.
CBI	Content-Based Instruction The use of standards-based lessons in math, science, social studies, and language arts as the materials for English language instruction.
Sheltered English Instruction	The use of specific materials and strategies to make instruction comprehensible to English learners. In ESL/ESOL programs, ELLs are grouped with an ESOL teacher for portions of the day (decreasing as ELLs gain in English proficiency) and are placed in general education classrooms as much as possible. When ELLs leave their general education classrooms to participate in ESOL instruction, it is referred to as "pull-out" ESOL. If the ESOL teacher meets ELLs in the general education classroom, providing English instruction in situ, it is referred to as "push-in" ESOL. When general education teachers adapt their subject area instruction to support ELLs, the practice may be called Sheltered English or Content-Based Instruction (CBI)—using the language of the subject lesson as the basis of the language lesson and providing "comprehensible" instruction. ESL/ESOL instruction may or may not make use of the student's home language as the basis for learning the new language. In reality, there are many variations in ESL/ESOL programs, schedules, and use of home language as they are influenced by the language resources of the teaching staff, the language diversity of the student population, and the philosophy of the administration.
SEI	Structured English Immersion ELLs who do not meet district definitions of "English proficient" are grouped together for intensive English language instruction for a defined block of time each day. Only English is used, and academic content is not introduced until students are sufficiently proficient in English to comprehend instruction.

FIGURE 8.4. Continued

Bilingual Education	Any instructional model in which a student's home language is the medium of instruction for a defined portion of the school day or week. There is an underlying assumption that the home language is valuable and should be maintained.
TBE	Transitional Bilingual Education An instructional model that makes use of the student's home language for instructional purposes for the shortest amount of time possible before the student transitions to English as the sole language of instruction.
Two-Way Immersion, Dual Language Program	Two-Way Immersion or Dual Language is a program in which two languages are used throughout the instructional day, and the status of each language (i.e., a majority language such as English and a minority language such as Spanish or Chinese) is used strategically. In the primary grades, subject area content is largely taught in the minority language. English-speaking students are immersed in the new language while minority language-speaking students establish academic knowledge in their home language. In the intermediate elementary grades, the language emphasis is switched: English is primarily the content area language and the minority language is used for enrichment and recreational classes. The goal of dual language immersion is that all students will attain bilingual fluency and cultural competence in both minority and majority societies. This program model is gaining popularity in communities with high numbers of same home language speakers (see http://www.cal.org/twi).

The generally accepted alternative to bilingual education has typically been Sheltered English Instruction. In this model, students are instructed entirely in English, but teachers are trained to use specific "sheltering" strategies to make the lessons understandable for students learning a new language—for example, clear speaking, providing visual representations of meaning, using predictable patterns of information and activities, providing multiple forms of presentation, using carefully sequenced question types, and creating alternative assessments. Sheltered English methods of instruction are methods of language teaching (see ESL, ESOL, and EFL in Figure 8.4) applied to subject area content lessons and activities (see CBI, Authentic Assessment in Figure 8.4). Sheltered English Instruction can be delivered in many types of school schedule plans: self-contained classrooms for students learning English, pull-out groups of ESOL instruction, push-in or team-teaching of ESOL with general education teachers, or all ESOL instruction can be provided by the mainstream, general education classroom teacher who uses appropriate ESOL teaching methods for English learners. In ESOL/Sheltered English Instruction, students' home languages are used to support content area learning informally or not at all, depending on the linguistic diversity and dispositions of the teaching staff.

Beginning in the 1980s, while bilingual education was encouraged through federal funding opportunities, political groups began to advocate for various forms of official language control. Voters in Dade County, Florida, passed an antibilingual ordinance (later repealed), and many states passed legislation citing English as the official language of that state. (Notably, Hawaii passed legislation citing both English and Hawaiian as the official languages of the state.) In 1998 California voters passed Proposition 227, an initiative eliminating bilingual education, and Arizona and Massachusetts voters passed similar legislation in 2002. A key part of each of these antibilingual education laws is the required implementation of a Structured English Immersion model of instruction. In this model, English learners are taught English language skills intensively for 1 year before joining mainstream classes with subject area content instruction (Clark, 2009).

In 2009 the Supreme Court took up the case of *Horne v. Flores*, a class-action suit claiming that English language learners were denied equal access to education because of insufficient funding to implement the program, an argument based on the finding in *Castaneda v. Pickard* that districts must provide adequate resources to comply with the "appropriate action" requirement of the law. The court ruled that the measure of "appropriate action" must be in student outcomes rather than specific funding levels, and that the lower courts had erred in not taking into account the changes that had been made in the English language instruction program (the implementation of Structured English Immersion). As of this writing, the complaint has returned to the lower courts for further review.

While state education policies are increasingly focused on the use of English as the sole language of instruction for students learning English, academic researchers and professional teaching organizations stress the effectiveness of including home languages (and community dialects) in students' English language instruction. They also emphasize the value added to society and economic competition by encouraging bilingual students to become fully literate in both languages.

Sandra, the student in the opening vignette, was likely to have been immersed in a mainstream English second grade with little or no language acquisition support. By the time Sandra reached high school, her English proficiency lagged behind that of her peers, and she says in her writing that she feels unsure of herself and believes that academic success is out of her reach. A longer excerpt of Sandra's writing shows us that she also lags behind her Spanish-speaking peers:

> I feel so uncomfortable when someone knows both Spanish and English and they don't make mistakes in either language. They say everything so right that my confidence goes down. It is like I don't even

want to talk anymore. I just want to crawl. When I am in a class full of people who only speak English, I feel out of my element.

In her writing, Sandra says she is unsure of herself in both Spanish and English and that she believes academic success is out of her reach. Her English language instruction program was not successful for her. At the same time, Sandra sees others in her classes who are proficient in both Spanish and English, and who are academically successful. How did they succeed?

Academic success for English learners is determined by many interactive variables, and it is often the very complexity of language issues that prevents many school leaders from fully participating in the planning, implementation, and evaluation of programs for English learners.

PRACTICES FOR INCLUDING ELLS IN SUCCESSFUL CLASSROOMS AND SCHOOLS

School leaders have the power to build inclusive practices for students learning English within any model of language instruction. In the article "Winning Schools for ELLs," Aleman, Johnson, and Perez (2009) list four characteristics of programs that have proven to be successful in producing high academic achievement for every demographic group of students they serve, including a population of 30% or higher of students learning English:

- High expectations for all learners
- Focus on conceptual understanding
- Culture of appreciation
- Broad base of leadership support

According to the article, to cultivate high expectations for all learners, teachers in award-winning schools hold their English learners to the same academic standards as all other students in the district. Teachers provide students with daily practice of challenging, engaging activities in which they build their skills in developing and expressing complex knowledge. Benchmark expectations are clearly communicated to students, and teachers actively collaborate in the supplemental support of any students who need additional practice, materials, or reteaching. Collaboration among teachers raises the overall rigor of instruction through shared practices, resources, and positive examples.

While using different curriculum materials and approaches, all teachers in award-winning schools focus on deep understanding of concepts, built through multiple experiences in different domains of learning. Students are

FIGURE 8.5. "Start Small, Start Now": Steps for School Leaders to Include Students, Their Languages, and Their Cultures

1. Respect student preferences for their name (American name or nickname), but know how to pronounce students' and parents' names in such a way that parents clearly understand you.
2. Say "hello" or "good morning" in the languages of the students in your school.
3. With the help of students, create signage, posters, banners, bulletin boards, and so on that include language and cultural information relevant to your school.
4. Meet with the librarians of your school and your community to find out what bilingual books are available for your students.
5. Search the Internet for age-appropriate language resources to share with students and their families.
6. Visit the grocery stores and other businesses in your school community to learn more about how community languages are used in public places.

required to use higher order thinking to carry out challenging tasks of explanation, discussion, and demonstration. Aleman and associates (2009) report, "As we observed classrooms, we heard student voices more often that teacher voices. . . . ELLs enjoy at least as many opportunities to contribute verbally as other students do" (p. 68). Surrounding the academic climate of these award-winning schools is a culture of appreciation for the language and cultural diversity of all students and their families. Appreciation for diverse languages and cultures can be seen and heard throughout these schools through posters, bulletin boards, assemblies, and classroom assignments. These schools all built their award-winning programs with caring, effective leadership. Goals are shared throughout the school "family," progress toward those goals is regularly reviewed as a team, and all positive growth is celebrated.

An award-winning program may take years to achieve, but school leaders can initiate and support beneficial practices on a small scale as they build momentum and consensus. Figure 8.5 presents small but significant steps that create a culture of inclusion and belonging for linguistically diverse students. These steps can be taken by one person or an entire school district.

CONCLUSION

Building an inclusive school culture for students who are learning English in school is a powerful move toward success for all students and their families. Students who feel a sense of belonging in school and who find work at school to be relevant in their lives are less likely to experience failure, lose hope, and drop out of school. Understanding the technical complexities of English language education empowers school leaders to find that the common goals of the school community foster good choices and shared understanding.

REFERENCES

Aleman, D., Johnson, J. F., Jr., & Perez, L. (2009). Winning schools for ELLs. *Education Leadership, 66*(7), 66–69.

Aud, S., Hussar, W., Planty, M., Snyder, T., Bianco, K., & Fox, M. (2010). *The condition of education 2010* (NCES 2010-028). Washington, DC: National Center for Education Statistics, U.S. Department of Education.

Bilingual Education Act, 20 U.S.C. § 880 (1968).

Brisk, M. E. (1998). *Bilingual education: From compensatory to quality schooling.* Mahwah, NJ: Erlbaum.

Brown v. Board of Education, 347 U.S. 483 (1954).

Castaneda v. Pickard, 648 F.2nd 989 (5th Circuit, 1981).

Civil Rights Act, 42 U.S.C. § 2000d *et seq.* (1964).

Clark, K. (2009). The case for structured English immersion. *Educational Leadership, 7*(66), pp. 42–46.

College Board. (2006). Sandra M.: Did I say it right, did it make sense? In *Words have no borders: Student voices in immigration, language, and culture* (p. 13). Retrieved March 31, 2011, from http://professionals.collegeboard.com/prof-download/words-have-no-borders-2009-cb-writing-comm.pdf

Elementary and Secondary Education Act of 1965 (ESEA). Pub.L. 89-10, 79 Stat. 27, 20 U.S.C. ch.70.

Equal Educational Opportunities Act, 20 U.S.C. § 1203 (1974).

Horne v. Flores, 129 S. Ct. 2579 (2009).

Keigher, A., & Gruber, K. (2009). *Characteristics of public, private, and Bureau of Indian Education elementary and secondary schools in the United States: Results from the 2007–08 schools and staffing survey. First look* (NCES 2009-321). U.S. Department of Education, National Center for Education Statistics. Retrieved March 31, 2011, from http://nces.ed.gov/pubs2009/2009321.pdf

Lau v. Nichols, 414 U.S. 563 (1974).

Martin Luther King Junior Elementary School Children v. Ann Arbor School District, 473 F. Supp. 1371. (E.D. Mich. 1979*).*

Mendez v. Westminster, 161 F.2d 774 (9th Cir. 1947).

Meyer v. Nebraska, 262 U.S. 390 (1923).

National Clearinghouse for English Language Acquisition (NCELA). (n.d.). *NCELA State Title III Information System.* Retrieved March 21, 2011, from http://www.ncela.gwu.edu/t3sis/

New Netherland. (n.d.). In *Wikipedia.* Retrieved March 31, 2011, from http://en.wikipedia.org/wiki/New_Netherland

No Child Left Behind Act of 2001, PL 107-110, 20 U.S.C. § 6301 *et seq.* (2002).

Plyler v. Doe, 457 U.S. 202 (1982).

U.S. Const., amend. XIV.

CHAPTER 9

Global Sensitivities: Students with Refugee Status

J. Lynn McBrien

On my first day in school, I was given a quiz. I did not even know English! I got one answer right. My teacher did not even try to talk to me about why I did so poorly. —Karin, 17, Iraq

I wish I could have skipped my whole first year here. I could not communicate, and I felt so alone. —Cai, 17, Vietnam

It is natural for students in the United States with immigrant/refugee status to feel excluded. Chances are, their first language was not English, and their cultural practices are different from the mainstream expectations of U.S. society. They may practice a non-Judeo-Christian religion. Refugee/ immigrant students may wear non-Western clothing; or, if they are trying to fit in, they may have only been able to afford clothing from a thrift shop that does not meet the standards of "in-crowd" students. Perhaps the girls attended a school where they would have received corporal punishment if they had arrived wearing nail polish or makeup. Perhaps these students have never had the opportunity to go to school at all, so the procedures taken for granted by native U.S. students—changing classes by bells, going to a cafeteria, waiting in line for the water fountain or bathroom, taking tests—bewilder them. In fact, they may have never seen a water fountain before coming to school.

I am amazed at the city lights, and I have lots of food to eat every day. In the camp I had to carry water in a bucket on my head from the well. Here it's right in the house. That's a big difference! —Shadia, 14, Liberia

In a land of such abundance, it is difficult for many teachers to imagine the fact that millions of children worldwide will never enter a school. For those who do, millions will attend classes under trees or in facilities that have no bathrooms, running water, meals, or textbooks, not to mention the technologies taken for granted in the United States, such as televisions and computers. This is true not only of refugees from war-devastated countries, but also of immigrants who have fled third-world poverty in hopes of providing a better future for their children. Refugee students come with the best of intentions, the highest of hopes, but they are as unfamiliar with what they will encounter as many teachers are with what these children and families have experienced in their past.

Teaching and supporting students who have immigrant/refugee status is not easy. Teachers and peers have to listen more carefully to understand them. Students who have immigrant/refugee status may not have the words they need to express themselves. They may need protection from peers (and adults) who discriminate against them. They may be struggling with past trauma as a result of war situations, or leaving behind close relatives or friends. They may be uncertain about a proper cultural response in the classroom. Refugee children are also likely to be behind academically because of language issues and/or lack of past educational experiences. The older the children are when entering a U.S. school, the less likely they are to have the cultural capital needed to understand concepts presented in middle or high school (especially with regard to U.S. history). However, heightened awareness and empirical examination of the experiences of students with refugee status has revealed information, characteristics, and strategies that improve the achievement of these students.

This chapter focuses on students who have refugee status who have been resettled in the United States and provides some information on undocumented and documented immigrants as well. The purpose is to explain key definitions, explicate major research about needs and concerns with these populations, raise awareness while energizing effective strategies, and include suggestions from research about ways in which to be successful with students who have immigrant/refugee status.

STUDENTS WITH REFUGEE, ASYLUM SEEKER, AND IMMIGRANT STATUS

The general definition of an *immigrant* is simple: Immigrants are any people who move from one country to settle in another. This broad definition, of course, includes refugees and undocumented immigrants. Yet, there are major differences between people who voluntarily choose to move to another country and who have followed their country's laws to do so, people who arrive clandestinely in another country and do not have legal documentation, and refugees or asylum seekers who are forced from their homeland due to fear of persecution for any number of reasons.

Refugees and Asylum Seekers

The United Nations defines *refugees* as people who, owing to well-founded fear of being persecuted for reasons of race, religion, nationality, membership in a particular social group, or political opinion, are outside the country of their nationality and unable or, owing to such fear, unwilling to avail themselves of the protection of that country (UNHCR, n.d.)

Refugees do not choose to leave their homeland because they want to, but because they must in order to protect themselves and their family members. Typical refugee situations result from political turmoil, civil war, and terrorist situations. Those fleeing such hostile situations have often encountered one or more traumatic situation that may include being imprisoned or tortured; witnessing violent acts, such as murder, torture, or rape; being detained as a child soldier; or enduring severe deprivations of food, water, or other basic necessities. Typically, those fleeing en masse due to political violence in their country are recognized as refugees, but there are exceptions.

The difference between refugees and asylum seekers often involves the process of flight. Broadly speaking, once citizens flee their native country because of persecution, they seek asylum in the country entered. Unless they have fled in large groups due to civil unrest (such as Somali or Sudanese civilians fleeing to Kenya to escape civil war), *asylum seekers* must present their case to the country to which they flee. If the authorities (in the United States, this is typically handled through the court system before an immigration judge) determine that the individuals meet the definition of a refugee, the asylum seekers may be granted refugee status (Wasem, 2006). According to the Department of Homeland Security, "an applicant for refugee status is outside the United States, while an applicant seeking asylum status is in the U.S., or at a U.S. port of entry" (Martin & Hoefler, 2009, p. 1).

Until their cases are decided, asylum seekers are often held in detention facilities along with convicted criminals. Although the Inter-American Commission on Human Rights (2009) reported that there have been some positive adjustments in unaccompanied minors' detention facilities, the reporter noted inadequate access to counsel, resulting in many children being left to represent themselves. If they lose their case, they are deported back to their country of origin. Only since July 2009 have women who sought asylum due to violent battering been allowed to qualify for asylum in the United States, although this qualification does not include women fleeing instances of female genital mutilation.

Most countries allow for only temporary settlement (although this arrangement can go on for 20 years or more). From temporary settlement, refugees can apply to be permanently resettled to a third country. Nine countries—the United States, Canada, Australia, Sweden, Norway, Finland, New Zealand, Denmark, and The Netherlands—host the majority of resettled refugees, although the UNHCR is working to find other willing countries. If they are fortunate, those applying may be granted a permanent resident status. The United States accepts far more than any other country for permanent resettlement, approximately two-thirds of the total yearly number. That number, however, is less than 1% of the world's total number of refugees.

People who have had to flee their countries ultimately face three resolutions. Refugees may be repatriated to their homeland if the situation causing their flight is dispelled. They may seek permanent resettlement in the country to which they fled, or they may request permanent resettlement to a third country. As noted, only a small number receive third country placement. Refugees awaiting resettlement endure many hardships. Millions live in refugee camps in which their housing may consist of tents or small, poorly constructed huts. They are dependent on the UNHCR and nongovernmental organizations (NGOs) to provide food, water, medical care, and education, all of which may be inadequate. Some countries can provide more stable temporary housing, but there are often restrictions on their ability to work and go to school, and as noncitizens, they do not have full protection of the country's laws.

Immigrants

Approximately 800,000 people constitute the "legal immigrants" to the United States annually (AILA, n.d.). Over half of these immigrants are "family sponsored": They are children, spouses, brothers, and sisters of U.S. residents. Refugees are also considered legal immigrants. Others include employment-based immigrants with skills considered desirable for the U.S. workforce.

Just under 12 million people living in the United States are classified as "unauthorized" or "undocumented" immigrants (Pew Hispanic Center, 2009). Nearly three-quarters of their children were born in the United States, and thus have U.S. citizenship. Seventy-six percent of unauthorized immigrants are Hispanic, with 56% coming from Mexico. They may cross the border illegally or overstay the terms of visas. Typical reasons for risking this status are the desire to be reunited with family members in the United States or to flee poverty, unemployment, crime, or violence in their home countries.

Unlike refugees and legal immigrants, unauthorized immigrants have reason to fear bureaucratic entities in the United States, as they can be prosecuted and deported if their status is discovered. As a result, they tend not to seek medical attention or social services, and they are targets for unfair labor practices and wages, as they cannot seek legal protection. However, current U.S. laws entitle undocumented children in K–12 to a free education, and schools may not ask families about their legal status when registering their children in school. An additional burden for many children of undocumented immigrants is that their parents may be migrant workers. This work requires workers to move with the crops as those crops need care or harvesting. As a result, children of migrant workers are not able to establish themselves in a single school for any significant period of time, and they juggle constantly changing locations, teachers, and curricula.

IMMIGRATION WITHIN A FRAMEWORK OF CHOICE

One way to frame immigration to the United States is to consider people's sense of choice in moving from the spectrum of no choice to full choice. This perspective has been argued from philosophical and practical viewpoints. As an example, a female Cuban refugee youth confided that she missed her friends, but that she no longer had to fear the loss of her father. She explained that he had disappeared most weekends and would return to their home bloody and bruised, having been taken and beaten by authorities because of his political dissent. Did the family have a choice? Arguably yes, the family could have remained in a state of persecution and violence. How much choice do undocumented immigrants living in a state of abject poverty and malnutrition have when they risk a dangerous border crossing, often relying on people smugglers who may be human traffickers? The answers are matters of debate, and how one answers may shape, in turn, how one responds to immigrants and refugees.

Generalizing is always problematic. Not only are there differences and exceptions between categories of immigrants, there are also significant differences within each group. For example, major economic, educational, and cultural differences existed between the first and third wave of Vietnamese refugees, and between those who fled Cuba in the early 1960s and those arriving today. Though imprecise, a lens of "choice" offers a way of understanding some of the challenges and fears that follow immigrants across border. The assessment in Figure 9.1 is based primarily on the degree of choice that one can exercise in coming into the United States. Figure 9.2 indicates general categories, as well as the resulting reactions to the immigration experience. These lenses provide a guide for assessing the characteristics and contextual factors surrounding student refugees and their families, and, hopefully, provide for a clearer understanding of their needs.

FIGURE 9.1. Range of Choice in Coming to the United States

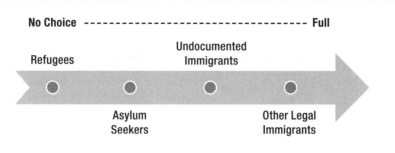

The School Experiences of Students with Immigrant/Refugee Status

Debate about immigration to the United States, especially illegal immigration, has been passionate in recent years. Opponents characterize undocumented people as bad characters who flood the country to take advantage of social services and jobs without paying taxes, learning the language, or embracing U.S. culture. Organizations such as the Anti-Defamation League (2009), the ACLU (2008), and other social justice organizations have countered the stereotypes with research demonstrating that immigrants want to learn English, pay taxes, contribute more to social services than they use, and are less likely to commit crimes than their native-born counterparts. Children of immigrants are frequently caught in the crossfire of these debates. Unless they arrived as unaccompanied minors, children of immigrants typically have little choice but to follow the decisions made by their parents or guardians. Yet they are frequently the target of stereotypes, prejudice, and discrimination by some U.S. peers and teachers. Students who are African refugees report that peers questioned whether they wore clothes or lived in jungles. Students who are Asian describe some teachers' assumptions that they will be top achievers in math and science. Children from Middle Eastern countries report frequent taunts by peers who call them "terrorists." Students face prejudice and discrimination in school from both peers and adults. Seventeen-year-old Karin, an articulate, accomplished young woman from Iraq, describes this experience as a result of her Muslim faith:

> It felt like I explained my scarf a million times every day. But [students] kept asking, "Why do you wear a scarf? Do you have to? Is there something wrong with your hair? Are you bald? Do you take it off when you shower?

FIGURE 9.2. Immigration Categories and Implications of Choice/No Choice

Classification	Issues of No Choice/Choice	Consequences/Challenges
Refugees	Often must flee with no preparation, as a result of warlike conditions. Flight is typically dangerous, and refugees may have to hide from governmental and illegal armies as well as thieves and wild animals. Have little choice in initial country of refuge; typically, it is the closest country to reach that might provide some safety. Temporary placement offers little to no choice in shelter, food/water, sanitation, medical care, education, and work. Camps are often unsafe from internal vandalism and violence as well as from outside illegal militia group raids. Those receiving third country resettlement are not given a choice of the country. The U.S. Family Reunification for Refugees is suspended at the time of this writing. Currently, the U.S. government provides funds per refugee for a limited number of months to pay for housing and food. During that time, they must learn enough English to find employment. Some refugees enter the country with high skills but must take low-wage jobs because their certifications are not accepted in the United States. Many enter with low skills.	Multiple traumas may result in psychological and/or physical conditions. Many suffer from post-traumatic stress disorder. Because they have not known who they can trust and they may have had to lie in order to get through bureaucratic issues (such as documentation, interviews, etc.), trust is a large issue with many refugees. Because they may have lived for months and even years in places where they were unable to work or have choices about meals, medical help, education, etc., many refugees suffer from "learned helplessness," a condition in which people believe that they cannot change their conditions, no matter what they do (Seligman, 1972). This condition can affect the physical, psychological, and social aspects of people's lives. Being underemployed for their skill level causes individual and familial/economic stress.
Asylum Seekers	Although they are fleeing situations that would define them as refugees, they typically take time to plan their escape. Must hide from authorities as they make their escape. Face detention, often in prison facilities, as they await the court's decision on their case. Risk deportation back to the country in which they were persecuted.	As people seeking to be recognized as refugees, face situations of trauma and trust as described above. Frequently they are not fully aware of their rights and the legal procedures they must navigate in order to receive a positive decision from an immigration judge.

FIGURE 9.2. Continued

Undocumented Immigrants	Typically, they must work out plans to enter the country illegally, so there is some choice in time. However, if they are working with smugglers, they must follow the timetable and plan of the smuggler.	Again, trauma and trust are major issues for this group of people.
	Risk uncertainty with a smuggler who may be a human trafficker that sells the immigrants into prostitution or sweatshop conditions.	As many flee to escape extreme poverty, they may suffer from malnutrition and other physical ailments.
	Risk dangerous crossing conditions in terms of inadequate water and food as well as possibility of confronting armed citizen patrols or government authorities.	They cannot access help from the government and are in constant danger of being discovered and deported. They often live in stress and fear.
Legal Immigrants	Obtain a visa (1) to be reunited with family, (2) because of employment, (3) after entering as a refugee or asylee, or (4) through an annual lottery (50,000 per year) not available to countries with high representation in United States. This process can take many years (U.S. Immigration Support, n.d.).	Even though the families may have had time to consider their move, this choice is not typically made by the children. Their migration preparation varies widely, depending on how their parents communicate the plans.
	People tend to need the assistance of an attorney, resulting in thousands more dollars in fees.	Although these children are less likely to have experienced physical or psychological trauma, they still face major adjustments in terms of such things as language, culture, and differences in schooling. They also grieve the loss of friends and family left behind.
	Must apply for legal permanent resident status (currently $1,010) and be certified by the Department of Homeland Security against prior medical, financial, or criminal issues that would cause denial of this status.	

After 9/11, kids started calling me "Saddam's sister." He was the reason my family had to leave our country! The way they were looking at us felt like, "You have done such a terrible thing to us and now we're going to take revenge," or whatever. We even got mean looks from teachers. My history teacher told our class that Islamic governments were corrupt and brainwashed people into the religion. When I tried to defend my religion, we argued. After class he told me that I shouldn't say things like that, so the class wouldn't hear those things. I said that everyone should know the truth. He said that I can keep that truth to myself.

Rather than mitigating Karin's ongoing social harassment, her teacher added to the mix of stress, anger, and fear. This is but one example illustrating the need for professional development on refugees for teachers and leaders in schools.

Experiences such as these can contribute to the lowering of academic motivation for students with refugee/immigrant status. Many children heard tales about how wonderful everything would be for them when they moved to the United States. Especially for those leaving situations of danger or great poverty, arriving to face discrimination can be demoralizing. Additionally, the rapid change to a highly technological, fast-paced school environment, in which the students may not be with other peers from their country, is a bewildering and exhausting experience. It is not uncommon for these children to fall asleep in class, not because they are uninterested, but because lack of a proper adjustment period is overwhelming. In addition to encountering all the new features of their lives, students with refugee/immigrant status are mourning the loss of relatives and friends they had to leave behind.

Figure 9.2 indicates the great variety of situations that immigrant children bring with them as they attempt to fit into the fabric of U.S. schools and society. Affecting most students across the categories are the difficulties they have trying to learn English and understand content areas. Cummins's (1981) research indicates that it takes 5–7 years for second language learners to acquire fluency in academic English, though they become conversant in 2 years or less (for a more in-depth discussion of challenges facing students who are English language learners, see Chapter 8). Yet, they are required to take standardized tests well before they are competent in a new language; frequently within the first year that they enter the U.S. school system.

Successful Inclusion of Students with Immigrant/Refugee Status

In the classroom, political opinions about immigration are immaterial. It is the obligation of all teachers to teach all students to the best of their ability and to care about them equally. If a student speaks Spanish and a teacher has issues with multilingualism, such issues must be left at home. If there there are students who are Muslim and a teacher accepts a stereotype equating Muslims with terrorists, it is important for the teacher to try to dispel it by getting to know these students as individuals. They may, in fact, be in the United States because their family was run out of their home country by terrorists.

Karin talked about her great love for school. Her family fled first to Iran, but was displaced again, to Pakistan, as a result of the first Gulf War. She recounted leaving her home before sunrise to arrive at a school that her parents told her she could no longer attend due to the financial burden. Her worried mother found her there hours later, and the teachers said that she could stay that semester for free because she was such a good student.

Yet, after her first day in a U.S. school, Karin returned to her family's apartment and said, "Mom, Dad, I quit! I'm not going to school anymore." In the short term, her rapid and discouraging experiences with language and prejudice crushed her motivation. However, she graduated at the top of her class winning numerous academic awards. She was awarded a 4-year scholarship to a woman's college where she completed her premed degree. After completing an internship at the Centers for Disease Control, she took a job as a research assistant at a "Southern Ivy" university. Karin is fluent in four languages. She is happily married and has a young son.

Karin is remarkable in her accomplishments. Success, however, is not unusual for refugee and immigrant children. What are some of the supports that help them rise above challenges that could defeat their goals and achievements?

Caring teachers are frequently cited as motivators for students with refugee/immigrant status (McBrien, 2009). Students in this study of adolescent girls' experiences in southern U.S. schools sometimes referred to teachers as a "second mother" or "second father." Students stated that teachers viewed as supportive were those who offered to explain concepts in more than one way, were patient, had a sense of humor, and did not embarrass them when they pronounced words wrong or made mistakes. Students also noted that teachers who had international experiences tended not to rely on stereotypes for categorizing students. One student described a teacher who had married a Liberian and visited the country frequently. As a result, the student said that this teacher did not express stereotypes that she heard from other teachers and peers.

IMPLICATIONS FOR SCHOOL LEADERSHIP

School leaders have an opportunity to build a school culture and community that is supportive and inviting to student refugees and their families. This opportunity aligns with requirements for supportiveness and inclusiveness for all students, but can also provide a "teachable moment" for highlighting the needs of this particular group. In addition to the many strategies for creating an authentically inclusive school setting, professional development activities can focus specifically on certain factors and support functions can be enhanced in some areas.

Overcoming Ethnocentricity

Of course teachers do not have to be well traveled to offer needed support to students with refugee/immigrant status. It is, however, helpful to be knowledgeable about world situations, both economic and political. It is important for teachers to be apprised of world situations by actively keeping up with current events. This can help them recognize areas from which refugees in their classrooms may be entering U.S. schools. Teachers can also gain valuable insights by attending community events that offer information about international situations, such as films, lectures, and intercultural events.

Honoring Privacy

Just as school systems cannot ask for social security numbers, they cannot ask questions about what brought their immigrant and refugee students to their schools. Igoa (1995) stated that some immigrant and refugee children feel a great need for privacy. They need time to work through their feelings of displacement and loss. Teachers can encourage them to use art—drawing, photography, stories—to work through this transition, assuring them that their work will not be shared without their permission.

Nurturing Sensitivity

Initially, all that teachers know about the students on their rosters is whether or not they are English language learners. Teachers may not know the circumstances, background, and degree of choice their students had with respect to coming to the United States. Sensitivity must be used in learning about immigrant and refugee students in order to gain their trust. For example, it is not appropriate to ask students to tell the class about their lives before coming to the United States unless they have gotten to know them well and know that they are comfortable doing so. This is because the students may have experienced major trauma prior to immigrating, and recalling it can provoke terrible memories.

It is important to be gentle with immigrant and refugee students who fall asleep or seem preoccupied in your class. The transition is daunting, and language immersion is tiring. On top of their school concerns, many immigrant children are enmeshed in family concerns. They may experience stress from parents who are struggling to learn the language and provide for their family. Immigrant children may feel pressure from hiding their identities. They may be placed in the position of translating adult information—bills, medical information, and legal terms—to their parents.

Advocating for Students

Teachers should be on the lookout for prejudice and discrimination against students who have refugee/immigrant status. In whatever ways are appropriate to the curriculum, all students can be taught about the refugee and immigrant experience. There are many elementary and high school level books and documentaries that can be used in the classroom to help U.S. students understand the challenges faced by these students. Simple gestures, such as just learning "hello" in the students' languages go a long way in helping the students feel welcomed.

Coordinating Within Schools

It is very important for regular classroom teachers to coordinate with ESOL teachers. ESOL classrooms are comprised of many students experiencing similar adjustment issues; thus, students will often bond with one another and with their ESOL teacher. As a result, the ESOL teacher can frequently provide regular classroom teachers with information that can help them assist their immigrant and refugee students. Too frequently ESOL teachers indicate that they feel segregated from routine school activities.

Coordinating with Outside Agencies

It would be helpful for teachers and administrators to learn about the social service agencies serving the international populations in their community. Often these organizations can provide important liaison services between families and schools, such as interpreters and cultural workshops for school, staff, and immigrant communities to orient them to school expectations. Community service providers can facilitate the vital link with parents who often struggle to be involved with their children's education because of employment demands, language issues, and/or cultural differences. There are numerous voluntary agencies (VOLAGs) that work with the State Department to resettle refugees, including the International Rescue Committee (IRC), U.S. Committee for Refugees and Immigrants, World Relief, Catholic Charities, and Lutheran Services. Torture treatment centers through the United States work with refugees who have endured traumatic experiences.

In addition, there are religious and secular agencies that aid in ongoing services needed by refugees and other immigrants. For example, Refugee Family Services outside Atlanta serves hundreds of refugees in the greater Atlanta area. Gulf Coast Jewish Family Services helps hundreds of refugees throughout Florida. Agencies like this are found throughout the country, and they typically provide numerous services that may include translation, school-family liaison services, after-school tutoring, cultural presentations, and more.

CONCLUSIONS

Although students who are refugees often need ELL instruction and face similar development stages and challenges faced by other children their age, they often bring a unique set of characteristics and experiences that force-fully shape their learning and social interaction. Research has shown that teachers who take the extra time to listen, understand, and get to know these students can make a major difference in their learning and their lives (Stewart, 2009). Research also indicates that students with refugee status who are supported and encouraged by teachers typically will work very hard to gain approval and succeed. In addition, teachers can gain a new and diverse world perspective by learning about lives and events that would otherwise remain unknown to them (Stewart, 2009).

Effective teachers typically show sensitivity and empathy for these students. However, even strong, caring, and dedicated teachers can benefit from additional professional development focused on students and their families who are refugees. School leaders, in turn, have a responsibility for creating a collectively supportive and inviting school setting for these students and their families. In most schools, knowledge, skills, and attitudes regarding student refugees and their families are uneven at best. Bringing the unique needs of this group of students to the forefront in professional development and community building can enact an authentically inclusive school community where students who are refugees can thrive.

REFERENCES

American Civil Liberties Union. (2008). *Immigration myths and facts.* Retrieved August 6, 2009, from http://www.aclu.org/immigrants/34870pub20080411.html

American Immigration Lawyers Association (AILA). (n.d.). *U.S. Immigration Policy on Permanent Admissions*. Retrieved March 31, 2011, from http://www.aila.org/content/default.aspx?docid=31895

Anti-Defamation League. (2009). *Curriculum connections: Myths and facts about immigrants and immigration*. Retrieved March 31, 2011, from http://www.adl.org/education/curriculum_connections/spring_2009/lesson2.asp /supplements/Myths and Facts.pdf

Cummins, J. (1981). Age on arrival and immigrant second language learning in Canada: A reassessment. *Applied Linguistics, 2*, 132–149.

Igoa, C. (1995). *The inner world of the immigrant child*. Mahwah, NJ: Erlbaum.

Inter-American Commission on Human Rights. (2009). *IACHR visits U.S. immigration retention facilities*. Retrieved August 4, 2009, from http://www.cidh.org/Comunicados/English/2009/53-09eng.htm

Martin, C. D., & Hoefer, M. (2009, June). Refugees and asylees 2008. *Annual Flow Report* (Department of Homeland Security). Retrieved July 30, 2009, from http://www.dhs.gov/xlibrary/assets/statistics/publications/ois_rfa_fr_2008.pdf

McBrien, J. L. (2009). Beyond survival: School-related experiences of adolescent refugee girls and their relationship to motivation and academic success. In G. Wiggan & C. Hutchinson (Eds.), *Global issues in education: Pedagogy, policy, school practices and the minority experience* (pp. 294–330). Lanham, MD: Rowman & Littlefield.

Pew Hispanic Center. (2009). *A portrait of unauthorized immigrants in the United States*. Retrieved July 27, 2009, from http://pewhispanic.org/reports/report.php?ReportID=107

Seligman, M. E. (1972). Learned helplessness. *Annual Review of Medicine, 23*, 407–412.

Stewart, J. (2009, April). *Transforming schools and strengthening leadership to support the educational and psychological needs of children affected by war*. Paper presented at the annual meeting of the American Educational Research Association, San Diego, CA.

United Nations High Commissioner for Refugees (UNHCR). (n.d.) *Refugees*. Retrieved July 27, 2009, from http://www.unhcr.org/pages/49c3646c125.html

United States Immigration Support. (n.d.) Home page. Retrieved August 5, 2009, from http://www.usimmigrationsupport.org/?gclid=CLz3gezljJwCFQa-sgodgiubXg

Wasem, R. E. (2006). U.S. immigration policy on asylum seekers. *CRS Report for Congress*. Retrieved August 4, 2009, from http://www.ilw.com/immigdaily/news/2006,0223-crs.pdf

Disrupting Heteronormativity: The Inclusion and Representation of Children Who Are LGBTQ and Their Families in Schools

Thomas Crisp

As a term, *heteronormativity* describes the processes through which social institutions and social policies reinforce the belief that human beings fall into two distinct sex/gender categories: male/man and female/woman. This belief (or ideology) produces a correlative belief that those two sexes/genders exist in order to fulfill complementary roles. . . . As a concept, heteronormativity is used to help identify the processes through which individuals who do not appear to "fit" or individuals who refuse to "fit" these norms are made invisible and silenced. (Queen, Farrell, & Gupta, 2005, p. 3)

CLARIFYING PERSPECTIVE (OR BEING PERFECTLY QUEER)

The purpose of this chapter is not to debate whether or not identifying as lesbian, gay, bisexual, transgender, or queer/questioning (LGBTQ) is a "good" or "bad" thing. Such discussions invoke conversations of morality, and this chapter is not focused on those issues. The chapter instead focuses on the reality of these students' lived experiences in schools and the commensurate responsibility of school leaders to provide a safe and inclusive environment. Rather than offer a vignette about one or more individual students, which could perpetuate rather than alleviate stereotypes, I provide a working definition of the key concept of heteronormativity as a foundation for shared understandings for the rest of the chapter.

This chapter aims to serve as a guide for school leaders to examine (mis)conceptions, key concepts, and theoretical and pedagogical approaches to inclusive classrooms and schools that work to disrupt heteronormativity and confront homophobia. In addition, examples throughout the chapter demonstrate how schools and society ignore the lived experiences of young people who are LGBTQ and the dire consequences that result for them and their families.

In 1980, Adrienne Rich argued that Western culture is permeated by the ideological assumption that all people are heterosexual and that this presupposition works actively (as well as implicitly) to make all others invisible. Building on this work, in 1991 Michael Warner coined the term *heteronormative* to describe the ways in which all social relations (e.g., media, institutions) work to reinforce and reinscribe the belief that heterosexuality is a "normal" or "natural" way of being. Although the term may initially seem complex, in the introduction to their volume *Interrupting Heteronormativity,* Queen, Farrell, and Gupta's (2005) definition of heteronormativity clarifies and highlights the all-consuming and pervasive way in which heteronormativity operates as a system to maintain an unjust status quo by effectively eliminating those who do not, cannot, or refuse to embody these labels. As an extension of this system, American classrooms and schools are habitually heteronormative mechanisms that perpetuate hierarchies of power and privilege for those who "fit" culturally privileged and established norms while simultaneously marginalizing children and families that are already disenfranchised and cast as deviant by mainstream society.

CAN WE TALK?:
TERMINOLOGY AROUND SEXUALITY AND SEXUAL IDENTITY

In this chapter a number of terms will be utilized to make particular points most effectively. In an effort to ensure that statements or positions are clear, it is essential to clarify how particular words or phrases will be used throughout this chapter. Delineating a shared set of terminology is also an essential consideration in fostering effective discussions with students, families, and colleagues about issues related to sexuality and sexual identity. The definitions for each of the terms below were not created exclusively for this chapter, but build upon, reproduce, and extend understandings held by many involved in the fields of gender studies and queer theory.

- *LGBTQ*—This is an umbrella modifier that stands for "lesbian, gay, bisexual, transgender, and queer/questioning" and is utilized to represent the people who self-identify as members of those populations. It is one of several popular modifiers (i.e., GLBT, LGBT, GLBTQ) but is selected for use here because it seems to be the most inclusive of these populations. Often, the "Q" is said to stand for either "queer" or "questioning," not both, but it is only by including both possibilities that this modifier can be its most inclusive. GLBTQ is a modifier used to represent a direct connection to the Stonewall Riots of 1969 by drawing attention to the "G" for gay liberation movement (e.g., see Cart & Jenkins, 2006), while the use of LGBTQ attempts to ensure that lesbian identities are not lost in the modifier. Sometimes, talk about "gay rights" privileges gay males at the expense of lesbian females, so situating lesbian ("L") as the primary identifier within the modifier LGBTQ serves to best keep lesbian existence visible. Although a single modifier is used to represent all people who are LGBTQ, it does not imply that self-identifying as "gay" is the same as self-identifying as "lesbian," "bisexual," "transgender," "queer," or "questioning"; there is variation across populations as well as within.[1]
- *Homosexual*—A person whose primary attractions are toward those who claim the same biological sex.
- *Heterosexual*—A person whose primary attractions are toward those who self-identify as the "opposite" sex.
- *Sexual Identity*—How one chooses to name oneself. Sexual identity is a term that allows for agency, in that a person is permitted to decide how they wish to be "named" (or "not named"—i.e., queer). To differentiate this term from notions of sexual orientation, often one will speak of how someone "self-identifies" as a person (i.e., "I self-identify as a gay male").
- *Sexual Orientation*—Sexual orientation is used to indicate the gender (or self-identity) of the objects of an individual's primary attraction. It is different from sexual identity in that sexual identity involves an individual's claiming of an identity, whereas orientation centers on an individual's attractions.
- *Normative*—The term *normative* is used to describe those identities or positions privileged by a particular society. In the case of Western culture, heterosexuality is an example of a "normative" identity.

- *Nonnormative*—This is a term used to describe those identities or positions traditionally marginalized by a particular society. In the case of Western culture, self-identifying as a transgender female is a "nonnormative" identity.
- *Lesbian*—A lesbian is a self-identified female who is primarily physically attracted to other self-identified females.
- *Gay [male]*—The term *gay* is sometimes used to refer generally to all people who are LGBTQ, but is more specifically used to name a self-identified male who is primarily physically attracted to other self-identified males.
- *Bisexual*—Bisexuality is often misunderstood as involving those who simply "can't make up their mind" as to whom they are attracted. In actuality, someone who self-identifies as a bisexual is attracted to people of multiple sexes. Individuals who self-identify as bisexual may be simultaneously attracted to multiple sexes across the life span or to one sex as opposed to others at particular times in life.
- *Transgender*—A transgender person is someone who is biologically classified as "male" or "female" but whose self-identity does not match their biological classification.
- *Queer*—Often used as a derogatory term, *queer* has been taken back by the LGBTQ community in recent years and is used to describe someone who cannot or who refuses to be categorized into any particular gender identity (i.e., "I'm not 'male' or 'female.' I'm queer").
- *Questioning*—This is a self-identity that can be taken on by those of any "biological sex" who are not ready to claim an identity (e.g., "I am a bisexual female") and who do not, for any number of possible reasons, identify themselves as "queer."

There are, of course, an abundance of other terms (including slang) that are worthy of attention, but limitations of space prohibit the full attention these deserve. Take, for one example, the term *drag*. Dressing in drag is the act of drawing attention to the performative nature of gender (Butler, 1990) by embodying the characteristics of the "opposite" sex. Although popularly linked to gay males, drag is most often performed by males who self-identify as heterosexual (Garber, 1997). The root of the term *drag* is debated, but many attribute it to William Shakespeare who, in a scene in which a male character entered dressed as a female character, wrote "dr.a.g" (*dressed as girl*: dr. a. g.) in the manuscript margins.

Another example would be the words *fag* or *faggot*. These derogatory terms are used to describe gay males and are also used to describe a bundle of twigs/sticks utilized for kindling. (In places like the United Kingdom, a "fag" is a cigarette.) The linkage of "fag" to gay males has an obscure history and has been linked by some scholars and wordsmiths to the Middle Ages or the Spanish Inquisition, where gay males were tied together and set on fire to serve as kindling for the burning of alleged witches (Johansson, 1981). Others have linked the term to the burning of gay males during twelfth- or thirteenth-century Britain, but these claims remain unsubstantiated (Johansson, 1981). Still others believe that the word is a uniquely American creation. Understanding the complicated history of words like this underscores the importance of raising awareness, breaking down stereotypes, and moving beyond mere "tolerance" of people who are LGBTQ. As much as one may wish that the use of these words in phrases like "that's so gay" or "he's a fag" indicates they have "evolved" or have "new meaning" for this generation of young people, these words cannot be divorced from their histories.

Finally, it is important to note the use of the term *sexual identity* as opposed to *sexual orientation* throughout this chapter. The difference might seem inconsequential, but one of the major goals of this chapter is to underscore a belief that language matters. What we do—and don't—say is vitally important, and each word we speak must be selected with thought and foresight. There is no room for carelessness because, minimally, children's perceptions of themselves and their families are at stake. Although "orientation" is still more commonly used, it suggests a positionality in relation to some "norm": How is this position oriented *in relationship to ___*? Because heterosexuality is the normative sexual identity in Western culture, use of the phrase "sexual orientation" indelibly links those with nonnormative identities to heterosexuality and implies a relationship between the two in which heterosexuality is the privileged position (i.e., "How am I oriented as compared to heterosexuality?"). Heterosexuality becomes the marker against which all others are measured.

The word *identity* is also used in this chapter because of the agency it affords all people. In talking about sexual identity, individuals are talking about how they choose to identify themselves at that time (Blumenfeld, 1994). It reveals "gender" and even "biological sex" to be social constructions and permits fluidity across gender categories, as opposed to limiting people to the binary categories of "male" or "female." Although one may self-identify as "male" today, an identity of "female" is not excluded as a possibility for tomorrow—or even tonight (Butler, 1990, 1993, 2004; Foucault, 1978; Stephens, 2002).

These definitions clarify and highlight the all-consuming, limiting, and omnipresent ways in which heteronormativity operates as a system that maintains a hegemonic status quo: Heteronormativity effectively eliminates those who do not, cannot, or refuse to embody or "take on" these labels.

PERPETUATING THE STATUS QUO IN SCHOOLS

The presuppositions that give heteronormativity its power work actively (as well as implicitly) to make all others invisible, marginalizing those who resist normative conceptions of sexuality. On the contrary, those who embody characteristics that "fit" into socially accepted and recognized categories (i.e., those who self-identify as "male" or "female" and "heterosexual") are often unaware of (or, at least, do not question) the privileges they are granted simply on the basis that they identify as "male," "female," or "heterosexual." This means that many in the population are unknowing participants who contribute on a daily basis to a system that sanctions inequality.

This may be off-putting or uncomfortable, but the following example serves as simply one of a myriad of ways in which heteronormativity is reified on a daily basis. Every time someone is asked to fill out a questionnaire (e.g., census, a visit to a doctor's office), ze[2] is usually asked to check a box indicating hir sex as "male" or "female." In schools, young people are regularly asked to indicate male or female when registering in a new school, joining a sports team, or taking a standardized test. There are millions of young people who simply check a box and move on without giving it much thought, but there are many others for whom these forms are a reminder of their invisibility in schools. Although there are certainly exceptions, as a vital part of this pervasive system, American classrooms and schools are heteronormative mechanisms that propagate hierarchies of power, automatically privileging those who "fit" the culturally privileged and established norms while simultaneously marginalizing children and families already disenfranchised and cast as deviant by "mainstream" society. Schools are training grounds that reflect the ways in which a particular society wants itself to be viewed: What is represented and taught in schools reveals what is (and is not) valued by society.

Statistics document that children and young adults who self-identify as "LGBT" struggle to find a place in American classrooms. These young people frequently feel marginalized, harassed, and unwelcome in schools that refuse to recognize their existence and are surely not inclusive. The findings of the 2009 *National School Climate Survey*, issued by the Gay, Lesbian, and Straight Education Network (GLSEN), indicate that 88.9% of respondents hear "gay" used negatively and 72.4% hear other homophobic slurs ("fag" or "dyke") frequently or often in schools. A staggering 61.6% of respondents report that they feel unsafe at school because of their sexual identity and 39.9% report that they feel unsafe because of their gender expression (Kosciw, Greytak, Diaz, & Bartkiewicz, 2010, p. xiv). These findings suggest that LGBT students are more than four times more likely than the general population of secondary school students to have missed a day of school because they felt unsafe and LGBT students who face high levels of in-school victimization are more likely to indicate they have no plans to pursue postsecondary education than their peers (p. xvii). According to another GLSEN survey in 2007, only the District of Columbia and 10 states (California, Connecticut, Iowa, Maine, Massachusetts, Minnesota, New Jersey, Vermont, Washington, and Wisconsin) have passed legislation that explicitly protects students who are LGBTQ from harassment and discrimination. Further, only five states (California, Iowa, Maine, Minnesota, and New Jersey) protect students based on gender identity and expression (Presgraves, 2008).

These statistics are startling and, coupled with recent anti-LGBTQ political measures (e.g., antigay marriage and antigay rights legislation like Proposition 8 in California, the continued support for the Defense of Marriage Act and Don't Ask, Don't Tell policy), suggest dramatic changes are required in order to alter the ways in which LGBTQ experiences are (dis)regarded in American schools and curricular materials (Crisp & Knezek, 2010). Although often overt, the marginalization of children who are LGBTQ and their families is frequently implicit, which makes it all the more insidious and difficult to transform. It may be helpful to focus on pervasive examples of how schools and society ignore the lived experiences of people and families who are LGBTQ-identified.

THE EVERYDAY STUDENT EXPERIENCES OF LGBTQ

School bathrooms and locker rooms are often categorized according to biological sex: "male" and "female." This leaves no space for those who do not identify themselves as a member of either of these groups. One assumption behind this type of separation is to minimize the potential for "opposite" sex interactions, explicitly supporting the misconceptions that (1) "boys" and "girls" are fundamentally (biologically) "different" and (2) all "boys" are attracted to "girls" (and vice versa). Simultaneously, then, it implicitly presumes that no sexual or romantic possibilities exist between members of shared gender identities.

Classrooms (as early as preschool or kindergarten) are filled with talk of "crushes" between students and yet these conversations rarely—if at all—involve two people who share the same gender identity. Often, phrases like "When you get married and have children . . ." are bantered about without any critical reflection as to the assumptions that accompany these types of expressions. The statement "When you get married and have children . . ." suggests, in part, that the children implicated in the phrase do (or will) self-identify as "heterosexual" and that all children who are granted the privilege of being able to marry (which, as of the writing of this chapter, again marginalizes people who are LGBTQ) will choose to do so. Such statements have tremendous power and weight because they reinforce ideological constructions of the ways in which "we" (society) want the world to look and operate: It is a heterosexual, sex-and-marriage scenario that reinforces heteronormativity at the expense of any who cannot or choose not to adhere to this path. These types of comments seem inconsequential because they reinforce what is too often taken for granted. However, it is precisely those notions that feel the most "real," safe, or like "common sense" that merit the most critical interrogation.

The literature read to (and read by) children rarely includes any space for queer identities (Crisp & Hiller, 2011). Instead, it represents and promotes monogamous coupling between a "male" and "female" either explicitly (such as those fairy tales in which a prince and princess fall in love and live happily ever after) or implicitly (the plethora of books that feature children who belong to families with married, heterosexual-identified parents). It is not difficult to generate an extensive list of texts, which represent normative gender identities and relationships, but it is often difficult to come up with a single book (let alone a range of titles) that represents queer identities and relationships. Those books that do feature characters with nonnormative gender identities often depict the queerness of their characters (such tropes as the tomboy or sissy) as a temporary or transitory aspect of an "innocent childhood," quickly disregarded as the protagonists enter puberty and "discover" the "opposite" sex (Abate, 2008; Flanagan, 2007).

Teachers, students, and administrators routinely identify themselves as heterosexual by talking about their husband/wife (or boyfriend/girlfriend) or by displaying photographs on their desk or wall. Although sharing pieces of personal lives may be an excellent way to bond with students, the stakes are higher (and it is much more complicated) for queer educators to share these pieces of themselves with others than it is for those who self-identify as heterosexual. People who are LGBTQ can still be fired from their jobs simply for self-identifying as LGBTQ. Often, teachers who are LGBTQ are told they cannot reveal their sexual identity to their students, a restriction that does not apply to those who self-identify as heterosexual. Asking people who are LGBTQ not to reveal their sexual identity is not only discriminatory, it is homophobic and reinscribes heteronormativity, both fostering and maintaining the assumption that all people self-identify as "heterosexual."

Sexual education and "health" courses center on rigidly defined "male" and "female" bodies and discussions of sexual activity almost exclusively involve heterosexual intercourse for the purposes of procreation. When discussions of masturbation, oral sex, or other acts do occur in schools, they are framed within an assumption of heterosexuality. It is essential to consider what "possibilities" are (not) offered to students and who is (not) being represented. As a more concrete illustration of what is meant here, recently, under the guise of science education, many teachers were taking their students to see a traveling exhibit of preserved human bodies.[3] Many of these teachers did not question the ways in which the display legitimized bodies: verifying existence through the inclusion of particular types of bodies and reinscribing the invisibility of others (i.e., Were any transgender bodies included?).

Often, the omission of LGBTQ issues is couched in a belief that teachers and administrators must provide a neutral environment by "checking their personal beliefs at the door." However, proponents of this position fail to recognize that schools, teaching, and curriculum are always politically and socially situated. One argument deployed in order to justify the exclusion of LGBTQ examples, discussions, and curriculum in classrooms is that their inclusion would be politically motivated, and that educators must take care to avoid politics in the classroom. This perspective fails to recognize that all teaching is political (Graff, 2000). There is no such thing as "neutral" teaching or a neutral school environment. Every act of teaching, whether an act of commission or omission, is a political act. Thus, keeping LGBTQ presence out of classrooms is not a "neutral" position at all; it is an *equally* political position as including people who are LGBTQ (just on the other side of the issue). To put it more bluntly, those involved in pedagogy who are not representing people who are LGBTQ are not being neutral, they are involved in an act of hostility against the children in their tutelage: telling them that they (or their caregivers or others whom they love) either do not matter or do not exist. Those who would argue that "I don't judge anyone, but homosexuality shouldn't be talked about in classrooms" may be confusing sexual *identity* with sexual *activity*— although some would like to conflate these terms, they are distinct and different. Heterosexual people are repeatedly represented in classrooms on a daily basis without any discussion of what is "done in the bedroom" and the same should be true for people who are LGBTQ-identified people. Those involved in public education are charged with the task of preparing students to live as members of a diverse society; not including representations of people who are LGBTQ in schools is tantamount to telling a child, "Your two daddies—those two people you love more than anyone else in the world—are bad/wrong/nonexistent." Anyone who approves of this message should not be involved in educating children.

BRINGING LGBTQ ISSUES TO THE FOREFRONT

Although the statistics reported earlier in this chapter may seem bleak, Kosciw and Diaz (2008) suggest supportive staff can serve to intervene on behalf of students who are LGBTQ. The ultimate goal is to help school leaders reimagine the inclusion of students and families who are LGBTQ by reshaping the contents of their classrooms and curriculum. Queer curriculum is not a unit of study to be piled onto an already overly demanding schedule (just as "African American history" should not be exclusively represented in February), nor is it about tolerance of the "other" (Blumenfeld, 1994; Blumenfeld & Raymond, 1993). It involves substantive epistemological shifts that can be impactful when embodied by individuals, but even more profound when embraced by an entire school.

The statistics presented earlier illustrate the imperative for bringing LGBTQ issues into curricular and pedagogical conversations. The LGBTQ population remains "the invisible minority" (McClean, 1997, p. 178) in classrooms and schools. Bringing about systemic change within a district, school, or individual classroom is challenging indeed and may seem impossible, but it has been and must continue to be done. School leaders have the responsibility to ensure their school is welcoming and safe for all students, and to be aware of the impact that the ongoing, everyday heteronormativity of school experiences has on students who are LGBTQ is a strong early step in this process. The remainder of this chapter will be devoted to ways of enacting change aimed at these purposes by addressing issues ranging from school/classroom policies, the classroom environment, language, texts and curriculum, and more. This is not an exhaustive list of strategies but rather offers a starting place for school leaders' consideration as they develop inclusive policies and practices that embrace students who are LGBTQ. School leaders are encouraged to begin by supporting the process of looking inward and reflecting on personal and professional assumptions, moving to an examination of current school policies, setting and modeling expectations, and reaching out to parents and caregivers. In addition, effective strategies for training and professional development as well as for maintaining a physically and psychologically safe environment can assist school leaders as they strive for inclusiveness.

An Educator's Responsibility: Looking Inward

The place to begin is always with ourselves; recognizing injustice or a need for change is a profound and important first step. Educators must examine their own presuppositions in order to begin to influence those around them. They must make explicit—and then critically examine—the theoretical positions and ideas that shape how they view the world. It is strongly suggested that school leaders participate in "antihomophobic" and "social justice" training and retreats. It is not enough to proceed armed only with good intentions. As Oscar Wilde said, "It is always with the best intentions that the worst work is done." Antihomophobic and social justice training and retreats are offered in many communities and in every state and can be easily located through an Internet search coupling the words *education* or *pedagogy* with terms like *antihomophobic, antiheterosexist,* or *antiheterosexism.*

In addition, school leaders are encouraged to talk with representatives from LGBTQ outreach organizations in nearby areas. Participating in antiheterosexist education retreats will not only deepen and strengthen their own understanding of LGBTQ issues, it will provide ideas for antihomophobic education and will connect leaders with other allies who are equally committed to issues of social justice related to LGBTQ identities. Building a support group, or circle of allies, may be vital in working to change the culture of the school or classroom. In this intimate circle of allies, it is important not to prejudge anyone and to always allow others the opportunity to change. It is sometimes surprising who may be the best ally.

A social note about the term *ally:* Calling oneself an ally is discouraged as presumptuous among many traditionally marginalized populations. Doing so makes an assumption about what/how a person thinks, acts, or influences those in their intimate circles. To be called an "ally" is a gift that can only be given by an "insider" from a particular population.

The work of self-discovery surrounding sexual identity is ongoing and continues throughout one's life. It is important that school leaders make space in a very busy and overloaded professional development training schedule to encourage such conversations and personal reflection. It is also important that school leaders are aware of the need for these reflective experiences to be sensitively facilitated by a person with knowledge and experience in LGBTQ and social justice issues. Therefore, all leaders, regardless of their own sexual identity, are encouraged to participate in this type of training and education.

Assessment of Policies and Processes

After initiating self-education and the creation of a circle of allies in this work, school people should then assess the policies in the school and classroom. In looking at them, it is important to take note of what type of antidiscrimination protections are in place (and who is held accountable to/for these protections) and which are absent (or who is left out). Does the school or district policy explicitly protect students and families on the basis of sexual and gender identity? If these words are absent from the policies, it could be that this population is not protected.

It is little wonder that multiple books for children who are LGBTQ children and young adults have been written to inform them of their legal rights. In *Sexual Orientation and School Policy: A Practical Guide for Teachers, Administrators, and Community Activists*, Ian K. MacGillivray (2004) provides the following sample diversity goal statement with beliefs:

Statement
Value Diversity and Promote Understanding
Beliefs
- All human beings have inherent worth.
- All students, regardless of race, ethnicity, gender, sexual orientation,[4] age, disability, or religion, deserve a quality education.
- [The school district] will not tolerate discrimination, intimidation, harassment, or violence based on race, ethnicity, gender, sexual orientation, age disability, or religion.
- Healthy school communities respect differences, welcome diversity, and promote cultural plurality.
- Racial, ethnic, and cultural diversity should be evident across all employee groups and central administration. (p. 199)

This example of a Values and Beliefs statement that is straightforward and has clear language is very appealing in its protection of all students, employees, and the school community more generally. Language similar to that of the beliefs statement may already exist in the district and school mission and vision statements. However, reviewing and clarifying language, and revisiting the language often in meetings and conversations, can bring the values to the forefront in decision making and action. School leaders can also facilitate a crosscheck or professional audit of how the Values and Beliefs statement of the school are truly reflected in the policies and practices of the school. Figure 10.1 is an example of a tool built around the previous vision and belief statements that clearly embraces inclusion. This tool can be used by a school leader as a review of where policy and practice coalesce in the school, and where there is room for further development. Two examples of practice are called for in this reflective process, however, a school leader may decide to collect additional examples of practice to evaluate the multiple ways the school does and wants to embrace the values and belief statements.

Modeling and Setting Expectations

The impact of school leaders cannot be underestimated in this regard. Setting expectations, using inclusive and affirming language,[5] and model-

FIGURE 10.1. Review of School Practices for Inclusion

Policy	Evidence in Practice	Area for Further Attention	Date Reviewed
Vision Statement: Value diversity and promote understanding	Practice 1:		
	Practice 2:		
Belief 1: All human beings have inherent worth.	Practice 1:		
	Practice 2:		
Belief 2: All students, regardless of race, ethnicity, gender, sexual orientation, age, disability, or religion, deserve a quality education.	Practice 1:		
	Practice 2:		
Belief 3: The school does not tolerate discrimination, intimidation, harassment, or violence based on race, ethnicity, gender, sexual orientation, age, disability, or religion.	Practice 1:		
	Practice 2:		
Belief 4: The school community respects differences, welcomes diversity, and promotes cultural plurality.	Practice 1:		
	Practice 2:		
Belief 5: Racial, ethnic, and cultural diversity is evident across all employee groups.	Practice 1:		
	Practice 2:		

ing inclusive "beliefs in action" are key tools in leadership. Through these tools, school leaders have the ability to influence those both "above" and "below" them in the school community. Educators at all levels can profoundly influence those within their immediate sphere: Superintendents can influence principals, principals can influence teachers, teachers can influence their students, and so forth. But that influence can flow in both directions with subordinates' attitudes and behaviors having equally powerful effects on superiors. Indeed, from the smallest of voices can come the most profound movements.

If a school leader cannot (or is not ready to) effect a districtwide change in policy, directly stating the expectations at the school or classroom level is

FIGURE 10.2. LGBTQ Criteria for Texts and Materials

Question or Criterion	Textbook	Portrayal of LGBTQ
How are people who are LGBTQ "positioned" in these texts? (Are they protagonists? Secondary characters?)		
How are people who are LGBTQ "depicted" within the text? (What are they like? In what ways do they reinforce or disrupt stereotypes?)		
How do you know these people/characters are LGBTQ? (Is it explicitly named in the text? Implied in illustrations?)		
Are these "quality" texts? (Why or why not?)		

Note. Adapted from "Being Versus Becoming: (Re-)reading the Curricular Inclusion of Gay Adolescent Literature," by T. Crisp and S. Knezek, 2010, *English Journal*, 99(3), 76–79.

an equally good strategy. Share those policies with students, send copies home to caregivers, and post (and revisit) those strategies throughout the school. Teachers honoring these policies within each classroom can initiate a synergy to perpetuate a schoolwide climate of inclusion and respect. In respect to classroom curriculum and instruction, including age-appropriate people who are LGBTQ and examples in the daily curriculum requires careful selection of texts and teaching strategies in a nurturing and respectful environment. Some criteria for texts and materials selection are offered in Figure 10.2.

Two additional considerations are paramount. First, silence is not an option. Silence about children who are LGBTQ and curricular examples can perpetuate the notion that certain topics are taboo. A derogatory comment made by a student or adult in the classroom or school can be used as a teachable moment. Inclusive and respectful language and behavior can send a clear message in the classroom and across the school. Second, singling out children who are LGBTQ or their families can have a detrimental effect. Pointing out that Marie has two mommies may set up the child for harassment. Just as the "Taco Night" is mostly ineffective in creating inclusive relationships and understanding between Hispanics and others, highlighting differences in a superficial ways is ineffective in promoting inclusion. Authentic inclusion requires genuine and routine engagement among students and faculty.

Another consideration in creating an inclusive environment for students who are LGBTQ is examining the rate at which these students are referred for special education services. Too often these students are incorrectly referred to special education either because their studies are seriously and adversely affected by factors related to their lack of fit in sexual categories or because they are assumed to need emotional help (Biegel & Kuehl, 2010). Accuracy in placement of these and all students is essential.

Reaching Out to Parents and Caregivers

An ongoing concern for school leaders is nurturing strong relationships with parents and caregivers of students with all sexual identities. In deciding whether or not to inform caregivers about LGBTQ-related policies, the suggestion here is that it is always important to keep these individuals informed and actively involved in school curriculum and the events occurring in classrooms. Be prepared to meet with parents and caregivers (preferably face-to-face) to discuss concerns, but do not assume that there will be issues with queer-inclusive curriculum. In many facets of school education (e.g., sexual education), parents and caregivers are given the option of "opting out" of a particular aspect of a school curriculum. Ideally, LGBTQ-inclusive learning environments do not focus on discrete "units" being taught, but are a daily part of the community and curriculum. This in itself makes "opting out" difficult—if not impossible. In addition, it is important to keep reminding those with concerns that this is not about *sex*, it is about *identity*. If the school or district would not allow students to "opt out" of curriculum depicting/representing African Americans, females, or other underrepresented groups, they should not be permitted to "opt out" of any queer-inclusive curriculum. Again, this is not about morality, it is about social justice.

Training and Professional Development

Inclusion of children who are LGBTQ and their families in the "fabric" of the school involves deep learning among many groups at the school. Child-to-child relationships and caregiver-to-caregiver relationships are as critical as those among teachers, staff, and students. Training and professional development that raises awareness, develops skills, and sets expectations can be focused on varied groups, including students, teachers, school staff, parents and caregivers, and community members.

Physical Environment, Psychological Safety

Much of the harassment of students who are LGBTQ occurs outside the classroom. Attending to students' physical and psychological safety can begin with tracking students through the day to identify any times, passages, or specific places in the school where they are vulnerable. Many of these areas of vulnerability can be addressed with simple changes. Within the classroom, simple changes in the way that we divide the class into groups can become more inclusive. Instead of girls against the boys, for example, teachers can count off or group by row or tables. Teachers can also listen to students who do not fit or refuse to fit into sexual categories, especially older students who can voice their preferences and offer suggestions.

The NEPC report *Safe at School: Addressing the School Environment and LGBT Safety through Policy and Legislation* (Biegel & Kuehl, 2010) offers a number of recommendations for maintaining safe environments for students who are LGBTQ. They highlight the importance of attending to bullying of all students and include recommendations for training and professional development targeted at helping student relationships at critical junctures such as athletics (p. 4). These recommendations reinforce a schoolwide initiative that clearly treats bullying and harassment as unacceptable behaviors and makes adults responsible both as models and monitors. The report suggests a model code that can guide educators in creating accessible and inclusive learning environments for students who are LGBTQ:

1. Adopt proactive rather than reactive initiatives.
2. Focus consciously on school climate in day-to-day planning, activities, assessments, and evaluations.
3. Commit to inclusive policies and shared values within our pluralistic society.
4. Strive to end discriminatory discipline practices and the inappropriate referral of students to special education, which can have a particularly negative impact on marginalized and disenfranchised groups.
5. Communicate guidelines and tenets for improving school climate to students, not just educators. They should also be taught directly in an age-appropriate manner, especially in the secondary grades.
6. Consider adopting one or more structured school-climate programs, which often provide—but are not limited to—opportunities for service learning, diversity education, and character education.
7. Consider adopting one or more specific initiatives that address such areas as bullying, hate violence, and at-risk youth generally.
8. Implement one or more LGBT-specific programs or activities at individual school sites, such as safe zones, gay-straight alliances, suicide-prevention programs, and wellness centers geared toward students of particular races or ethnicities. (Biegel & Kuehl, 2010, pp. 10–12)

CONCLUSION

School leaders can initiate substantive change on a local level by taking the steps outlined across this chapter. They can begin the process of disrupting heteronormativity and creating spaces for children who are LGBTQ-identified and their families in schools and classrooms. If the work to be done within any local context feels overwhelming or daunting, it may help to remind themselves that ultimately, this work is not optional. People who are LGBTQ need to see themselves represented in schools: Their self-esteem, their self-worth, and their lives depend upon it.

NOTES

1. Throughout this chapter, the modifier employed will vacillate between LGBT (lesbian/gay/bisexual/transgender) and LGBTQ (lesbian/gay/bisexual/transgender/queer or questioning). This is because there are times in which the use of the "Q" (queer or questioning) is not applicable, as, according to the tenets of queer theory, each of us is ultimately "queer." As a result, there are moments in which it makes sense to "strategically essentialize" (Spivak, 1993, pp. 3–9) and specifically demarcate LGBT-identified people as a separate group as opposed to including all who would be considered a part of the broader modifier of LGBTQ.

2. Here, gender-neutral language is invoked—the use of words like *ze* (as opposed to *he or she*) or *hir* (as opposed to *his or her*) represent attempts by queer theorists and scholars to begin disrupting the heteronormativity of language.

3. The word *guise* is used here because, although these exhibits are marketed as being about knowledge and science, there is little or no information or "science" presented: It is more about exhibitionism, voyeurism, and the macabre than it is about gaining any scientific understanding of the human body.

4. Here is an example of the use of the more popular term *sexual orientation*. Consider, instead, the term *sexual identity*.

5. Some examples of gender-neutral language are used throughout this chapter, for example, *ze* as opposed to the gendered *he* or *she* and *hir* as opposed to *him* or *her*.

REFERENCES

Abate, M. A. (2008). *Tomboys: A literary and cultural history*. Philadelphia: Temple University Press.

Biegel, S., & Kuehl, S. (2010). *Safe at school: Addressing the school environment and LGBT safety through policy and legislation*. Boulder, CO: National Education Policy Center. Retrieved October 3, 2010, from http://nepc.colorado.edu/publication/safe-at-school

Blumenfeld, W. J. (1994). *Homophobia: How we all pay the price*. Boston: Beacon Press.

Blumenfeld, W. J., & Raymond, D. (1993). *Looking at gay and lesbian life*. Boston: Beacon Press.

Butler, J. (1990). *Gender trouble: Feminism and the subversion of identity*. New York: Routledge.

Butler, J. (1993). *Bodies that matter: On the discursive limits of sex*. New York: Routledge.

Butler, J. (2004). *Undoing gender*. New York: Routledge.

Cart, M., & Jenkins, C. A. (2006). *The heart has its reasons: Young adult literature with gay/lesbian/queer content, 1969–2004*. Lanham, MA: Scarecrow Press.

Crisp, T., & Hiller, B. (2011). *"Is this a boy or a girl?": Re-thinking gender representation in Caldecott medal-winning literature*. Paper presented at the fifth annual Children's Literature Symposium, University of South Florida, Sarasota-Manatee.

Crisp, T., & Knezek, S. (2010). Being versus becoming: (Re-)reading the curricular inclusion of gay adolescent literature. *English Journal, 99*(3), 76–79.

Flanagan, V. (2007). *Into the closet: Cross-dressing and the gendered body in children's literature and film*. New York: Routledge.

Foucault, M. (1978). *The history of sexuality: Volume I. Introduction*. New York: Random House.

Garber, M. (1997). *Vested interests: Cross-dressing and cultural anxiety*. Routledge: New York.

Graff, G. (2000). Teaching politically without political correctness. *Radical Teacher, 58*, 26–30.

Johansson, W. (1981). The etymology of the word "faggot." *Gay Books Bull, 6,*16-18, 33

Kosciw, J. G., & Diaz, E. M. (2008). *The 2007 national school climate survey: The experiences of lesbian, gay, bisexual and transgender youth in our nation's schools*. New York: GLSEN.

Kosciw, J. G., Greytak, E. A., Diaz, E. M., & Bartkiewicz, M. J. (2010). *The 2009 national school climate survey: The experiences of lesbian, gay, bisexual and transgender youth in our nation's schools*. New York: GLSEN.

MacGillivary, I. K. (2004). *Sexual orientation and school policy: A practical guide for teachers, administrators, and community activists*. Landham, MD: Rowman & Littlefield.

McClean, M. M. (1997). Out of the closet and onto the bookshelves: Images of gays and lesbians in young adult literature. In T. Rogers & A. O. Soter (Ed.), *Reading across cultures: Teaching literature in a diverse society* (pp. 178–198). New York: Teachers College Press.

Presgraves, P. (2008). *2007 National school climate survey: Nearly 9 out of 10 LGBT students harassed*. Retrieved October 9, 2008, from http://www.glsen.org/cgi-bin/iowa/all/news/record/2340.html

Queen, M., Farrell, K., & Gupta, N. (2005). Editors' introduction. In K. Farrell, N. Gupta, & M. Queen (Eds.), *Interrupting heteronormativity*. Syracuse, NY: Syracuse University Press.

Rich, A. C. (1980). Compulsory heterosexuality and lesbian existence. *Journal of Women's History, 15*(3), 11–48.

Spivak, G. C. (1993). *Outside in the teaching machine.* New York: Routledge.

Stephens, J. (2002). *Ways of being male: Representing masculinities in children's literature.* New York: Routledge.

Warner, M. (1991). Fear of a queer planet. *Social Text, 9* (4), 3–17.

CHAPTER 11

Creating a Culture of Respect: Gender Perspectives

Janice R. Fauske

Cheree entered the AP Calculus class to find that she was one of only three young women enrolled. The teacher, Mr. Fletcher, was very friendly and welcomed each of the women to the course: "I am so glad to finally have some girls in the course." After taking roll and talking about the course assignments, Mr. Fletcher excitedly announced that he wanted to be sure that the "girls" succeeded so he had assigned a male tutor to each. Cheree was assigned Tommy. Over the course of the semester, she and Tommy met several times to study. In fact, they began dating. Cheree became more and more stressed before each test. Even though she studied regularly and could do the problems at home, Cheree could only manage a C in the course despite earning straight As in prerequisite math courses. Cheree went to Mr. Fletcher to ask if he could go over her mistakes. Mr. Fletcher could not do this, however, because he never saw her calculations. He only accepted final answers on a list of 1–10 problems for each test. Cheree never took the AP Calculus test.

Cheree was also taking AP Chemistry and had Tommy as her lab partner. They were two of a group of six students (four boys and two girls) who worked together in the large group to plan experiments and study. The lab experiments were then conducted in groups of two, and results compared across groups before preparing lab reports for their teacher, Mr. Minx. Cheree enjoyed the group meetings and the lab work. She was able to ask questions freely and to watch others work. The collaboration on lab work was very helpful. Cheree earned an A in AP Chemistry and went on to earn college credit for General Chemistry on the AP exam.

Much has been studied and written about gender in schools and its impact on learning. Differences in learning preferences and achievement between males and females have been explored along dimensions of age and subject, and study has continued into those same differences within postsecondary programs. The impact of stereotypes and hostile environments has been explored, and same-sex classrooms and schools have been assessed. This chapter summarizes these studies and describes their potential effects on young women and men. Strategies for teachers and school leaders for addressing gender and sex-based bias are presented as well.

Before beginning to explore and summarize what we claim to know about gender influences in schools, consider the assumptions that frame the study and data collection surrounding gender. First, the term *gender* is used throughout these studies when the deciding factor for how data are categorized is the *sex* of the student. However, gender differs from sex. Masculine gender, for example, can be expressed by both males and females. Thus much of what is described in the literature as gender actually refers to sexual difference. Second, much of what is studied as *gender* is based on traditional notions of heterosexual males and females. The data assume a set of shared characteristics among young men and young women, yet sexual identity is a more complex social consideration than whether someone was born a male or female (Butler, 1993; for a fuller discussion of sexual identity, see Chapter 10). Nevertheless, heterosexual students comprise a large percentage of the overall student population, and there is little doubt that stereotypes about these populations exist.

In fact, stereotypes about the sexes are ingrained and unquestioned in schools. Consider, for example, the continued use of the term *girls*. Hackman (2002) notes that the women's movement has "taught us the power of language and the important role accurate, empowering language plays in social change" (p. 61) and the continued, common use of the term *girls* undermines efforts to change stereotypes. In this chapter, the term *female* is used in place of girls unless directly quoted.

Sandra Bem's (1993) pivotal book *The Lenses of Gender: Transforming the Debate on Sexual Inequality* captures much of what defines traditional views of gender over time, and particularly the Western evolution of gender stereotypes. She questions why "women and men, as groups, played such different and unequal roles in virtually every society" (p. 30), and cites the Binet Intelligence Quotient test and its bias toward White males as but one example of how bias has emerged (p. 7). Historically, males have been privileged to attend schools, while it was optional for females, and still is in many countries (World Bank, 2001). Bem (1993) further describes gender polarization that has produced binary interpretation of masculine and feminine characteristics and the concept of androgeny that distorts these interpretations, concentrating more on individual characteristics than on examining superficially created lenses of masculinity and femininity (pp. 25–26). Nevertheless, schools continue to superimpose the polarized lenses of male and female in numerous ways, including an emphasis on gathering data and comparing male and female students' achievement and behavior.

Keeping these observations and limitations in mind, what can be learned from the study of gender or sexual difference in schools? Knowledge about educational patterns and trends that show differences or similarities in learning and achievement for young men and women can inform curricular, professional development, and leadership decisions. The intent of this book is to focus energy and attention on what can be done to make schools authentically inclusive—to focus on the positive, the future. Yet, making schools more inclusive also requires that we focus on the barriers that are an inherent part of the system of schooling (Pivik, McComas, & Laflamme, 2002). This chapter will not, nevertheless, consider illegal and/or sexually biased acts of violence, although there is much evidence to show that sexual misconduct in a variety of forms including criminal misconduct is fairly common in schools. The intent here is not to diminish the seriousness of these horrific crimes against children, but to focus on cultural elements and patterns of gender bias that regularly interfere with learning. These elements and patterns may not be criminal but do contribute to ways of thinking that "permit" certain negative behaviors to persist rather than be extinguished. The role of school leaders is to question and replace the behaviors that perpetuate gender bias of all kinds.

GENDER, COURSE TAKING, AND ACHIEVEMENT

Historically, studies have shown that in the elementary grades young women achieve at higher levels than young men. Studies show that females make higher grades and have better behavior (Buchmann, DiPrete, & McDaniel, 2008). "Today, from kindergarten through high school and even in college, girls get better grades in all major subjects, including math and science" (Perkins, Kleiner, Roey, & Brown, 2004, p. 4). Other studies show that males do better in science and females in reading, and that other factors, such as socioeconomic status, as well as race, influence scores (Buchmann et al., 2008). Some researchers maintain that these differences are simply a reinforcement of tendencies rather than biological differences between the sexes, and that the culture of the students' upbringing magnifies these differences over time; for example, if boys are more active, parents reinforce this tendency with physical activities, and if girls are more verbal, parents talk to them more (Elliot, 2010, p. 33).

In fact, some studies report that there is a new set of stereotypes engendered: "Thirty years of political insistence that gender doesn't matter has had the ironic effect of reinforcing gender stereotypes" (Sax, 2008, p. 36). Sax maintains that widely publicized studies about the problems faced by girls in schools, such as How Schools Shortchange Girls (AAUW, 1992), have created lower expectation for girls' performance among educators and among the girls themselves, especially in math and science. Thus, female students themselves may perpetuate the stereotype that they struggle with math and science. For example, female students report more stress and less efficacy associated with certain science courses, which may be a result of educators responding to and operating under the persistent stereotype that females struggle in math and science courses (Cavanagh, 2008). Even the president of Harvard, Lawrence Sumners ("The AAUP's Committee on Women Responds," 2005; Wilson, 2005) mentioned that innate gender-based differences in math and science could be one reason for fewer females in those career fields. He was chastised later by faculty and the AAUP for these remarks. Nevertheless, the Sumner incident is a powerful example of how pervasive the stereotype regarding an absence of females in math and science has become. Clearly, this stereotype is pervasive, widely accepted, and influences young females. Yet, assessment of girls' cognitive abilities as equal to boys' points to other reasons for the low number of female students in advanced math and science courses and careers.

A number of studies report differences between females and males in performance in math and science. Sadker and Sadker (1994) concluded that females benefited from single-sex classes and from specific kinds of instruction in math and science courses that was less competitive. There is also evidence that same-sex teachers favor females over males and that, conversely, the lack of male teachers is detrimental to males in all subject areas, including math and science (Buchmann et al., 2008; Sokal, Katz, Chaszewski, & Wojick, 2007). Recent studies show conversely that females and males have essentially equal cognitive abilities in science and math (Buchmann et al., 2008). In fact, several studies show that females now take more advanced placement, college preparatory, and related courses than do males, and they get better grades (Bae, Choy, Geddes, Sable, & Snyder, 2000; Buchmann et al., 2008; Catsambis, 2005; Gallagher & Kaufman, 2005). Other studies show, however, that although female students take more advanced placement courses in language, literature, and history, males continue to take more advanced placement courses in math and science (Moore & Slate, 2008). The prevailing knowledge is that females and males have comparable cognitive abilities in science and math but that female enrollment in advanced courses tends to be in those outside of math and science. The question of why this pattern prevails remains largely unanswered.

Although achievement statistics show gains for females overall, the study of women has often ignored "the [specific] experiences and issues of women of color, lesbian and bisexual women, poor and working-class women, or women with disabilities" (Hackman, 2002, p. 61). Researchers point particularly to the influence of the interaction between ethnicity and gender as one determinant of both female and male enrollment in advanced placement courses. Ojeda and Flores (2008), for example, concluded that Mexican American cultural expectation overrode the influence of gender for females, evidenced in their not choosing advanced math and science courses. Other studies indicate that enrollment percentages for minority students in AP courses continue to lag behind those of White students (Moore & Slate, 2008). Thus gender is not isolated as a factor influencing enrollment in AP courses.

Graduation rates show a definite trend toward young women attending and completing college. The proportion of women earning a bachelor's degree in the United States has grown from 35% in 1960 to 58% in 2005 (Buchmann et al., 2008; Snyder & Dillow, 2007). Although there are several indicators that sexual differences for enrollment in advanced courses as well as graduation from college are ameliorating, questions remain about why participation in science and math courses continues to lag.

Challenges for Males

Some researchers are concerned about trends for males and are calling for more sophisticated studies of possible sexual differences in cognitive or development skills in young people (Entwistle, Alexander, & Olson, 2007). They cite patterns that indicate possible development or cognitive challenges to males in the education system. Males are more likely to start kindergarten late, repeat kindergarten, show learning disorders, or be held back in elementary grades (Buchmann et al., 2008; Entwistle et al., 2007). The challenges for males in the schools are well summarized by Tyre (2008):

> While there was no difference between boys and girls on intelligence tests, boys trailed girls on almost every other measure. Boys were responsible for the majority of discipline problems and accounted for more than 70 percent of the students assigned to special education. While their classroom performance was about the same in the early years, by fifth grade girls had higher marks across all four core subjects—reading, writing, science, and math. . . . (p. 1)

These findings provide important considerations for teachers and school leaders working with students of both genders. Tyre (2008) goes on to further highlight gender differences:

For Every 100 GIRLS

. . . enrolled in kindergarten, there are 116 boys.

. . . enrolled in high school, there are 100 boys.

. . . enrolled in public gifted and talented programs, there are 94 boys.

. . . who graduate from high school, there are 96 boys.

. . . suspended from public school, there are 250 boys.

. . . expelled from public school, there are 335 boys.

. . . diagnosed with a special education disability, there are 217 boys.

. . . diagnosed with a learning disability, there are 276 boys.

. . . diagnosed with a speech impairment, there are 147 boys.

. . . diagnosed with emotional disorders, there are 324 boys.

. . . enrolled in college, there are only 77 men.

. . . who earn an associate's degree there are only 67 men.

. . . who earn a master's degree there are only 62 men. (p. 41)

Single-Sex Classes and Schools

Segregated classes for males and females have been studied by a variety of practitioners and researchers. Single-sex science courses, for example, have been found to be beneficial for young women's performance (Sadker & Sadker, 1994; Sadker & Zittleman, 2005; Stewart, 2009). Similarly, single-sex classes have benefited young, African American males (Horton, 2010), although the interaction of single race as well as single sex in impacting this success is not clear. The Urban Prep Academy, an all–African American school for males in the Englewood area of Chicago open since 2006, reports that all 107 students graduated and all of its graduates are college bound in 2010 (Horton, 2010). Clearly, something is working well in this school for low-income African American males. *Separated by Sex: A Critical Look at Single-Sex Education for Girls* (AAUW, 1998) summarized existing research on single-sex classrooms and concluded that the findings were inconclusive. Jaqueline Woods (Woods & Dylinski, 2002), director of the American Association of University Women (AAUW) in 2002, observed, "Once the findings were adjusted for student socioeconomic status, pre-enrollment ability, selectivity of the school and other variables, the differences diminished or disappeared" (p. 4). Yet, in a point-counterpoint article with Woods, Dylinski argues that single-sex classes and schools are beneficial to girls in a number of ways:

> girls report feeling at ease in discussing personal items in class, less fear of peer sanctions when erring, less fear of asking questions, less fear of appearing "smart," and, significantly, less peer pressure to engage in high-risk behaviors. . . . [Critics] maintain, however, that the strengths of these schools stem from smaller class sizes, good teachers, high academic expectations—anything but the single-sex environment itself. It's a view that simply doesn't wash with reality, students at the Philadelphia High School for Girls will tell you. (p. 4)

Both the Urban Prep Academy and the Philadelphia High School for Girls are examples of successful environments for single-sex students from low-SES backgrounds. It is difficult to determine the impact of the single-sex factor in these schools, but anecdotal evidence reported from experiences at these schools suggests a dynamic that enhances student behavior and performance.

Throughout the literature on single-sex classes, numerous examples of beneficial impact on students, particularly female students, have been presented. For example, Leonard Sax (2008), speaking for the National Association for Single Sex Public Education (NASSPE), criticizes the AAUW report *Where the Girls Are: The Facts About Gender Equity in Education* (2008) and argues that the report's focus on achievement ignores such facts as the number of females taking physics classes continuing to drop over the past 20 years. Sax argues "that single-sex classrooms can advantage girls without disadvantaging boys, and vice versa" (p. 29). He further asserts that single-sex schools directly affect the course choices made by females and males:

> Girls at girls' schools are several times more likely to study subjects such as computer science, physics, and engineering, compared with girls attending coed schools. Boys at boys' schools are more than twice as likely to study subjects such as art, poetry, and advanced Spanish as boys of comparable ability attending coed schools. (p. 29)

Indeed, single-sex classes and schools are on the rise. In 2006, 33 states offered "gender-exclusive public school classes, with New York and Ohio having the most such programs" (Lewis, 2006, p. 73). Lewis reports that Title IX had prevented single-sex courses, however, "except in choir, sex education, and physical education classes" and that the No Child Left Behind Act (NCLB) opened the door for "federal funds to be used for innovative programs that will boost achievement, including single-sex schools and classes" (p. 72). Similarly, Sax (2008) supports this increasing trend toward single-sex classes:

> Six years ago, when we launched the organization, 11 public schools in the United States offered single-sex classrooms. Right now, 392 public schools offer single-sex classrooms. For the school year that starts this fall, more than 500 will offer single-sex classrooms. (p. 29)

Lessons from These Studies and Trends

We know that achievement data may not tell the whole story about the influence of sexual difference on learning in classrooms. We know report after report claims that girls exhibit a greater level of confidence, take more risks, and are motivated to continue in math and science courses when in single-sex courses. We know that the kind of teaching in physics that works with males differs from what works with females (Nelson & Sanders, 2004; Sax, 2008). It seems that single-sex classes and schools encourage a number of behaviors that are conducive to effective learning and create situations that are optimal for certain groups of students.

One explanation for the impact of single-sex classes is that females in mixed-sex courses are negotiating social ecologies and relationships as a part of constructing their learning experiences in the classroom (Walshaw, 2001). Walshaw (2001) describes girls in math courses as living in a "slippery space" (p. 490) where they create a discourse of knowledge and power when they are sure of the content and move to discourses of femininity when uncertain or in doubt (p. 488). This pattern exemplifies Gilligan's (1993) argument that women have different ways of knowing than men, and that women see the world in terms of relationships and connections while men see the world from a perspective of autonomy. Thus constantly negotiating these slippery spaces while simultaneously negotiating relationships with males and teachers can be detrimental to learning.

GENDER NEUTRAL IS GENDER NULL

Studying the discourse of participants as a means of understanding how relationships are negotiated within social context reveals how they simultaneously construct themselves and are coconstructed through language (MacNaughton, 1998; Wade, Fauske, & Thompson, 2008; Walshaw, 2001). The study of actual utterances within the classroom context offers a rich source of data that act as a window into individual perceptions that goes beyond analysis of test scores, who takes what AP courses, and graduation rates. Yet much of the debate around influences of sexual difference on student learning centers on those kinds of statistics.

The American Association of University Women (AAUW) has been influential in shaping the discussion of the female experience in schools through three widely read reports. The first, *How Schools Shortchange Girls* (1992), concludes that, in addition to schools negatively impacting girls academic performance, harassment of young women in schools is commonplace and that creating a safe place for students to report harassment is essential: "An integral part of successfully preventing sexual harassment in schools includes providing an environment in which students feel comfortable talking to adults about harassment and in which students know that staff members will take their complaints seriously" (p. 6). The AAUW defines harassment broadly, going beyond the US DOE more restrictive definition of sexual harrassment, which is behavior "so severe, persistent, or pervasive that it affects a student's ability to participate in or benefit from an education program or activity, or creates an intimidating, threatening, or abusive educational environment." The AAUW definition of *harassment* has been criticized by the Foundation for Individual Rights in Education (FIRE) as being too broad and including "constitutionally protected expression, such as any unwanted sexual comments, jokes, gestures, or looks" that are protected as freedom of speech (Schroeder, 2006, p. 73). Thus, Schroeder concludes that the AAUW report (1992) misinforms teachers and students about what constitutes sexual harassment, and he notes that the report includes as the reason that some girls do not report sexual harassment is because they do not see it as a big deal. What is offensive to one student is not offensive to another. The emergent questions are (1) which definition should be supported in schools, and (2) how do schools and school leaders balance protection of free speech with individual sensitives?

The second report, *Separated by Sex: A Critical Look at Single-Sex Education for Girls* (1998), claims that responding to potential sexual harassment by creating single-sex classes is not supported by data. The third report, *Where the Girls Are: The Facts About Gender Equity in Education* (2008), argues that both male and female students, but girls in particular, have improved in educational performance. This report also acknowledges the influence of race and socioeconomic status on performance and states that "understanding disparities by race/ethnicity and family income level is critical to understanding girls' and boys' achievement" (p. 3). Overall, the three AAUW reports sensitize educators and parents to the potential problems that girls seem to face in schools. Some themes across the reports appear contradictory, such as the conclusion, that single-sex classrooms can help girls learn in the first report but little support for single-sex education in the second report. In fact, evidence documenting the effects of single-sex classrooms is inconclusive but promising anecdotally. These reports in total have focused attention on the influence of being female in schools but have also caused educators to examine practices that could be detrimental to either girls or boys. The third report offers an optimist assessment of girls' performance in schools, but introduces more directly the interactive effects of being female with race and socioeconomic status. All of these considerations contribute to a more thoughtful examination of practice.

Overall, educators are left with many unanswered questions and disagreements about the influences of sexual difference on student performance. Further, indicators for student *performance*, which tend to rely on standardized test scores and related numerical data, may not capture the "whole picture" of student *learning*. Therefore, the remainder of the chapter acknowledges the influence of sexual difference and offers strategies for creating a supportive environment based on the belief that all students must be treated with respect and included. To that end I describe an environment that invites dialogue and facilitates examination of gender-based stereotypes.

The language used in many of the studies of gender bias in classrooms show schools by default support the creation of a gender-neutral environment (Nelson & Sanders, 2004). The assumptions that underlie advocating for such an environment include creating a neutral space for inviting dialogue among students and encouraging openness in exploring unwelcomed and desirable behaviors (Pierce, 2005/2006; Reeder, 2005). Although the strategies offered in these studies can be helpful, creating a gender-neutral environment presupposes that school personnel as well as students recognize their potential biases and can think beyond their own limiting stereotypes. Such a goal is ambitious to say the least and requires substantial professional development of staff at all levels, especially frontline teachers, and consistent training and behavioral expectations of students. It is good but maybe not enough. A gender-neutral environment aims to ignore gender and make it null. Therefore, creating a gender-neutral environment based on the binary categorization of masculine and feminine may be shortsighted and inadequate. Consider a gender-positive school environment that focuses more on embracing gender differences than on political correctness and what not to do. Gender-positive behaviors enhance inclusion and social justice. In addition, a gender-positive environment acknowledges that interpretations of gender among students and school personnel are complex; sexual identities and orientation cannot be assumed.

STRATEGIES FOR GENDER-POSITIVE ENVIRONMENTS

Student to Student

Just as inclusion among groups defined in other ways, expectations for student-to-student relationships are pivotal and require direct intervention and training. Pierce (2005/2006) describes findings from a study of life in high schools:

> Once inside individual classrooms, students work hard to follow tacit codes for appropriate behavior among assembled peers . . . this unspoken but de facto student culture . . . dominates students' experience of school. Because this finding reveals so much about students' social compromise and so little about their engaged learning, it seems that classroom teachers hold the surest, most immediate power to reclaim and reform classrooms from sites of student accommodation to sites of active and even enjoyable accomplishment. (p. 1)

Pierce and others (AAUW, 1992) highlight the powerful role of teachers and call for structured dialogue among students that provides a space for addressing relationships, for sharing problems, and for reinforcing appropriate behaviors. However, care must be taken to avoid perpetuating gender- and sex-based stereotypes, which requires specific skills and training for students as well as for teachers. Dialogues among students can be assessed by how well they promote three skills for students:

1. Think critically about the basis of real and perceived male-female differences.
2. Understand the variety of factors that influence individuals' behavior, in addition to their sex.
3. Reduce their reliance on gender stereotypes to predict and interpret behavior. (Reeder, 2005, p. 115)

Schools have many vehicles for these dialogues, including such programs as communities of caring, targeting expected behaviors and participatory citizenship. Student-based mentoring programs also provide an avenue for promoting thoughtful interaction and respect.

Teacher to Student

In addition to creating spaces for dialogue, teaching strategies and instructional decisions can impact interaction between sexes. Take the opening scenario, for example, with two differing strategies, one more competitive and the other more collaborative. Note that both teachers have good intentions and are ostensibly supportive of young women taking science and math. Nelson and Sanders (2004) conducted a study of high school physics teachers in which the teachers were questioned about perception of their own teaching. Many teachers claimed to be aware of potential biases and to actively avoid gender-based bias, yet case after case of observation showed another story. One teacher asked to be observed so that he could demonstrate his perceived lack of bias. The report from his observer noted: "Taking into account the class's gender representation, the teacher had spent 80 percent of his time responding to boys and 20 percent to girls" (p. 75). The teacher was shocked and began changes in teaching to correct this pattern. In the next observation, the teacher thought that the female response time would be well over 50%, yet the report was exactly 50:50 (p. 75). This story illustrates how deeply ingrained our patterns of interaction with females and males are. Teachers tend to ask males deeper questions, give them more wait time, and call on them more often in the sciences (p. 76). This holds for both male and female teachers. Simple strategies for calling on females as often as males, asking both sexes tough questions, and preventing interruptions from other students can be very helpful in eliminating bias. In addition, structuring learning activities in less competitive formats can promote more risk taking and greater confidence among those who shy away from overt competition, both males and females.

Some specific strategies for addressing challenges faced by male students include adding learning activities that call on physical or spatial abilities, using examples and materials that incorporate male interests, and offering more visual stimuli (King, Gurian, & Stevens, 2010). Eliot (2010) promotes providing male students with more opportunities for interaction with men, teachers, parents, community speakers, and other volunteers. Eliot also advocates taking stereotypes, both male and female, and teacher biases seriously. For school leaders, infusing these strategies and approaches into teacher-to-student interaction requires providing ongoing, focused professional development opportunities.

Actions For School Leaders

Because sex stereotypes are deeply ingrained and often unexamined, they can be easily perpetuated in the school community. We know that modeling gender-positive behaviors is important to creating a gender-inclusive environment. As a school leader, self-examination of one's beliefs is the beginning of moving beyond those stereotypes to becoming authentically and consistently inclusive. Figure 11.1 lists a set of questions that can guide self-assessment and plans to build a gender-positive environment.

A much more extensive self-assessment, the Bem Sex Role Inventory (Bem, 1974), is available online and offers more detailed information about beliefs and perceptions about sex roles and gender.

SCHOOL-LEVEL MODELING

The implications for establishing school-level expectations include providing professional development opportunities as well as modeling across the adults in the school. Studies show that both school climate and student achievement are enhanced in schools where teachers go beyond their formal duties to build relationships with students (DiPaola & Tschannen-Moran, 2001; Meier, 2002). DiPaola and Hoy (2005) described this level of behavior as "exemplary and caring behavior that surpasses minimal expectations" (para. 2). These expectations for adult modeling of caring behavior are not specifically targeted for addressing gender bias, but can be helpful across the board in setting expectations for interaction between the sexes. Adults' schoolwide modeling expected behaviors can set a standard that creates an ethic of caring and allows the "best self" in both sexes to emerge. DiPaola and Hoy (2005) suggest several strategies for school leaders, ac-

FIGURE 11.1. Self-Assessment of Gender- and Sex-Based Biases

Questions	Responses (examples)	Gender-Positive Plan of Action
Do I treat males and females differently in my professional work?	(something as simple as holding a door or as complex as expecting women to do more work)	
Do I expect gendered behaviors from my colleagues? My employees?	(women should make coffee, take notes, be more or less emotional)	
How do I portray males and females in the language I choose?	(ladies and gentlemen, girls and boys, moms and dads)	
Do I promote stereotypes by attending to certain groups or activities over others?	(Sadie Hawkins dances, supporting boys' sports over girls' sports)	
How do I respond to gender differences in expression of sexual identities?	(female athletics, male dancers, LBGT club meeting/members)	

knowledging that implementing these expectations for model behavior will take time. They call for leading by example, reinforcing the behaviors when observed, focusing on informal as well as formal exchanges, establishing orientation or mentoring programs to help newcomers adopt the modeled behaviors, and nurturing a positive professional environment. School leaders can also offer seminars for parents to engage in dialogue. Adults in the lives of students have tremendous impact on the choices that students make, and adults modeling ethical and caring behavior across the sexes can have a powerful impact on young people.

REFERENCES

American Association of University Women (AAUW). (1992). *How schools shortchange girls*. Washington, DC: AAUW & National Education Association.

American Association of University Women (AAUW). (1998). *Separated by sex: A critical look at single-sex education for girls*. Washington, DC: AAUW Educational Foundation.

American Association of University Women (AAUW). (2008). *Where the girls are: The facts about gender equity in education*. Washington, DC: AAUW Educational Foundation.

The AAUP's Committee on Women Responds to Lawrence Summers. (2005, July/August). *Academe, 91*(4), 1–2.

Bae, Y., Choy, S., Geddes, C., Sable, J., & Snyder, T. (2000. *Trends in educational equity of girls and women.* Washington, DC: National Center for Educational Statistics.

Bem, S. L. (1974). The measurement of psychological androgyny. *Journal of Consulting Clinical Psychology, 42,* 155–162. Retrieved March 31, 2011, from http://www.mindgarden.com/products/bemss.htm

Bem, S. L. (1993) *The lenses of gender: Transforming the debate on sexual inequality.* New Haven, CT: Yale University Press.

Buchmann, C., DiPrete, T. A., & McDaniel, A. (2008). Gender inequalities in education. *Annual Review of Sociology, 34,* 319–337.

Butler, J. (1993). *Bodies that matter: On the discursive limits of sex.* New York: Routledge.

Catsambis, S. (2005). The gender gap in mathematics: merely a step function? In A. M. Gallagher, J. Kaufman (Eds.), *Gender differences in mathematics: An integrative psychological approach* (pp. 220–245). Cambridge, UK: Cambridge University Press.

Cavanagh, S. (2008). Stereotypes of mathematical inferiority still plagues girls. *Education Week, 28(1),* 9.

DiPaola, M., & Hoy, W. (2005). Organizational citizenship of faculty and achievement of high school students. *High School Journal, 88(3),* 35–44.

DiPaola, M. F., & Tschannen-Moran, M. (2001, September). Organizational citizenship behavior in schools and its relationship to school climate. *Journal of School Leadership, 11,* 424–447.

Eliot, L. (2010). The myth of pink and blue brains. *Educational Leadership, 68(3),* 32–36.

Entwisle, D. R., Alexander, K. L., & Olson, L. S. (2007). Early schooling: the handicap of being poor and male. *Sociology of Education, 80(2),* 114–138.

Gallagher, A. M., & Kaufman, J. C. (Ed.). (2005). *Gender differences in mathematics: An integrative psychological approach.* Cambridge: Cambridge University Press.

Gilligan, C. (1993). *In a different voice.* Cambridge, MA: Harvard University Press.

Hackman, H. (2002). Girls in the middle. *Multicultural Education, 10(2),* 61.

Horton, A. (2010). Academy of achievers. *Jet, 117(16),* 16–19.

King, K., Gurian, M., & Stevens, K. (2010). Gender friendly schools. *Educational Leadership, 68(3),* 38–42.

Lewis, A. (2006). Single sex classes. *The Education Digest, 72(3),* 72–73.

MacNaughton, G. (1998). Improving our gender equity "tools": A case for discourse analysis. In N. Yelland (Ed.), *Gender in early childhood* (pp. 149–174). London: Routledge.

Meier, D. (2002). *In schools we trust.* Boston: Beacon Press.

Moore, G. W., & Slate, J. R. (2008). Who's taking the advanced placement courses and how are they doing: A statewide two-year study. *The High School Journal, 92(1),* 56–57.

Nelson, S. C., & Sanders, J. (2004). Closing gender gaps in science. *Educational Leadership, 62(3),* 74.

Ojeda, L., & Flores, L. Y. (2008). The influence of gender, generation level, parents' education level, and perceived barriers on the educational aspirations of Mexican American high school students. *The Career Development Quarterly, 57*(1), 84–95.

Perkins, R., Kleiner, B., Roey, S., & Brown, J. (2004). *The high school transcript study: A decade of change in curricula and achievement, 1990–2000*. Washington, DC: National Center of Educational Statistics.

Pierce, K. M. (December 2005/January 2006). Posing, pretending, waiting for the bell: Life in high school classrooms. *The High School Journal, 89*(2), 1–15.

Pivik, J., McComas, J., & Laflamme, M. (2002). Barriers and facilitators to inclusive education. *Council for Exceptional Children, 69*(1), 97–107.

Reeder, H. M. (2005). Exploring male-female communication: Three lessons on gender. *The Journal of School Health, 75*(3), 115–117.

Sadker, D., & Zittleman, K. (2005, March/April). Gender bias still lives. *Principal, 84,* 18–22.

Sadker, M., & Sadker, D. (1994). *Failing at fairness: How America's schools cheat girls.* New York: Macmillan.

Sax, L. (2008). Where the girls aren't: What the media missed in the AAUW's report on gender equity. *Education Week, 27,* 42, 36.

Schroeder, K. (2006). Not really harassed. *The Education Digest, 71*(7), 73–74.

Sokal, L., Katz, H., Chaszewski, L., & Wojick, C. (2007). Good-bye, Mr. Chips: male teacher shortages and boys' reading achievement. *Sex Roles 56,* 9–10, 651–659.

Snyder, T., & Dillow, S. (2007). *Digest of Educational Statistics 2006.* Washington, DC: National Center for Educational Statistics, U.S. Department of Education, U.S. Government Printing Office.

Stewart, W. (2009, May 29). Single-sex schools boost girls' science, study finds. *The Times Educational Supplement,* 4841.

Tyre, P. (2008). Boy trouble. *Instructor, 118*(2), 35–37, 39–41.

Wade, S., Fauske, J., & Thompson, A. (2008). Prospective teachers' problem solving in online peer-led dialogues. *American Educational Research Journal, 45*(2), 398–442.

Walshaw, M. (2001). A Foucauldian gaze on gender research: What do you do when confronted with the tunnel at the end of the light? *Journal for Research in Mathematics Education, 32*(5), 471–492.

Wilson, R. (2005). Science, math, bubble gum, and dreams. *The Chronicle of Higher Education, 51,* (49), A48.

Woods, J., & Dylinski, S. (2002). Is single-sex education a proven strategy? *American Teacher, 87*(1),4–6.

World Bank. (2001). Engendering development: Through gender equality in rights, resources, and voice. *World Bank Policy Research Report Series.* New York: Oxford University Press.

CHAPTER 12

Schools That Make a Difference for Children in Poverty

Judy F. Carr

Craig Gillette is an Associate Superintendent of Schools in a high-poverty school district in the Northeast. Recently, in working with a group of teacher leaders representing schools throughout the district, he finished a presentation on the district's initiatives to improve student learning—standards and assessments, high-quality teachers and leaders, data and reporting—and then added the qualification, "but of course we can only expect so much with the students we have in this district."

FROM A CULTURE OF POVERTY TO A "GEOGRAPHY OF OPPORTUNITY"

According to the Children's Defense Fund (2010), one out of five children in America is poor, and one in twelve children lives in extreme poverty, defined as a household income of half or less of the annual poverty level of $22,050 for a family of four. They also note that 70% of children living in poverty have one or more parents who work. Moreover, almost as many children living in the suburbs are as poor as children living in urban areas, and large numbers of rural students also live in poverty, which underscores the importance of not framing poverty as an urban issue alone.

> Thirty-five percent of rural students live below the poverty level . . . and 45 percent of public school students in remote rural areas attend a moderate-to-high poverty school, a percentage that was only topped in large numbers in large and mid-size cities, where 66 and 49 percent of students, respectively, attend

moderate-to-high-poverty schools. Both of these numbers are higher than their counterparts in urban areas. (Bryant, 2010, pp. 54–55)

The majority of high-poverty schools experience "savage inequalities" with regard to resources and opportunities that have a negative impact on learning and on performance (Kozol, 1992). Not the least of these are the low expectations too many teachers and administrators hold for their students who are socioeconomically disadvantaged (McKinney, Flenner, Frazier, & Abrams, n.d.). When teachers and administrators hold low expectations for students, it can create a Pygmalion effect, or self-fulfilling prophecy (Rosenthal & Jacobson, 1992). Because teachers do not expect students who are socioeconomically disadvantaged to perform well, there is an "expectation gap" (Quaglia, Fox, & Corso, 2010), and it is not a surprise that they, in fact, do not perform well (Jensen, 2009).

This kind of *deficit thinking*, thinking that puts greater emphasis on what is perceived to be missing, as opposed to *asset-based thinking*, thinking that focuses on what is believed to be possible (Cramer & Wasiak, 2006), is one of several "equity traps" identified by McKenzie and Scheurich (2004). *Equity traps* are patterns of thinking and behavior that foreclose the possibilities for creating equitable schools, and they are typically reinforced among administrators and teachers through formal and informal communication, and the subtle and sometimes not-so-subtle sharing of assumptions and beliefs about children and families who live in poverty. Such deficit assumptions are closely tied to a "culture of poverty" thesis (Lewis, 1959; Payne, 2005) that attributes socioeconomic problems to deficiencies in the individual, although, as Prins and Shafft (2009) point out, empirical evidence may not support this view:

> Poor individuals are thought to have a set of psychological traits and dispositions that are *unlike* those of the middle and upper classes and that they pass these on to their children, creating an "intergenerational cycle of poverty". . . . The view that poverty is a lifestyle or permanent state, however, is not supported by empirical evidence. (pp. 2284, 2295)

Nevertheless, framing the problem as the individual's continues to be a prevalent view in many schools due at least in part to the continuing popularity of the work of Ruby Payne (2005) defining a "culture of poverty" despite the fact that the conceptualization of poverty on which her work is based has recently been called into question (Gorski, 2006, 2008; Kunjufu, 2006).

In contrast, structural explanations identified by Prins and Schaffft (2009) "attribute poverty to economic and structural factors such as job

scarcity, low wages, weak social safety nets, inadequate schools, and prejudice and discrimination" (p. 2283). Helping students who live in poverty
perform well requires "reforms that narrow the vast socioeconomic inequalities in the United States" (Rothstein, 2008, p. 10), and expansion of
the local "geography of opportunity" (Prins & Schafft, 2009, p. 2283) for
students who are socioeconomically disadvantaged and their families.

Expanding the local geography of opportunity requires close examination of what is and what is not happening within the walls of the school.
Skrla, Scheurich, Garcia, and Nolly (2004) describe the process of an "equity audit" to highlight and address inequities that may exist in the school,
and they propose looking at 12 indicators in three broad categories of practice where inequities typically are found in terms of patterns of overrepre-
sentation and underrepresentation:

- Teacher quality—teacher education, experience, mobility, appropriate certification or lack thereof
- Program equity—special education, gifted and talented education,
  academic progress of students in bilingual education, and student
  discipline
- Achievement equity—state achievement test results, high school
  completion rates, completion of college prep curriculum, and higher level assessments such as SAT and ACT

Are students who are socioeconomically disadvantaged underrepresented in
advanced placement classes? Are they overrepresented in special education
or behavioral referrals? When patterns such as these persist, lack of equity
has a negative impact on the experience and the performance of children
who live in poverty. It is essential to expand the geography of opportunity
to assure that all students, especially children who live in poverty, have the
opportunities they need to succeed in school and in life.

It is also essential to consider this question: What percentage of administrators, teachers, and staff in the school truly believe that students who live
in poverty can learn at least as well as those who do not? If the response is
less than 100%, that is, if even one adult in the school does not believe that
all students can learn well, then initiatives designed to improve the performance of this group of students may be compromised. It is important for all
members of the school community to listen for and directly confront deficit
thinking and the language of diminishment, negative references within the
school to individual students or groups of students and/or their families. At
the same time school leaders can model assets-based language and actions
(Benson & Scales, 1998) and actively focus on the extent to which schools
do make a difference in the learning and the lives of children who live in

poverty. Teachers and administrators can examine their own belief systems for any traces of negative assumptions and language regarding students who are socioeconomically disadvantaged and their potential for learning.

SCHOOLS THAT MAKE A DIFFERENCE

Making a difference is a process of building from our high points, a process of making real our shared beliefs about the ability of *all* students to learn well, *all* teachers to teach in effective, responsive ways, and *all* leaders to guide the process with passion and persistence. In *It's Being Done* (2007) and *How It's Being Done* (2009), Karin Chenoweth details schools across the United States that have demonstrated that children in poverty can achieve high standards when teachers and principals refuse to write them off and instead show how thoughtful instruction, high expectations, and careful consideration of each child's needs can result in remarkable improvements in student achievement, across subgroups. In crafting a school's response to children in poverty, there are many positive examples to draw from, as demonstrated by examples given below.

Some California elementary schools serving largely low-income students score as much as 250 points higher on the state's academic performance index than other schools with very similar students (Williams et al., 2005).

Douglas Reeves (2004) in his 90/90/90 study examined schools where 90% of the students were eligible for free and reduced lunch, more than 90% of the students were from ethnic minorities, and more than 90% of the students met or achieved high academic standards, according to independently conducted tests of academic achievement.

The School District Effectiveness Study (Cawelti, 2003) located whole school districts in the United States that have accomplished substantial gains districtwide in student achievement and determined what strategies had been employed to accomplish these gains. Two criteria were used to choose districts for the study: (1) The district served a large number of students from low-income families, and (2) all or most of the schools had increased achievement (as measured by standardized tests) for 5 years prior to the study. Cawelti and Protheroe (2003) identified the following common characteristics across these districts, factors that are attributed to their success in improving the performance of all students, particularly students who live in poverty:

Identifying and moving toward key indicators of success
Aligning curriculum, horizontally and vertically
Managing information systems efficiently

Administering benchmark tests
Using item analysis data
Restructuring for accountability
Using site-based budgeting
Engaging in team planning for improvement
Having central office leaders facilitate processes
Using best practice teaching strategies in specific disciplines
Managing classrooms to focus on learning

In workshops across a myriad of school districts and at national conferences, the author asked participants to review summaries of approaches to
which the educators in the schools featured in Karin Chenoweth's books
(2007, 2009) attribute the turnaround of performance by students in their
schools. Invariably, very similar themes emerge. Their responses illustrate
that we know what needs to be done to improve the experience and learning
of children who live in poverty. In the vast majority of high-poverty schools
in the United States, however, systems of strategic response incorporating
the approaches central to these themes are not being implemented. These
systems of strategic response can be represented graphically as a set of congruent relationships among the essential elements, as shown in Figure 12.1.
While this is a powerful systems-based model for high-quality experience
and learning for all learners, it encompasses essential strategies identified
by Cawelti (2003), Chenoweth (2007, 2009), Gorski (2008), and Reeves
(2004) as being effective in schools that make a difference for children living
in poverty.

A Focus on the Individual Learner

Each of the parts of the model shown in Figure 12.1 is interdependent
with the others and the primary focus of each part is on each learner. Thus,
for example, while the curriculum-instruction-assessment triangle of alignment is very common, at least since the days of Ralph Tyler (1949), maintaining at the same time alignment with the needs *and* the strengths of each
learner is less evident in practice in many schools.

Curriculum Is Directly Aligned with Standards

Even in schools and districts where state or national standards have
been explicitly incorporated in the local written curriculum, it is common
to see instruction guided by textbooks or past practice rather than by the
careful selection of materials, resources, and engagements needed to support students in learning well what the curriculum specifies they need to

FIGURE 12.1. Center for Curriculum Renewal Logo: Student-Centered, Standards-
    Based Learning

Note. From *Improving standards-based learning: A process guide for educational leaders* (p. 2)
by J. F. Carr and D. E. Harris, 2009, Thousand Oaks, CA: Corwin Press.

learn (Schmoker, 1996). The written curriculum, when well crafted, serves
as a commitment to children and their families of what they will have the
opportunity to learn.

Instruction Is Strategic

Strategic instruction is differentiated, incorporates research-based strategies (Marzano, Pickering, & Pollock, 2001), and provides gradual release
of responsibility from the teacher to the student (Fisher & Frey, 2008). This
is not simply a matter of moving from whole-group to small-group instruction, though that is an important shift as well. Too often, particularly in
elementary school classrooms, well-intentioned teachers break students into
small groups but then have all groups do the same activities, just in a different order. This practice does provide a heightened level of engagement for
students, but is little more than activity management, not differentiated instruction. Differentiation of instruction (see also Chapter 4 of this volume)
is based on assessed strengths and needs of students and is tailored to create
building blocks from where they are to where they need to go to attain the

desired learning results. Figure 12.2 distinguishes strategically differentiated instruction from instruction that is not strategic.

Because children who are socioeconomically disadvantaged may not have had experiences that their peers who are more economically advantaged may have had (Cawelti, 2003; Chenoweth, 2007, 2009; Children's Defense Fund, 2010), it is especially critical that the strengths and needs of these learners be identified and that the precious time available for their instruction be targeted. In addition, when instruction is strategic, teachers make conscious choices to use research-based approaches for all subject areas, such as those identified by Marzano and colleagues (2001) and others, as discussed in Chapter 4. Teachers also make intentional decisions about approaches to instruction specific to the subject matter, such as implementing the Standards of Practice for Mathematics identified in the Common Core State Standards (2010). For their part, students need opportunities to see the teacher model or demonstrate new material, to try out new learning through guided feedback from the teacher, to work in collaboration with peers, and to engage in independent practice using new skills on their own (Fisher & Frey, 2008). The design of instruction becomes a process of creating the building blocks to take all students from where they are individually to where they need to be in terms of the learning at hand.

Assessment Supports Student Learning, Instructional Improvement, and Accountability

To support students in improving their learning requires assessment *for* learning (Black & William, 1998; Chappuis, 2009; Jones, Carr, & Ataya, 2006; Stiggins, Arter, Chappuis, & Chappuis, 2004) in which students receive explicit feedback about their learning in relation to their learning goals. They also periodically participate in summative assessments (classroom, school, district, state) that provide a sense of where they are in relation to the expectations they need to meet—an assessment *of* learning. For example, the Brazosport School District that was part of the Cawelti (2003) study uses frequent, short, 4-question assessments to gauge student progress as part of what they call their "8-step instructional process." Other schools and districts use such strategies as benchmark assessments, quarterly assessments, writing exemplars, and item analysis from state assessments to improve instruction and chart progress.

Data Is Used to Improve Instruction

In schools where children who live in poverty succeed, use of data is not merely a systems exercise. Data provide essential information about each

FIGURE 12.2. Strategic Differentiation of Instruction

Strategic Differentiation	Not Strategic	Examples of How Stragic Differentiation Can Be Implemented
Instruction is based on assessment and identified skill needs and strengths in relation to performance indicators.	Instruction is based on assumptions about students' strengths and needs.	Analyze state and local assessments. Analyze ongoing classroom work.
Students are grouped and regrouped based on skill needs and strengths.	Students are grouped by activities, themes, centers, learning style, or because they "get along with one another."	Use templates to appply data for strategic grouping of students.
Materials and activities are chosen to be "building blocks" to the needed learning.	Materials and activities are in the order presented by the publisher and are not differentiated based on individual skill needs	Share activities and strategies with colleagues. Directly tie activities to skill needs. Decide which activities and materials are likely to have the most impact on skills acquisition and in what order? (Scaffolding)
Center activities are different for different groups based on skill needs (e.g., different levels for the same skill, different skills for different groups).	Same center activities for all students.	Connect resources to performance indicators, skills, learning needs/levels.
Group formation changes regularly based on assessment information and newly identified skill needs.	Once students are assigned to groups, the groups stay the same for an extended period of time.	Use templates to help organize assessment data and identify group membership based on skill needs.
Students set goals in relation to their strengths and needs identified through assessment.	The teacher knows the learning focus but the student does not.	Share standards/performance indicators with students, often as "I can" statements. Post objectives. Use student goal setting sheet with space for teacher and student input.

student for the purpose of improving learning. This leads, for example, to principals meeting regularly with individual teachers and asking them to set goals for each student in relation to the data available, to set targets at key milestones throughout the year, and to identify and implement key strategies to support students in attaining the targets (Piercy, 2006). Even more important is that students know what their own targets are, what they have learned well, what the teacher expects, and what they can do to improve (Quaglia et al., 2010). Data from state assessments are disaggregated by subgroups (Cawelti & Protheroe, 2003) and used to identify strategies to assure all students perform well.

Supervision and evaluation create environments of clear expectations, differentiated professional development, and ongoing professional dialogue for best practices in support for the learning of children who live in poverty.

If teachers are to implement best practices to support engaged learning and high performance for children who live in poverty, they need the experience of evaluation, supervision, and professional development that are differentiated based on their strengths and needs (Glickman, Gordon, & Ross-Gordon, 2007).

The school's clear vision is translated into "look fors" (Mooney & Mausbach, 2008) that make concrete and specific the practices that are expected to be used routinely (Hall & Hord, 1987) in every classroom in the school, such as practices identified in this and other chapters throughout this book. The "look fors" then provide a firm foundation for preconference dialogues and classroom observation during formal evaluation of teachers; they guide how resources are expended for professional development; and they are the focus on continuous dialogue among teachers and administrators working together in professional learning communities (DuFour & Eaker, 1998) about what they see in their data, what they see in actual practice throughout the school, what is to be celebrated, and what changes need to be made. This dialogue is strongly connected to ongoing inquiry involving classroom walk-throughs (Downey, Steffy, English, Frase, & Poston, 2004) and educational rounds (City, Elmore, Fiarman, & Teitel, 2009) in which principals, teachers, and others collect data about classroom practice. Eisner (2002) recommends that the principals should spend a minimum of a third of their time in classrooms conducting short walk-throughs to collect data about actual practices throughout the school. At the least, it is essential that administrators commit to and schedule specific time to spend in classrooms.

Increasingly, teachers are also involved in learning walks to share in the collection of such data to be used for school improvement and collegial dialogue, not as part of summative teacher evaluation. Sometimes feedback is given to individual teachers, but increasingly the data from walk-throughs support dialogue about patterns of practice (Carr & Harris, 2009; City et

FIGURE 12.3. Assessment Questions for Building Systems of Strategic Response

Focus	Questions
The learner is the focus.	Are curriculum, instruction, and assessment tied to the strengths and needs of each individual learner? Is positive language used by adults in discussion of students? Are learning goals identified for each student? Do all students know what their own targets are, what they have learned well, what the teacher expects, and what they can do to improve? Are all students fully and actively engaged in learning?
Curriculum is directly aligned with standards.	Are the written curriculum, the taught curriculum, and the assessed curriculum all directly aligned with standards? Are materials, resources, and learning engagements intentionally selected to support students in learning the aspects of the standards they need to learn next?
Instruction is strategic.	Is instruction differentiated based on assessment data regarding the strengths and needs of each learner? Are research-based instructional strategies consistently in routine use in each classroom? Do all teachers consistently practice gradual release of responsibility?—"I do, we do, you do."
Assessment provides ongoing feedback about learning and students know where they stand.	Do students receive ongoing feedback about their learning in relation to standards (assessment *for* learning)? Do students periodically participate in summative assessments (classroom, school, district, state) that provide a sense of where they are in relation to the expectations they need to meet (assessment *of* learning)?
Data is used to improve instruction.	Do administrators meet regularly with teachers to use data to set goals for individual students? Are data from state and other assessments disaggregated by subgroups and used for program design and improvement?
Supervision and evaluation and professional development support educators through clear expectations and ongoing dialogue.	Have "look fors" been created to make concrete and visible the school's vision of best practices? Are the "look fors" used to guide teacher evaluation, classroom walk-throughs, and allocation of time and resources for professional development? Do administrators spend at least a third of their time in classrooms collecting data about patterns of practice throughout the school? Are teachers engaged in ongoing dialogue about student work, student performance data, and patterns of practice data?
Resources, policies, and communication support the success of children who live in poverty.	Are resources equitably provided to support the success of students who are economically disadvantaged (and all other students)? Are systems of communication designed to communicate within and beyond the school? Do policies support the high expectations for students who live in poverty?

al., 2009) across classrooms, the setting of goals for schoolwide change, and the celebration of accomplishments in relation to goals previously set. Combined with dialogue about student performance data and along with examination of student work (Blythe, Allen, & Powell, 1999), classroom walk-throughs and the review of patterns of practice data set the context for strategic professional development. This context is differentiated for the needs of new and experienced teachers and that differentiation effectively builds the repertoire of knowledge and skills needed to teach effectively students who are socioeconomically disadvantaged.

RESOURCES, POLICIES, AND COMMUNICATION SUPPORT THE SUCCESS OF CHILDREN WHO LIVE IN POVERTY

Historically, children who live in poverty have received the least qualified teachers, the least material resources, and the least access to upper level courses and experiences (Kozol, 1992). Communication with families is often limited by schools, which expect parents to come to the school rather than taking the school to them (Epstein, 2001). Policies too often have not been in place to assure high-quality education for children living in poverty. Schools that make a difference for children in poverty have in place policies and practices that explicitly and intentionally support high expectations and positive outcomes for students who are socioeconomically disadvantaged. The tool shown in Figure 12.3 presents questions educators can use to assess and implement processes and practices to support fair and strategic approaches to the education of children who live in poverty. This tool can be used to identify a school's strengths, to identify needs, and to guide ongoing attention to the needs and the strengths of students who are socioeconomically disadvantaged, their teachers, and the administrators who make manifest their belief that all students can learn well.

REFERENCES

Benson, P., & Scales, P. C. (1998). *A fragile foundation: The state of developmental assets among American youth.* Minneapolis, MN: The Search Institute.

Black, P., & William, D. (1998). Inside the black box: Raising standards through classroom assessment. *Phi Delta Kappan, 80*(2), 139–148.

Blythe, T., Allen, D., & Powell, B. (1999). *Looking together at student work.* New York: Teachers College Press.

Bryant, J. A., Jr. (2010, November). Dismantling rural stereotypes: One-size-fits-all solutions don't meet the needs of ignored and misunderstood rural schools. *Educational Leadership, 68*(3), 54–57.

Carr, J. F., & Harris, D. E. (2009). *Improving standards-based learning: A process guide for educational leaders.* Thousand Oaks, CA: Corwin Press.

Cawelti, G. (2003) *What do we know: Benchmarking to eliminate the achievement gap.* Philadelphia: Laboratory for Student Success (LSS), Mid-Atlantic Regional Educational Laboratory at Temple University.

Cawelti, G., & Protheroe, N. (2003). *Supporting school improvement: Lessons from districts successfully meeting the challenge.* Arlington, VA: Educational Research Service.

Chappuis, J. (2009). *Seven strategies of assessment for learning.* Portland, OR: ETS Assessment Training Institute.

Chenoweth, K. (2007). *It's being done: Academic success in unexpected schools.* Cambridge, MA: Harvard Education Press.

Chenoweth, K. (2009). *How it's being done: Urgent lessons from unexpected schools.* Cambridge, MA: Harvard Education Press

Children's Defense Fund. (2010). *State of America's children 2010 report.* Washington, DC: Childen's Defense Fund. Retrieved August 28, 2010, from http://www. childrensdefense.org/child-research-data-publications/data/state-of-americas-children-2010-report.html

City, E., Elmore, R., Fiarman, S., & Teitel, L. (2009). *Instructional rounds in education.* Cambridge, MA: Harvard Education Press.

Common Core State Standards Initiative. (2010). *Common Core State Standards.* Retrieved March 31, 2011, from http://www.corestandards.org/assets/CCSSI_Math%20Standards.pdf

Cramer, K. D., & Wasiak, H. (2006). *Change how you see everything through asset-based thinking.* Philadelphia: Running Press.

Downey, C., Steffy, B., English, F., Frase, L., & Poston, W. (2004). *The three-minute classroom walk-through: Changing school supervisory practice one teacher at a time.* Thousand Oaks, CA. Corwin Press.

DuFour, R., & Eaker, R. (1998). *Professional learning communities at work: Best practices for enhancing student achievement.* Bloomington, IN: National Educational Service and Alexandria, VA: Association for Supervision and Curriculum Development.

Eisner, E. (2002). *The arts and creation of mind.* New Haven, CT: Yale University Press.

Epstein, J. (2001). *School, family, and community partnerships: Preparing educators and improving schools.* Boulder, CO: Westview Press.

Fisher, D., & Frey, N. (2008). *Better learning through structured teaching: A framework for the gradual release of responsibility.* Alexandria, VA: Association for Supervision and Curriculum Development.

Glickman, C., Gordon, S., & Ross-Gordon, J. (2007). *Supervision and instructional leadership: A developmental approach.* New York: Pearson.

Gorski, P. C. (2006). The classist underpinnings of Ruby Payne's framework. *Teachers College Record.* Retrieved March 31, 2011, from http://www.tcrecord.org

Gorski, P. C. (2008). The myth of the "Culture of Poverty." *Educational Leadership,* 65(7), 32–36.

Hall, G., & Hord S. (1987). *Change in schools: Facilitating the process.* Albany: State University of New York Press.

Jensen, E. (2009). *Teaching with poverty in mind: What being poor does to kids' brains and what schools can do about it.* Alexandria, VA: Association for Supervision and Curriculum Development.

Jones, P., Carr, J. F., & Ataya, R. L. (Eds.). (2006). *A pig don't get fatter the more you weigh it: Classroom assessments that work.* New York: Teachers College Press.

Kozol, J. (1992). *Savage inequalities: Children in America's schools.* New York: HarperCollins.

Kunjufu, J. (2006). *An African centered response to Ruby Payne's poverty theory.* Chicago: African American Images.

Lewis, O. (1959). *Five families: Mexican case studies in the culture of poverty.* New York: Basic Books.

Marzano, R., Pickering, D., & Pollock, J. (2001). *Classroom instruction that works.* Alexandria, VA: Association for Supervision and Curriculum Development.

McKenzie, K., & Scheurich, J. J. (2004). Equity traps: A construct for departments of educational administration. *Educational Administration Quarterly, 40*(5), 601–632.

McKinney, S. E., Flenner, C., Frazier, W., & Abrams, L. (n.d.). *Responding to the needs of at-risk students in poverty.* Retrieved March 31, 2011, from http://www.usca.edu/essays/vol172006/mckinney.pdf

Mooney, N., & Mausbach, N. (2008). *Align the design: A blueprint for school improvement.* Alexandria, VA. Association for Supervision and Curriculum Development.

Payne, R. K. (2005). *A framework for understanding poverty.* Highland, TX: aha! Process.

Piercy, T. (2006). *Compelling conversations: Connecting leadership to student achievement.* Englewood, CO: Lead and Learn Press.

Prins, E., & Schafft, K. A. (2009, September). Individual and structural attributions for poverty and persistence in family literacy programs: The resurgence of the culture of poverty. *Teachers College Record, 111*(9), 2280–2310.

Quaglia, R. G., Fox, K. M., & Corso, M. J. (2010, November). Got opportunity? [Closing opportunity gaps]. *Educational Leadership, 68*(3). Retrieved March 31, 2011, from http://www.ascd.org/publications/educational-leadership/nov10/vol68/num03/Got-Opportunity.aspx

Reeves, D. B. (2004). *Accountability in action: A blueprint for learning organizations* (2nd ed.). Englewood, CO: Advanced Learning Press.

Rosenthal, R., & Jacobson, L. (1992). *Pygmalion in the classroom: Teacher expectation and pupils' intellectual development.* New York: Irvington.

Rothstein, R. (2008). Whose problem is poverty? *Educational Leadership, 65*(7), 8–13.

Schmoker, M. (1996). *Results now: How can we achieve unprecedented improvements in teaching and learning?* Alexandria, VA: Association for Supervision and Curriculum Development.

Skrla, L., Scheurich, J., Garcia, J., & Nolly, G. (2004). Equity audits: A practical leadership tool for developing equitable and excellent schools. *Educational Administration Quarterly, 40*(1), 133–161.

Stiggins, R., Arter, J., Chappuis, J., & Chappuis, S. (2004). *Classroom assessment for student learning: Doing it right—using it well.* Portland, OR: ETS Assessment Training Institute.

Tyler, R. W. (1949). *Basic principles of curriculum and instruction.* Chicago: University of Chicago Press.

Williams, T., Kirst, M., Haertel, E., et al. (2005). *Similar students, different results: Why do some do better? A large-scale survey of California elementary schools serving low-income students.* Mountain View, CA: EdSource.

Part IV

FACILITATING SYSTEMS OF SUPPORT

The two chapters in this part emphasize the interconnectedness of the school community and fluidity of that relationship, recognizing that the school community is a living, changing, and dynamic entity. The role of data and implications for systemic decision making are explored. In Chapter 13 Tary Wallace describes ways that research has shown to extend and strengthen our inclusive practices by employing measurement and research skills to gather, analyze, and interpret data for effective program design and evaluation. Consistent and meaningful data usage that guides decision making, the development of systems of support, and the building of communities of effective practice are outlined. In Chapter 14, the final chapter, Julia M. White and Phyllis Jones summarize key themes of the preceding chapters to provide a multidimensional framework school leaders can use to identify and assess their own schools' commitments to inclusion. Leaders who recognize and support inclusive practices in schools implement systems that convey clear expectations for processes and practices, respond to the needs of adults working with diverse learners, and provide information about what is working and what is not, what should stay the same and what changes are needed. In addition, this chapter provides processes, examples, and tools for systems used by schools that are doing the work of fully including all students, of providing rich and appropriate experiences for all students, of assuring high performance of all students. The role of data and implications for systemic decision making are explored.

CHAPTER 13

Using Data to Build and Analyze Systems of Inclusive Practices

Tary Wallace

Principal Levin feels a strong sense of satisfaction and joy after re-viewing numbers showing that attendance has increased across all demographic groups within the school. Increasing attendance was one of the top three goals in the latest school improvement plan. It was so important that multiple program initiatives were directed at increasing attendance. The satisfaction yields to dismay with the real-ization that budget constraints will allow only one of the initiatives to continue in the coming year. Because all of the initiatives were started simultaneously, the data cannot clearly indicate which of them was most related to the increase in attendance or if they were equally re-lated across the demographic groups. How will the decision of which initiative to continue be made? Will it be the cheapest, the most popu-lar with teachers or with central administration? Principal Levin knows that students' lives will be impacted by this decision and she wishes there was better information with which to make it.

Schools dedicated to inclusive practices use data to make decisions as-suring the best possible experience and outcomes for all students. A decision-making process that involves consideration of data from multiple sources is more robust and helps to make decisions more transparent and meaningful. This chapter describes the skills and strategies important for school leaders making decisions about inclusive school policies and practice. It develops an appreciation of how a school leader can capitalize upon best practice research data in informed decision making. An example illustrates building a stronger awareness of issues by reviewing the database, and the chapters examine how such a review can support making more knowledgeable decisions. The examples offered relate to key research data about achievement and inclusion. The chapter also presents a system for using data that will generate meaningful conversations and guide data-based decisions in inclusive schools.

DATA USE TODAY

School leaders are using data regularly at more points along the continuum of school life (Creighton, 2007; Goldring & Berends, 2009). There are also many more efforts to evaluate assessment and/or accountability systems at state and district levels (Fuhrman, 2003). While evaluation of programs and systems has occurred for centuries, the more widespread use of achievement and other data for making judgments about programs is changing. Schools must now include all students in their standardized assessments that provide data for the evaluations and report data more widely and publicly than ever before. From whole-school reform models to decisions about the instructional placement of individual students, data are used more effectively without a "one-size-fits-all" perspective (Tomlinson, 1999). School leaders are constantly called upon to apply data and make judgments about adopting programs or strategies at their schools and districts. Effective school leaders refrain from equating value with higher performance test scores only in value-added models, and instead make distinctions among a variety of value-added measures that contributes to a healthier, more successful learning environment (Ainscow, 2005; Theoharis, 2010).

CAPITALIZING ON THE BEST PRACTICE RESEARCH BASE

In order to facilitate and make informed decisions based on data, school leaders and their staff members need to access and critique existing best practice research and policy through local and national databases. This can be achieved in the following ways:

- Locating and interpreting best practice research, including databases and empirical findings
- Managing and critiquing the information generated in the databases
- Using findings to inform practice and advocate for change when appropriate

Locating and Interpreting Best Practice Research

One source of data for decision making in schools is the study of best practice. Staying current with professional journal subscriptions, professional organization memberships, adding to the school's professional library, attending conferences or workshops, and encouraging teachers to do the same will naturally contribute to the current knowledge of best practice research. Other proactive ways that school leaders may stay current are cohosting a local conference, developing collaborative relationships with colleges of education and becoming designated as a professional development school (National Association for Professional Development Schools, 2008), exploring funding opportunities for school-based projects that allow systematic inquiry of a particular school issue, and joining newsgroups and electronic mailing lists for professional organization peer groups, policymaking groups, or research institutes sharing recent developments in the field. Such partnerships and initiatives can support the consideration of a wide range of databases of best practices (Galletta & Jones, 2010; Lefever-Davis, Johnson, & Pearman, 2007; Shirley et al., 2006).

Managing and Critiquing Reports and Databases

School leaders need skills to evaluate reports and databases and to act as a filter for managing the abundance of data that are generated around school policy and practices. There are so many sources and so much data available that managing the information can draw heavily on time and energy. It is vital that school leaders build capacity among other administrators and teachers in their school to help with this endeavor (Baker & Richards, 2004; Creighton, 2007; Goldring & Berends, 2009; Popham, 2006). Skillful use of integrated data management and analysis software is essential, especially when a school leadership team wants to ask a specific question of the data. State departments of education, local districts, and professional organizations are valuable sources of training in creating data management systems. Results of applied educational research, surveys, and evaluation research is supporting the use of data management systems to make sense of the prolific amounts of data on school practices (U.S. Department of Education, 2007; Wayman, Stringfield, & Yakimowski, 2004). The secured, electronic data management system operated by inclusive school leaders will contain a variety of current and longitudinal data that is easily accessed by school personnel who need it. It would contain the comprehensive store of data needed for decision making at levels as broad as the district and beyond to as narrow as the individual student.

The data would be current, accurate, and efficiently accessed for day to day use as well as yearly reporting needs. The system would have the capacity to aggregate and disaggregate data as needed to ensure appropriate inclusion of all students in the many assessment and evaluation activities continuously occurring within and across schools. The system would allow coordination and dissemination of data coming from national, state, and local entities and would support the stream of information that goes out to students, teachers, other school personnel, local and district administrators, and a variety of other stakeholders.

Once data are managed in a way that is meaningful for the decision to be made at the school level, it is then important to interpret the findings. When interpreting findings from data sets, school leaders draw on skills that are built during their professional training and augmented with seminars, workshops, and on-the-job experience. Skills in interpretation of findings that they acquired will help ensure they are relying on the best available information to support decision making.

Using Findings to Inform Practice and Advocate for Change

Did Principal Levin consult empirical research literature on attendance when the school improvement initiatives were designed? There is a variety of information available that the task force likely used to support initiative designs. For example, one recently published article reviewing literature on school refusal, or problematic school nonattendance motivated from within the child and including such factors as truancy and/or school phobia, found that the groups of greatest concern in attendance initiatives are underrepresented in research studies (Kearney & Albano, 2007; Lyon & Cotler, 2007). Was the attendance initiative task force aware of the report on drop out prevention from the What Works Clearinghouse at the U.S. Department of Education, Institute of Education Sciences (available from http://ies.ed.gov/ncee/wwc/reports/Topicarea.aspx?tid=06)? As the principal and the task force were preparing to make the decision on which initiatives will continue, they might have read the meta-analysis reporting effectiveness of school-based initiatives on problem behavior and, specifically, the findings on types of initiatives that most affect nonattendance (Wilson, Gottfredson, & Najaka, 2001). Clearly, as school leaders make sense of data generated from a variety of sources, the application of such findings create an explicit rationale for school-based decision making.

USING DATA TO SUPPORT SCHOOL-BASED DECISION MAKING: AN EXAMPLE OF RESEARCH ON BEST PRACTICES FOR STUDENTS WITH DISABILITIES

The following example of appraising the data on school inclusion and student achievement demonstrates the power of a review of best practice research in supporting a school leader to make more informed decisions.[1] There is a myth about inclusion and student achievement that presumes students without disabilities who learn alongside students with disabilities are negatively impacted (Cole, Waldron, & Massoumeh, 2004). Research published in the last decade has challenged this view and actually points to the increased academic achievement of students who are typically developing as well as students who learn differently. This is important data for school leaders to be aware of in school-based decision making about creating opportunities for greater inclusive experiences across the school. Much of the developing research base on inclusion and student achievement relates to the inclusion of students with disability labels; it shows a mostly positive trend, but highlights the complexity of researching school inclusion and achievement and the need to appreciate the many school-level factors that also come into play (Dyson, Farrell, Polat, Hutcheson, & Gallannaugh, 2004).

Rouse and Florian (2006) help to clarify the discussion about inclusion and student achievement when they recall the difference between achievement and performance. *Achievement* is concerned with the progress made by learners over time and often measured by standardized tests. *Performance* relates more broadly with how a student actually performs in a particular activity and is often tied to curriculum standards. Bearing this in mind, many students who present and learn differently for a variety of reasons may demonstrate high levels of achievement (based on baseline data), but not perform at grade-level competency on a curriculum standard. This reality challenges current school accountability measures that are focused primarily upon performance data and calls for accountability measures that include elements of student achievement and of student performance.

Fortunately, much of the developing research base does pay attention to student performance as well as achievement, reinforcing that inclusive schools do not adversely impact either achievement or performance of students without disabilities. Cole and colleagues (2004) demonstrate that students without disabilities in inclusive settings made more significant academic progress in reading and mathematics tests than students in traditional classrooms. Likewise, the results of a study by McDonnell and colleagues (2003) show that students without disabilities enrolled in inclusive classrooms were more likely to make gains in reading scores, although there was no notable difference in math, language and spelling. They also demonstrate that students who have Individual Education Plans (IEPs) successfully complete IEP objectives in general education settings. Similarly, Rea, McLaughlin, and Walther-Thomas (2002), who also focused upon students with disabilities, found that students placed in inclusive settings scored higher on standardized tests than their peers in more restricted environments. Carter, Sisco, Brown, Brickman, and Al-Khabbaz (2008) based their research on student engagement rather than on achievement or performance. They found that specific instructional formats were associated with slight positive differences in academic engagement for students with and without disabilities, including, one-to-one instruction followed by small-group and independent seatwork. Thus both students with and those without disabilities benefit from inclusive instructional settings.

As mentioned, this small research base on inclusion and student achievement has been slow to develop but has highlighted school-level characteristics of effective inclusive schools that go beyond disability issues to focus upon teaching and learning for all students who may present and learn differently. The first large national study on inclusion and student achievement was conducted in the UK. Dyson and colleagues (2004) used student data analysis and case study methodology to study high- and low-achieving schools that were highly inclusive and less inclusive. They found that there was variation in the achievement of schools with similar levels of inclusivity; some of the highly inclusive schools were classed as high achieving, and some fell into the category of low achieving. Dyson et al. highlight other school-level factors that are critical to how successful a school is when being highly inclusive and facilitating high student achievement. They found that other student demographic factors, which include gender, race, student family income, and the application of the chosen models of pedagogical provision, are critical in appreciating why a highly inclusive environment obtains high student achievement. Their findings indeed support one of the key tenets of this book, that the debate on school inclusion should transcend disability and be about all students in a diverse school community.

In their case studies of highly inclusive, high-achieving schools, Dyson et al. (2004) found a common pedagogical model that was evident across schools that are both highly inclusive and had high student achievement for all students. The model prescribes flexibility of grouping, customization of provision to individual student needs, and careful individual monitoring in a context of schoolwide initiatives for raising attainment of all students. Paradoxically, case studies of low-achieving schools also showed elements of such a pedagogical model, but the translation into effective practice was compromised in these schools (due to a variety of reasons). This suggests that school leaders who want to promote greater inclusion with high student achievement are vigilant about the quality of the implementation of any pedagogical processes and strategies. Just having the strategies present in a school will not lead to a highly inclusive and high-achieving school. School leaders can be proactive in promoting the quality translation of pedagogy into classroom and school practices to support higher student achievement.

The presence of students with behavior issues who disrupt lessons and cause high levels of teacher stress, however, have a significant impact on the learning of others (Dyson et al., 2004). Not all students who demonstrate behavior issues in the classroom have labels of emotional and behavior issues, but all students with behavior issues present a challenge to successful student inclusion and achievement. This clearly highlights the need for school leaders to pay constant attention to supporting positive behavior across the school, as well as to collecting and analyzing data regarding challenging behaviors in order to respond in a contstructive and informed way.

Rouse and Florian (2006) carried out a similar study in the UK to explore the relationship between inclusion and student achievement. They also adopted a case study methodology that recognized that the realization of inclusion can vary across different schools, thus supporting the influence of other school-level factors on student achievement and levels of inclusion. Their study shows that the presence of students with disability labels does not have a negative impact on the achievement of students who do not have disability labels. Indeed, they found that many teachers and school leaders they interviewed believed that the strategies they employ to include students with disability labels contribute to the improved achievement for all students in the school.

It can be argued that the research base on inclusion and student achievement is still in the earliest stage of development, with many methodological challenges as the complex dynamics of diverse school communities are studied. However, what school leaders can appreciate in current small- and large-scale studies is the promising direction that the data point to. In addition, the lessons learned from the current database drives the need for school leaders to nurture and review the careful application of a sensitive pedagogical model that is reviewed and developed in an ongoing way. Having this level of knowledge would enable a school leader to orchestrate meaningful conversations and engage in ongoing program analysis of inclusive practices across the school community.

USING DATA TO CREATE MEANINGFUL CONVERSATIONS AND DATA-BASED DECISIONS IN INCLUSIVE SCHOOLS

School leaders can facilitate collegial discussion that is informed by existing data in order to support shared appreciation and ownership of decisions about instructional program operations and results. In addition, school leaders can collect, analyze, interpret, and report school-based achievement data to support schoolwide decision making (Goldring & Berends, 2009; Hamilton et al., 2009; Popham, 2006). Such data include standardized test scores in addition to a wider array of informaton concerning the whole-school community (teachers, parents, students) to provide a rich portrayal of the many facets of inclusive schools that contribute to success. Leaders of inclusive schools encourage the participation of diverse voices in the conversations about and the practice of data collection and analysis, interpreting, and making sense of findings (National Alliance for Partnership in Equity, n.d.; Nicolaidou, Sophocleous, & Phtiaka, 2006; Riehl, 2000). In addition to the formal data, Principal Levin also uses her excellent professional wisdom and experience, the information from her casual observations and personal communications from stakeholders, as well as systematically collected empirical information, to make meaningful school decisions. Historically, program analysis in schools has often been informal and based on a variety of ways of knowing that may not be strategic means of gathering data and conducting program analysis. Consider, for example, the common "ways of knowing" (Ary, Jacobs, & Sorensen, 2010, p. 2; Fraenkel & Wallen, 2009, p. 4; McMillan & Schumacher, 2006; Slavin, 2007) illustrated in Figure 13.1 that are often used for making decisions in schools.

Strategic analysis is required to answer questions such as the one facing Principal Levin in the scenario at the start of this chapter. Using a logic model (Chen, 1990; Patton, 1997) is a powerful approach for school leaders in developing, analyzing, and supporting exemplary models and systems of inclusive practices in schools. A logic model documents achievements, organizes data, and helps to define any variance between the planned program and the actual program. Figure 13.2 illustrates such a logic model.

While the application of this logic model is recursive rather than linear, it can be used to document a sequence of actions, leading from the resources through impact. Consider the example below in which the model is used to frame internal review of inclusive practices in a school:

- *Resources/Inputs*—What are the human, fiscal, organizational, and community resources (materials, time, money, people, expertise, conceptual model) available to build and implement inclusive practices in the school?
- *Activities*—How are the resources, processes, tools, events, technology, and actions actually planned for, implemented, and delivered? What actually happens in practice?
- *Outputs*—What are the direct products and results of the implementation of the inclusive practices in the school? What are the student results? What growth has occurred?

FIGURE 13.1. Multiple Ways of Knowing and Sources of Data

Ways of Knowing	Cautions
Sensory experience	May be incomplete and not dependable.
Personal experience	Limited to our lived experiences (shaped by sex, race, and other factors); sometimes we make mistakes in our observations; our experiences may not apply to new contexts or different situations. Inclusivity caution: Personal experience may not include experience with diverse cultures or groups of people.
Agreement with others	Even though many, many people may be thinking the same thing, it could still be incorrect. Inclusivity caution: Others may not always be aware of knowledge or perceptions of diverse others to either agree or disagree with them.
Expert opinion	Experts can be wrong and various experts can disagree; an opinion suitable in one context may not be suitable in another. Inclusivity caution: Members of typically nonincluded communities may be less likely to be included in expert pool.
Tradition	May have been the best answer at one time but may not be the best answer at this time; may keep us from acknowledging flaws in current ways and keep us from being open to new ways that would serve us better at this time Inclusivity caution: Nonincluded groups may not have been fully represented in traditional knowledge base.
Logic and the application of inductive and deductive reasoning	Used in isolation or inappropriately can also be flawed and lead to poor conclusions. Inclusivity caution: Exclusion of subgroups may be part of the faulty premises from which conclusions are drawn.

- *Outcomes*—What are the specific changes in the teachers' and students' behavior, knowledge, skills, status, and levels of functioning?
- *Impact*—What fundamental intended and/or unintended changes occurred for students, teachers, and systems as a result of the inclusive practices?

Sometimes, school leaders find it efficient to simplify this logic model to guide dialogue among practitioners about the relationships among inputs,

FIGURE 13.2. Logic Model for School Decision Making

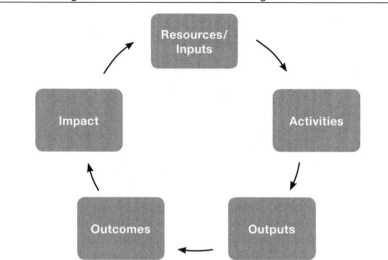

processes, and outputs. Using language more common to the school setting, questions and data sources specific to inclusive practices can be identified, related to resources and conditions, programs and practices, and results as shown in the sample chart in Figure 13.3.

Using the preceding Logic Model of questions and data sources, Principal Levin might then generate the specific questions and data sources needed to determine which initiative to continue in her school, in order to most likely continue the school's trend of increased attendance across demographic groups. For example, she might generate a table showing her specific questions in relation to specific data collection methods she will use to engage her school's leadership team of teachers and parents in dialogue and decision making. The table might look something like Figure 13.4.

With data such as these, the school principal and leadership team can analyze the data, engage in collegial dialogue about findings, and make recommendations with relative confidence. Such dialogue and reflection on and about practice (Schön, 1983) is critical inquiry that takes place in multiple contexts—study groups, teacher teams, departments, grade-level teams, professional learning communities, building leadership or restructuring teams. Dialogue grounded both in best practice data and data emerging from local systems of effective data gathering and analysis leads to just the sort of "better information" Principal Levin wished for in the scenario at the start of this chapter for making decisions that positively impact the lives of students.

FIGURE 13.3. School-Based Example of the Use of a Logic Model

Data Sources	Resources and Conditions	Programs and Practices	Results
Answers to possible questions	What are the resources provided? To what extent does the allocation of time, people, and resources align with our intentions for inclusive practices? To what extent do the resources support inclusive practices?	What are we actually doing in classrooms and at the school and district levels to implement inclusive practices? Do teaching, learning, assessment, and policies align with our expectations for inclusive practices? What inclusive practices are in place?	Are results equivalent across all groups in the school? What do students know? What are students able to do?
Current research	What studies have results related to these questions?	What practices and programs have been identified as effective?	What verifiable results have these programs and practices produced?
Classroom data sources	Demographic data. Units designed. Materials used—quantity, quality, accessibility, and equity of material. Vertical and horizontal alignment. Equity issues. Nature of communication with parents and community.	Completion of in-class work. Participation in out-of-class assignments and projects. Observation. Artifact analysis. Access to qualified teachers and materials. Frequency of classroom assessment and feedback to students about their learning.	Student work. Classroom assessment, observation, rubrics, checklists. Departmental exams.
School district data sources	Policies and procedures. Demographic data: free or reduced lunch. Community employment figures. Nature and frequency of professional development —relationship to intentions for inclusive practices. Organization of the school day. Certification of staff, years of service at school, variety of positions. Safe facilities.	Survey. Implementation of policies and procedures. Mobility rate. Survey of quality of professional development.	Scholastic awards. Retention rates. Comparative data among subgroups to school, district, state, national, and international results. Admission to and performance in postsecondary education. Performance in workforce.
State data	State funding. State laws and regulations.		State assessments.

Note. Adapted with permission from *Succeeding with standards: Linking curriculum, assessment, and action planning* (pp. 60–61) by J. F. Carr and D. E. Harris, 2001, Alexandria, VA: Association for Supervision and Curriculum Development.

FIGURE 13.4. Examples of Questions, Data Sources, and Dialogue

Question	Literature Review Regarding Impact of Each Initiative	Surveys	Student Forums	Teacher Forums	Parent Forums	Document Review	Demographic Data for Participants in Each Initiative/All Initiatives	Results Data for Participants in Each Initiative/All Initiatives
Resources and Conditions								
*What resources are required for each initiative?	X	X		X		X		
*What percentage of students from each subgroup have participated in each initiative?						X		
Programs and Practices								
*What are the perceptions of participants and others about each initiative?		X	X	X	X	X		
*To what extent has each initiative been implemented with fidelity?		X	X	X	X			
Results								
*What does the literature show to be the impact of each initiative?	X							
*What are the attendance results for students who participated in each initiative?							X	X

212

NOTE

1. This section was contributed by Dr. Phyllis Jones.

REFERENCES

Ainscow, M. (2005). Developing inclusive education systems: What are the levers for change? *Journal of Educational Change, 6*, 109–124.

Baker, B. D., & Richards, C. E. (2004). *The ecology of educational systems: Data, models, and tools for improvisational leading and learning.* Upper Saddle River, NJ: Pearson.

Ary, D., Jacobs, L. C., & Sorensen, C. (2010). *Introduction to research in education* (8th ed.). Belmont, CA: Wadsworth.

Carr, J. F., & Harris, D. E. (2001). *Succeeding with standards: Linking curriculum, assessment, and action planning.* Alexandria, VA: Association for Supervision and Curriculum Development.

Carter, E. W., Sisco, L. G., Brown, L., Brickman, D., & Al-Khabbaz, Z. A. (2008). Peer interaction and academic engagement of youth with developmental disabilities in inclusive middle and high schools. *American Journal of Mental Retardation, 113*(6), 479–494.

Chen, H. T. (1990). *Theory-driven evaluations.* Thousand Oaks, CA: Sage.

Cole, C. M., Waldron, N., & Massoumeh, M. (2004). Academic progress of students across inclusive and traditional settings. *Mental Retardation, 42*(2), 136–144.

Creighton, T. B. (2007). *Schools and data: The educator's guide for using data to improve decision making* (2nd ed.). Thousand Oaks, CA: Corwin Press.

Dyson, A., Farrell, P., Polat, F., Hutcheson, G., & Gallannaugh, F. (2004). *Inclusion and pupil achievement* (Research Report 578). London, UK: Department for Education and Skills.

Fraenkel, J. R., & Wallen, N. E. (2009). *How to design and evaluate research in education* (7th ed.). New York: McGraw-Hill.

Fuhrman, S. (2003, September). *Redesigning accountability systems for education* (CPRE Policy Brief RB-38). Philadelphia: Consortium for Policy Research in Education, University of Pennsylvania.

Galletta, A., & Jones, V. (2010). "Why are you doing this?" Questions on purpose, structure, and outcomes in participatory action research engaging youth and teacher candidates. *Educational Studies, 46*(3), 337–357.

Gay, L. R., Mills, G. E., & Airasian, P. (2009). *Educational research: Competencies for analysis and applications* (9th ed.). Upper Saddle River, NJ: Pearson.

Goldring, E., & Berends, M. (2009). *Leading with data: Pathways to improve your school.* Thousand Oaks, CA: Corwin Press.

Hamilton, L., Halverson, R., Jackson, S., Mandinach, E., Supovitz, J., & Wayman, J. (2009). *Using student achievement data to support instructional decision making* (NCEE 2009-4067). Washington, DC: National Center for Education Evaluation and Regional Assistance, Institute of Education Sciences, U.S. Department of Education. Retrieved March 31, 2011, from http://ies.ed.gov/ncee/wwc/publications/practiceguides/

Kearney, C. A., & Albano, A. M. (2007). *When children refuse school: A cognitive-behavioral therapy approach* (2nd ed.). New York: Oxford University Press.

Lefever-Davis, S., Johnson, C., & Pearman, C. (2007). Two sides of a partnership: Egalitarianism and empowerment in school-university partnerships. *The Journal of Educational Research, 100*(4), 204–210.

Lyon, A. R., & Cotler, S. (2007). Toward reduced bias and increased utility in the assessment of school refusal behavior: The case for diverse samples and evaluations of context. *Psychology in the Schools, 44*(6), 551.

McDonnell, J., Thorson, N., Disher, S., Mathot-Buckner, C., Mendel, J., & Ray, L. (2003). The achievement of students with developmental disabilities and their peers without disabilities in inclusive settings: An exploratory study, *Education and Treatment of Children, 26*(3), 224–236.

Mcmillan, J. H. & Schumacher, S. (2006). *Research in education: Evidence-based inquiry* (6th ed.). Boston: Pearson.

National Alliance for Partnership in Equity. (n.d.). *System-building standards for educational reform: An equity perspective.* Retrieved March 31, 2011, from http://www.napequity.org/pdf/standards.pdf

National Association for Professional Development Schools. (2008). *What it means to be a professional development school.* Retrieved from http://www.napds.org/9%20Essentials/statement.pdf

National Forum on Education Statistics. (2004). *Forum guide to building a culture of quality data: A school & district resource.* (NFES 2005-801). U.S. Department of Education. Washington, DC: National Center for Educational Statistics.

Nicolaidou, M., Sophocleous, A., & Phtiaka, H. (2006). Promoting inclusive practices in primary schools in Cyprus: Empowering pupils to build supportive networks. *European Journal of Special Needs Education, 21*(3), 251–267.

Patton, M. Q. (1997). *Utilization-focused evaluation: The new century text.* Thousand Oaks, CA: Sage.

Popham, W. J. (2006). *Assessment for educational leaders.* Boston: Pearson.

Rea, P., McLaughlin, V., & Walther-Thomas, C. (2002). Outcomes for students with learning disabilities in inclusive and pull-out programs. *Exceptional Children, 68,* 203–222.

Riehl, C. J. (2000). The principal's role in creating inclusive schools for diverse students: A review of normative, empirical, and critical literature on the practice of educational administration. *Review of Educational Research, 70*(1), 55–81.

Rouse, M., & Florian, L. (2006, November). Inclusion and achievement: Student achievement in secondary schools with higher and lower proportions of pupils designated as having special educational needs. *International Journal of Inclusive Education, 10*(6), 481–49.

Schön, D. (1983). *The reflective practitioner.* New York: Basic Books.

Shirley, D., Hersi, A., MacDonald, E., Sanchez, M. T., Scandone, D., Skidmore, C., & Tutwiler, P. (2006). Bringing the community back in: Change, accommodation, and contestation in a school and university partnership. *Equity Excellence in Education, 39*(1), 27–36.

Slavin, R. E. (2007). *Educational research in the age of accountability*. Boston: Allyn & Bacon.

Theoharis, G. (2010). Disrupting injustice: Principals narrate the strategies they use to improve their schools and advance social justice. *Teachers College Record, 112*(1), 331–373.

Tomlinson, C. A. (1999). Mapping a route toward differentiated instruction. *Educational Leadership, 57*(1), 12–16.

U.S. Department of Education. Office of Planning, Evaluation, and Policy Development. (2007). *Teachers' use of student data management systems to improve instruction.* Washington, DC: U.S. Government Printing Office.

Wayman, J. C., Stringfield, S., & Yakimowski, M. (2004). *Software enabling school improvement through analysis of student data* (Report No. 67). Baltimore: Center for Research on the Education of Students Placed at Risk.

Wilson, D. B., Gottfredson, D. C., & Najaka, S. S. (2001). School-based prevention of problem behaviors: A meta-analysis. *Journal of Quantitative Criminology, 17*(3), 2001.

CHAPTER 14

Creating School Systems of Inclusive Leadership

Julia M. White and Phyllis Jones

Opportunity, thoughtful language, informed dialogue, notions of belonging, communities of caring, ethical pedagogy, data-driven best practices, advocacy, challenging the status quo, reflective teaching, purposeful curriculum, and social justice are some of the recurring key themes of the preceding chapters. They combine to provide a multidimensional framework for identifying, assessing, and enhancing a school's commitment to inclusion. Inclusive school communities also value the contribution of collaborative practices among teachers, parents, other professionals, and the students themselves. This chapter highlights how this framework for inclusion is enacted in schools and explicates the crucial role school leaders have in facilitating greater inclusive practices by engaging in envisioning the future, active development, sustained reflection, and continuous development. The chapter begins with a story of two teachers enacting these themes while coteaching:

> Margaret is a first-grade teacher who is certified in both Elementary Education and Exceptional Student Education. She is assigned as an exceptional student education teacher at an elementary school in a medium-sized district in the southeastern United States and coteaches with Sarah, a general education teacher. Margaret recently won a national award for her inclusive practice. Approximately half of the students in their class have disability labels, while other students are identified as English language learners, receive free and reduced lunch, and/or have been labeled as "gifted and talented" and require additional assignments and instruction to keep them engaged in their schoolwork. Related services such as speech, occupational, and physical therapies are presented in the classroom, incorporated into lessons

216

and recess/physical education class. All students say the Pledge of Allegiance and sing "America the Beautiful" every morning in American Sign Language. Students are not stigmatized for their "ADHD behaviors," as all students have access to koosh balls, time on the classroom trampoline, weighted vests, chewlery, and other sensory integration tools. Instruction is project based and students work in cooperative groups when it is appropriate. Margaret and Sarah engage in thoughtful planning with related services personnel, the school data coach, and their paraprofessional to produce standards-based, differentiated, hands-on lessons in which students are actively engaged in their own learning. Working together and helping peers are encouraged, and bullying and putting down peers is not allowed. Margaret and Sarah have spent considerable time teaching students to resolve conflict and their collaborative teaching is creative and flexible. They talk about their class as a holistic whole with individual students contributing to the community in positive ways. Margaret leads curriculum planning and teaching in math, while Sarah does the same in literacy. Differentiation is a natural element of the classroom and students move in and out of groups depending upon learning strengths, preferences, needs, and interests. When one walks into their classroom, one walks into a controlled cacophony of excited learning. There is a waiting list of parents of all races throughout the district who want their children in this classroom.

Margaret and Sarah demonstrate dispositions that promote meaningful inclusion; they have a strong vision of an equitable classroom. They talk about their work being connected with social justice in the community and envision an inclusive world; they construct a classroom in which their collective vision for including all children is realized, and they explicitly value and respect each student. Moreover, they work to disseminate what they have learned through their experiences to other teachers in their own school, throughout the district, and through national presentations. Theoharis and Causton-Theoharis (2008) identify three critical dispositions required for inclusive leadership in schools and classrooms: (1) taking a global theoretical perspective; (2) possessing a bold, imaginative vision (i.e., thinking globally and acting locally); and (3) embracing a sense of agency (p. 236). Consider the role of these teacher leaders in relation to the dispositions they demonstrate and the influence that they might have in the school.

Margaret and Sarah's classroom is a model of inclusive practice; one of the tenets of their work is "making differences ordinary" (McLeskey & Waldron, 2006, p. 272). They do this through their work with the first-grade inclusion team (teachers, paraprofessional, speech and occupational therapist) who provide push-in services for all students, so that all students can benefit from the classroom activities that they structure. They are doing on a small scale what Ferguson (2004) calls "systemic inclusion," making "the full continuum of supports available to the full range of students" in their classroom (p. 279).

Although Margaret and Sarah have been change agents and have achieved inclusion in their classroom, it is limited to their classroom. Their story illustrates that the translation of policy into practice is variable across the nation, state, district, and school. Theirs is the only classroom in this school that is cotaught full-time, and is one of only a few in which related services are pushed in. Each year there are anxious days and weeks about whether the coteaching program Margaret and Sarah lead with such expertise will continue. This model of inclusive teaching appears fragile, rather than a stable and sustained schooling provision. Sindelar, Shearer, Yendol-Hoppey, and Lieber (2006) found that innovative practice is less likely when schools and districts are not committed to the initiative, or when they are overly invested in high-stakes assessment. Thus schools that are fully invested in inclusion organize themselves in ways that sustain best practices.

> Dr. William Henderson Elementary School, formerly Patrick O'Hearn Elementary School, in Boston, is a national model for inclusive education. Because of the leadership of its principal, William Henderson (retired June 2009), this school fully includes all students in its rigorous, standards-based curriculum. The student body reflects the diversity of Boston; one-quarter of the students have disability labels; and most of the students qualify for free or reduced lunch. The school routinely performs at the top in the statewide assessment system. Henderson, principal at this school for over 20 years, ran his school much like Margaret and Sarah run their classroom. Related services are pushed in, each classroom is cotaught by a certified general and special educator, and the curriculum is addressed cooperatively, via a project-based approach, and adapted to the needs of each student. Children's stories are honored and families are integral to the success of this school. All staff receive professional development in inclusive practice. Funds are allocated to ensure that services follow students into the general education classroom. Staff's schedules are organized so that there is time to review data and to collaborate in lesson planning.

Inclusive practice is an increasingly important systemic educational issue that is also a social, human rights issue. The research base on systemic approaches for developing greater inclusive practice in schools includes elements related to visionary leaders. These leaders collaborate with faculty, staff, students, and families to create caring learning communities staffed by skilled, responsive teachers who provide equitable access to meaningful content through effective program models, curricular adaptations, and evidence-based instructional practices (Friend & Pope, 2005; Kluth & Straut, 2003; Lipsky & Gartner, 1996, 1998). Kluth and Straut (2003) and Lipsky (2003), recognizing the positive mandate of NCLB that all students have equitable access to meaningful content through the general education curriculum, assert that content area standards can be a catalyst to educational reform, if the standards are developmental and flexible and if schools use a wide variety of assessment tools to monitor student progress. Another systemic approach to developing and maintaining inclusive practice is the use of appropriate funding levels and formulas, as well as flexible use of the funds in general education placements (Lipsky, 2003; Lipsky & Gartner, 1996; Power-Defur & Orelove, 1997).

Schools across the nation are giving life to these systemic changes. Henderson Elementary School has a decades-long commitment to inclusive education. Ryndak, Reardon, Brenner, and Ward (2007), in their study of a southeastern state school district's efforts at implementing and sustaining inclusive practice, identify that there must be a common vision and understanding among stakeholders and that efforts toward systemic change take between 5 and 10 years, and during this time the level of commitment must go beyond professional development. At his school, beginning in 1989, Dr. Henderson enacted "social justice leadership" by resisting tracking and segregation and creating a school culture that eliminated marginalization (Theoharis, 2007). He was enacting the three dimensions of inclusive leadership outlined by Theoharis. The principal did this through empowering teachers to have ownership in school decision making through a school-based management group, the School Site Council, consisting of six parents, five staff members, and the principal. This council makes budget, policy, and hiring decisions. Shared governance and decision making yields ownership, and ownership yields commitment to and sustainability of innovative practice. The hiring decisions are crafted around their commitment to inclusive practice. Budget decisions are based on flexible allocations of "program" funding (e.g., special education, Title I) so that categorical programs are blurred and an array of services and supports are provided to students in common spaces. The delivery of content, focus on student skill development, and the achievement of all students becomes the responsibility of all professionals in that common space. Issues of accountability, assessment, and student progress in the curriculum are also the responsibility of all who inhabit this common space. The staff at Henderson engage in almost constant data analysis, examining student performance on standardized assessments to inform choices of effective instructional strategies and using curriculum-based assessment to chart the progress of students in the standards and their growth in achievement. Inclusion can mean academic success as federal mandates define it. For example, of 82 elementary schools in Boston, 20 made annual yearly progress (AYP) in English language arts and 32 made AYP in math. Henderson Elementary was one of the schools that made AYP in English language arts, and the school does not have any needs improvement or restructuring status.

> Margaret and Sarah were part of a small group of six general and exceptional education teachers from two elementary schools, one assistant principal, two university professors, a district specialist, and a state inclusion technical assistance provider called Sunshine District Advocates. The mission of this small group was to connect educators within Sunshine District who share a commitment to inclusion for all students. They were committed to modeling, through their own actions and words, respect for all individuals. This group proactively sought to provide nonjudgmental guidance and support for greater inclusive practices within their schools and the district, while taking risks in their understandings and practices in inclusive education. This group met monthly for 3 years. During this time, core members presented at state and national conferences, conducted workshops on inclusive instructional strategies, and initiated a peer-mentoring program involving students from an elementary, middle, and high school. Members worked to recruit other teachers and administrators, although only a few more teachers attended the meetings and no additional administrators. Meetings were held monthly, right after school. No principal ever attended a meeting, including Margaret and Sarah's principal. The group tried to have an inclusion-based book study approved as a district professional development, but this did not happen. While all of the members of this group were committed to promoting greater inclusive practice within their schools, this grassroots effort at engaging other teachers and administrators in thinking and talking about inclusion was a constant tension among members of the Sunshine District Advocates. Eventually, the group captured the interest of the principal, which led to a systemwide school audit of inclusive practices occurring during the following year. However, the principal left the school and eventually Sunshine District Advocates ran its course and the group no longer meets.

The absence of school leaders at these grassroots efforts and inclusive support collaboratives exemplifies a common flaw that impedes the development of inclusionary practices and creating an inviting, supportive school culture. Leaving the responsibility for inclusion to teachers alone discounts the influence of school leaders that emerges from knowledge and awareness of best practice, development of shared vision and goals, and an understanding of how best to support teachers and staff. Social justice leaders enact school reform by raising student achievement; improving school structures through desegregating marginalized student populations, increasing academic rigor, and shared accountability; empowering staff and building human capacity; and building relationships with students, families, and community to create a strong, safe, respectful school culture (Theoharis, 2007). While Margaret and Sarah were social justice leaders in their classroom and tried to do this in the broader school district community, they were ultimately teacher leaders in isolation. Such isolated inclusive initiatives are effective but have limited ability to influence change on a district, or sometimes even school, level.

In a school district not too far away from Margaret and Sarah, there is an Associate Superintendent of Schools who is committed to developing meaningful inclusive practices. Miranda has been in her position for 6 years and came to the district from another state that practiced more sustained inclusive practices. Miranda has systematically led a districtwide initiative around developing greater inclusion and demonstrates the power of ongoing systemic development. In 2006 the district embarked on a districtwide audit of inclusive practices that focused upon vision and leadership, policy and systems, and instructional practices. The districtwide team created an action plan based on the current strengths and needs that emerged through the audit. The action plan was shared with all schools across the district and instigated many initiatives related to greater inclusive practices in and across schools. Miranda was able to utilize the action plan when making decisions about resource provision and organizational changes. In the subsequent years she has made several key staffing decisions that have allowed her to create a team of district specialists who are also committed to developing greater inclusion and who are able to support the translation of the district vision to school practice. Four years later the inclusive audit was revisited, beginning with a recap on the earlier action plan and progress to date.

In reflecting on what occurred in the 4 years to lead to this change, several key developments stand out:

- District resources were strategically distributed according to the goal of increasing successful learning for all students (Sharma & Desai, 2008).
- The district curriculum, instructional, ELL, and ESE specialists began to work across special and general education to provide collaborative professional development. Such collaborative work has been highlighted as one of the key components of effective inclusion (Naidu, 2008).
- There has been a sustained focus upon ongoing collaborative professional learning related to effective pedagogy for all students. Darling-Hammond (2010) earmarks this as an essential piece in creating schools where all students learn and progress.
- It became an expectation of all district personnel not only to consider the least restrictive environment in the first instance for all student placements but to actively work together to make this happen. The number of segregated provision sites had been reduced from over 80 to 11 with all students across the district accessing general education curricula.
- Miranda has continuously communicated her beliefs about inclusion and has been willing to engage in conversations with school leaders about complex school site issues. She has engaged in the process of "visioning" suggested by Villa and Thousand (2003) as an effective way of enacting the change envisioned for the future.

In 2010 the team celebrated the progress that had occurred over the last 4 years. This opportunity to reflect on the developed inclusive policies and practices across the district also highlighted areas that needed further nurturing. It demonstrates that inclusion is an ongoing process that requires constant reflection and vigilance from school and district leaders as well as teachers. The rigorous ongoing evaluation of inclusive practices supports the development of robust systems of support for teachers and students (Villa, Thousand, & Nevin, 2008). One of the areas highlighted in the 2010 audit was the need to develop greater collaboration with families and to support school developments that meaningfully include parents in the inclusive discourse. Another was the need to highlight good practice across the district and more explicitly celebrate the progress of students in inclusive environments.

Following the 2010 audit the district team created a new action plan that built upon the positive changes that had occurred but framed the district's position to continue to champion and purposefully plan for greater inclusive practices. This large urban school district has a visionary leader who is committed to promoting high expectations for all students in communities of learning that are diverse and reflective of their local context. Miranda demonstrates social justice leadership and appreciates that inclusion is an ongoing process that requires continuous attention to equitable access to a general education curriculum in supportive learning communities.

Social justice leadership cannot exist in a vacuum; the implementation and sustainability of school reform, of inclusive schooling, depends on school leaders working in concert with key stakeholders to create caring communities of learning through the following practices:

1. Visionary leadership
2. Use of evidence-based practice
3. Rethinking assessment
4. Fostering democratic classrooms and community
5. Creative allocation of resources and supports

Rose (2010) reminds us that school leaders support inclusion by being continuously aware of injustice and being vigilant on contexts and causes of marginalization in schools. Figure 14.1 is a tool that can be used by school leaders to interrogate how their schools are enacting inclusive practice. Based on Kluth's (2005) Is Your School Inclusive?, this tool provides guiding questions to help administrators, lead teachers, and other school leaders move toward implementing, sustaining and evaluating inclusive schooling (see also Ferguson, Kozleski, Fulton, & Smith, 2005; Kluth, Biklen, & Straut, 2003; Kluth & Straut, 2003; Lipsky & Gartner, 1998; McLeskey & Waldron, 2006; Ryndak et al., 2007; Theoharis & Causton-Theoharis, 2008; Villa & Thousand, 2005; Working Forum on Inclusive Schools, quoted in Peters, 2004).

Leaders who recognize and support inclusive practices in schools implement systems that convey clear expectations for processes and practices, respond to the needs of adults working with diverse learners, and provide information about what is working and what is not, what should stay the same and what changes are needed.

As leaders engage in these essential processes, they can be seen to be the weavers of whole cloth, the cloth of belonging. Indeed, picture the fabric tweed: The different colored threads are elaborately woven together to make a beautiful piece of cloth. The richness and strength of the tweed is dependent upon how the various threads come together and support each other. The more prized pieces of tweed are the ones that integrate many different threads to produce an elaborate whole. Every strand is interwoven and belongs to the whole, contributing to the fabric's strength and inherent beauty. The same concept intertwines the very idea of inclusive schools, cleaving them to the whole, and creating schools where the systems, envi-

FIGURE 14.1. Evaluation of Inclusive Practice Use

Practice	Questions for Leaders
	Visionary Leadership Committed to Social Justice
	Do school leaders help all stakeholders understand and share a vision of inclusive education?
	Is this vision articulated throughout the school community and in all school documents, including policy statements?
	Is staff supported as they take risks and try new approaches?
	Are staffing decisions based on this shared vision of inclusive education?
	Do school leaders help all stakeholders understand that school reform for inclusion takes time to implement and sustain?
	Use of Evidence-Based Practice
	Are collaborative teaching strategies, such as cooperative learning groups and peer tutoring, used in classrooms?
	Is student-centered, inquiry-based learning implemented in classrooms?
	Is instruction differentiated to engage students and offer choices in ways they can best learn and express what they learn?
	Are learning environments managed though the principles of Universal Design for Learning?
	Are a range of curricular adaptations and modifications offered to all learners?
	Do all students have access to the general education curriculum in general education settings?
	Does staff collaborate for service delivery (e.g., speech therapists and teachers collaborate to provide services in the general education classroom; special educators and content area educators coteach)?
	Is qualitative research honored as empirical research that can inform instruction?
	Are appropriately high standards held for each student?
	Rethinking Assessment
	Is assessment authentic and curriculum based to scaffold levels of student learning?
	Are a wide variety of assessment tools used throughout the school?
	Are assessments used not only as a school accountability policy tool, but also as a tool to target effective instructional strategies to improve student performance?
	Are standardized assessments used not only to rate student performance but also to chart student progress in the standards and to provide students with ongoing feedback about their learning?

FIGURE 14.1. Continued

Practice	Questions for Leaders
	Fostering Democratic Classrooms and Community
	Are all individuals in the school treated with dignity and respect?
	Is there a culture of shared governance and decision making?
	Is collaboration among students, staff, families, and the community facilitated by school leaders?
	Do lessons draw on students' prior experiences to maximize student strengths and knowledge?
	Do students participate in decisions around classroom rules, curriculum, activities, and environment?
	Are student groups dedicated to equity and acceptance welcomed at school (e.g., Gay-Straight Alliances)?
	Are parents involved as partners in decisions around school and learning activities?
	Is the school considered a community center where groups meet and activities occur outside of typical school hours?
	Creative Allocation of Resources and Supports
	Is professional development ongoing and relevant to inclusive practice?
	Is time allocated and scheduled for coplanning and collaborative work?
	Are funding decisions made in ways so that an array of services are provided to all students?
	Are materials and supports available to any student who requires assistance or extension?

Adapted with permission from *Is Your School Inclusive?* by P. Kluth, 2005, http://www.paulakluth.com/readings/inclusive-schooling/is-your-school-inclusive/

ronment, and processes every school leader facilitates and champions evolve into a tightly interlaced whole. Schools where the students and teachers become the individual threads of the whole create a final fabric that is intricate in design and woven with care, where everyone knows they belong and can thrive.

REFERENCES

Darling-Hammond, L. (2010). *The flat world and education.* New York: Teachers College Press.

Ferguson, D. (2004). The real challenge of inclusion: Confessions of a "rabid inclusionist." In S. Danforth & S. Taff (Eds.), *Crucial readings in special education* (pp. 276–282). Upper Saddle River, NJ: Pearson.

Ferguson, D., Kozleski, E., Fulton, M., & Smith, A. (2005). *On . . . transformed, inclusive schools: A framework to guide fundamental change in urban schools.* Denver, CO: National Institute for Urban School Improvement.

Friend, M., & Pope, K. (2005). Creating schools in which all children can succeed. *Kappa Delta Pi Record, 41*(2), 58–61.

Kluth, P. (2005). Is your school inclusive? In *Paula Kluth: Toward more inclusive classrooms and communities* [Web site]. Retrieved March 31, 2011, from http://www.paulakluth.com/readings/inclusive-schooling/is-your-school-inclusive/

Kluth, P., Biklen, D., & Straut, D. (2003). Access to academics for all students. In P. Kluth, D. Straut, & D. Biklen (Eds.), *Access to academics for all students: Critical approaches to inclusive curriculum, instruction, and policy* (pp. 1–32). Mahwah, NJ: Erlbaum.

Kluth, P., & Straut, D. (2003). Towards standards for diverse learners: Examining assumptions. In P. Kluth, D. Straut, & D. Biklen, (Eds.), *Access to academics for all students: Critical approaches to inclusive curriculum, instruction, and policy* (pp. 33–48). Mahwah, NJ: Erlbaum.

Lipsky, D. K. (2003). The coexistence of high standards and inclusion. *School Administrator, 60*(3), 32–35.

Lipsky, D. K., & Gartner, A. (1996). Inclusion, school restructuring, and the remaking of American society. *Harvard Educational Review, 66*(4), 762–796.

Lipsky, D. K., & Gartner, A. (1998). Taking inclusion into the future. *Educational Leadership, 56*(2), 78–81.

McLeskey, J., & Waldron, N. (2006). Comprehensive school reform and inclusive schools. *Theory Into Practice, 45*(3), 269–278.

Naidu, A. (2008). Collaboration in an era of inclusion. In C. Florin, & M. G. John Lian, (Eds.), *Reform, inclusion and teacher education* (pp. 30–42). New York: Routledge.

Peters, S. (2004). *Inclusive education: An EFA strategy for all children.* Paper prepared for the World Bank Disability Group. Retrieved March 31, 2011, from http://siteresources.worldbank.org/EDUCATION/Resources/278200-1099079877269/547664-1099079993288/InclusiveEdu_efa_strategy_for_children.pdf

Power-Defur, L., & Orelove, F. (1997). *Inclusive education: Practical implementation of the least restrictive environment.* Sudbury, MA: Jones & Bartlett.

Rose, R. (2010). *Confronting obstacles to inclusion: International responses to developing inclusive education.* New York: Routledge.

Ryndak, D., Reardon, R., Brenner, S., & Ward, T. (2007). Transitioning to and sustaining district-wide inclusive services: A 7-year study of a district's ongoing journey and its accompanying complexities. *Research & Practice for Persons with Severe Disabilities, 32*(4), 228–246.

Sharma, U., & Desai, I. (2008). The changing role and responsibilities of school principals relative to inclusive education. In C. Florin & M-G. John Lian (Eds.), *Reform, inclusion and teacher education* (pp. 153–169). New York: Routledge.

Sindelar, P., Shearer, D., Yendol-Hoppey, D., & Lieber, T. (2006). The sustainability of inclusive school reform. *Exceptional Children, 72*(3), 317–331.

Theoharis, G. (2007). Social justice educational leaders and resistance: Toward a theory of social justice leadership. *Educational Administration Quarterly, 43*(2), 221–58.

Theoharis, G., & Causton-Theoharis, J. (2008). Oppressors or emancipators: Critical dispositions for preparing inclusive school leaders. *Equity & Excellence in Education, 41*(2), 230–46.

Villa, R. A., & Thousand, J. S. (2003). Making inclusive education work. *Educational Leadership, 61*(2), 19–23.

Villa, R. A., & Thousand, J. S. (2005). Organizational supports for change toward inclusive schooling. In R. Villa & L. Thousand (Eds.), *Creating an inclusive school* (2nd ed., pp. 57–80). Arlington, VA: Association for Supervision and Curriculum Development.

Villa, R. A., Thousand, J. S., & Nevin, A. I. (2008). *A guide to co-teaching: Practical tips for facilitating student learning* (2nd ed.). Thousand Oaks, CA: Corwin Press (Joint Authorship).

About the Contributors

Rebecca Burns is an assistant professor of ESOL (English for Speakers of Other Languages) in the College of Education at the University of South Florida, Sarasota-Manatee. Her primary research interest is the role of knowledge about language (linguistics and its applications) in preservice and in-service teacher education and its impact on student achievement in the classroom. Her field experiences include teaching middle school language arts in California and Colorado and administering child care programs in a rural farmworker community in Florida. She teaches teacher preparation ESOL courses at the undergraduate and graduate levels.

Marie Byrd-Blake is an assistant professor in the Department of Childhood Education and Literacy Studies at the University of South Florida, Sarasota-Manatee. A native Floridian, she received her B.S. and M.S. in Elementary Education from Florida State University and Florida International University, respectively, and her Ed.D. in Educational Administration and Supervision with a minor in Curriculum and Instruction from Florida International University. Marie has a strong background in urban school education; her current research entails utilizing this in schools to study the variables leading to the enhancement of academic achievement of students from high poverty, high risk and culturally diverse communities. She is also the founder and academic advisor of the USF Sarasota-Manatee student organization PRIDE (Promoting, Recruiting, Increasing Diverse Educators).

Judy F. Carr is codirector of the Center for Curriculum Renewal (http://www.curriculumrenewal.com). She works as a consultant to schools, districts, state agencies, and other educational organizations with a focus on leadership development and coaching, and systems design for standards-based curriculum, instruction, and assessment design and implementation. Until recently, she was also on the faculty in the College of Education at the University of South Florida, Sarasota-Manatee, where she taught in the Educational Leadership Program. In 1995 she was recipient of the Second Annual Vermont ASCD Outstanding Education Leadership Award.

Thomas Crisp is an assistant professor of reading at the University of South Florida, Sarasota-Manatee, where he teaches graduate and undergraduate courses in children's and young adult literature and literacy education. His research primarily focuses on queer and gender theories; children's and young adult literature; issues of social justice; and children's media, toys, and culture. His professional writing can be found in edited anthologies and journals like *Children's Literature in Education*, *Children's Literature Association Quarterly*, *English Journal*, *The Horn Book Magazine*, and *The Lion and the Unicorn*. He is currently the book reviewer for the *Florida Reading Journal*.

Janice R. Fauske is a professor in Educational Leadership and Policy Studies at the University of South Florida, Sarasota campus. Before joining the USF faculty, she worked as the assistant commissioner for Academic Affairs of the Utah State Board of Regents, as a faculty member and administrator at Weber State University, as founding dean of the School of Education at Westminster College, and associate professor and doctoral advisor in Educational Leadership and Policy at the University of Utah. Her teaching expertise includes teaching and learning for school leaders, leadership, organizational change, and qualitative research methods. Her research interests include organizational learning and change, effects of collaborative governance on teaching and learning in schools, and teaching in educational administration programs.

Phyllis Jones is an associate professor in the department of Special Education at the University of South Florida (USF). She taught and was an administrator in schools in the UK for 15 years before she became a faculty member in the College of Education at Northumbria University (UK) for 5 years. Her master's degree is from Durham University (UK) and her doctoral work was completed with professor John Swain at Northumbria University. She is the author of *Inclusion in the Early Years: Stories of Good Practice*, coeditor of *A Pig Don't Get Fatter the More You Weigh It: Classroom Assessment That Works*, and coauthor of *Collaborate Smart*. She is published widely in international journals related to inclusion, low-incidence disabilities, online pedagogy in professional learning, and also teacher education for teachers of students with low-incidence disabilities. She directs the SAGE (Successfully Accessing General Education) OSEP grant at USF. Phyllis was the first UK recipient of the joint AACTE/UCET travel fellowship and was awarded the Outstanding Undergraduate Teaching Award (2004–05) at USF.

Jenni Menon Mariano is an assistant professor of Educational Psychology at the University of South Florida, Sarasota-Manatee. She studies positive youth development including the development of noble purposes in adolescence and in the transition to adulthood. Jenni completed here Ph.D. in Child and Adolescent Development from the Stanford University School of Education in 2007, where she was a member of Willam Damon's research group at the Center on Adolescence. Prior to this she taught and worked internationally in Canada, China, and Europe. This work included coordinating a countrywide peace-building program in Bosnia-Herzegovina in response to the United Nations International Decade for a Culture of Peace and Non-Violence for the Children of the World (2001–2010).

J. Lynn McBrien is an assistant professor in Educational Foundations at the University of South Florida, Sarasota-Manatee. She teaches graduate and undergraduate courses in social foundations. Dr. McBrien received her B.S. in Secondary Education and English from Clarion University, her M.A. in English from Purdue University, and her doctorate in Educational Studies from Emory University. She was a Rotary International Fellow and received a post-graduate diploma in Anglo-Irish Literature at Trinity College in Dublin, Ireland. She also received the 2011 USF Women in Leadership and Philanthropy Faculty Research Award for humanitarian work and research in Uganda and Emory University's Humanitarian Award in 2005 for her work with resettled refugees in Georgia. Her primary research and publications focus on resettled refugee students and their families in the United States, protracted refugee settlements and education, and teaching former child soldiers. She also conducts action research on new media in higher education.

Tary Wallace is an assistant professor of Educational Measurement and Research in the College of Education at the University of South Florida, Sarasota-Manatee. She teaches classroom assessment and foundations of measurement and research courses. Her research interests are chiefly in the area of classroom assessment practices that impact student achievement and attitudes.

Julia M. White is an assistant professor in the Department of Teaching and Curriculum and director of the Inclusive Education Program at the University of Rochester (NY). She received her doctorate in special education from Syracuse University and teaches disabilities in schools and teaching and learning in inclusive classrooms. White's research is grounded in social justice for communities and individuals that are typically stigmatized and segregated. Her research interests include inclusive education teacher preparation and practice, educational policy, and the cultural representations of disability. The recipient of a Fulbright Teacher Exchange grant and later a Fulbright fellowship in the Slovak Republic, she studied schooling and inclusion as a human right, specifically as it pertains to children from Romani communities.

G. Pat Wilson is an associate professor of Reading at the University of South Florida, Sarasota-Manatee, and teaches graduate and undergraduate courses in literacy and instruction. She conducts research into reading and composing processes of children, with a focus on children's navigation and use of symbol systems in print and multimodal text. This has led to authored/coauthored articles published in *The Kappan*, *Language Arts*, *English Education*, *Journal of Early Childhood Teacher Education*, *Literacy Teaching and Learning*, *Reading Teacher*, and the *Journal of Literacy Research*. She has also coauthored chapters in edited books on topics in literacy and instruction. She has been a member of the steering committee for the Children's Literature Symposium since its inception and cochair since 2009.

Index